The Law of Virtual Worlds and Internet Social Networks

To my wife Fadime, daughters Melike-Grace and Medine-Rose
and in memory of my mother Muriel.

The Law of Virtual Worlds and Internet Social Networks

ANDREW SPARROW

GOWER

Published by
Gower Publishing Limited
Wey Court East
Union Road
Farnham
Surrey
GU9 7PT
England

Gower Publishing Company
Suite 420
101 Cherry Street
Burlington
VT 05401-4405
USA

www.gowerpublishing.com

British Library Cataloguing in Publication Data
Sparrow, Andrew Peter.
The law of virtual worlds and Internet social networks.
1. Electronic commerce--Law and legislation. 2. Virtual corporations--Law and legislation. 3. Intellectual property infringement. 4. Online social networks--Law and legislation.
I. Title
343'.09944-dc22

ISBN: 978-0-566-08850-6 (hbk)
ISBN: 978-0-7546-9204-1 (ebk)

Library of Congress Cataloging-in-Publication Data
Sparrow, Andrew Peter.
The law of virtual worlds and Internet social networks / by Andrew Sparrow.
p. cm.
Includes index.
ISBN 978-0-566-08850-6 (hbk.)
1. Internet--Law and legislation. 2. Shared virtual environments--Law and legislation--Great Britain. 3. Online social networks--Law and legislation--Great Britain. I. Title.
KD667.C65S68 2009
343.09'944--dc22

2009033045

Mixed Sources
Product group from well-managed forests and other controlled sources
www.fsc.org Cert no. SA-COC-1565
© 1996 Forest Stewardship Council
FSC

Printed and bound in Great Britain by
MPG Books Group, UK

Contents

About the Author

Andrew Sparrow is a national award winning Solicitor and founder of Lecote Solicitors, a niche commercial law firm concentrating on New Media, Internet and IT Law.

He was one of the first Solicitors in the United Kingdom to recognise and pursue the legal issues relating to online business. Andrew is author of seven books on Commercial Internet Law, published internationally.

In a national poll conducted in 2004 and supported by the then Department of Trade and Industry, he was acknowledged as one of 100 individuals in the United Kingdom who had contributed most to the development of the Internet in the previous decade. Andrew speaks on legal issues relating to the commercial Internet, around the world.

He can be contacted at:

Lecote Solicitors
In association with Rochman Landau
Accurist House
44 Baker Street
London
W1U 7AL
Tel: 020 7544 2424
Email: andrewsparrow@lecote.com
www.lecote.com

Praise for Andrew Sparrow's Previous Books

Music Distribution and the Internet

It is a book no one in the field would want to miss ...

Emerald Journal – Library Review

The great advantage of the book is that it deals with the issues in a comprehensive and logical manner. This book is a vital part of a commercial lawyer's armoury when acting for clients who operate websites for the sale of products and services.

Law Institute Victoria

How well, and from that how effective are legal decisions and interpretations in the field, is something Sparrow touches upon and something that readers will readily identify with ... Sparrow has added an attractive topical work to the current literature. It is a book no one in the field would want to miss.

Stuart Hannabus, Aberdeen Business School, writing for *Library Management Journal*

In his new book, Sparrow attempts to offer insights into the legal aspects of conducting music-related business online ... few other books about online music offer any analysis of matters such as advertising, regulations, electronic payment systems or international conflicts of laws.

Jeremy de Beer, Law Professor at the University of Ottawa

Film and Television Distribution and the Internet

The minefield of rights clearances, new rights definitions and global distribution possibilities comes with a price. And that price is knowledge ... this book is both an examination of the legal issues and a handbook in actually launching a film or TV programme into the new digital world. It could not be more timely.

Peter Buckingham, Head of Distribution and Exhibition, UK Film Council

This book is a handy introductory guide to some of the major legal and technical issues involved in marketing and distributing audiovisual content via the internet ... In short, this is a useful book for those seeking some initial guidance to the headline issues and represents good value for money.

Graeme Fearon, *Entertainment Law Review*

CHAPTER 1 Introduction: The Advent of the Avatar

If you believed that there are no laws which govern Internet social networks and virtual worlds this book should persuade you otherwise. There is law, and a good deal of it. Why would there not be? If one considers the degree of sophistication these environments comprise, the sheer wealth of content that resides within them, and the fact that they are, in the last analysis, human interactions with all the flaws that may bring, it becomes clear that they cannot exist on a parallel plane, immune from the rigours of legal governance.

It is hoped that, at the very least, the issues featured in this book will prompt the reader to think about how the law should properly control people's use of the environments.

It is the premise of this book that virtual worlds and social networks have a long term future. It is written in the belief that we are only at the beginning of the story of the Internet and what it will accomplish in terms of shaping our lives.

The book is not intended as an academic review of how virtual worlds might be regarded in society. It is rather an attempt to distil what is known or which might reasonably be supposed to be the laws which must impact on in-world activity and serve as a form of handbook to guide the reader through these fascinating communities.

We cannot yet fully assess the impact Internet social networks and virtual worlds will have both on society and the manner in which individuals share information and communicate. At first view, virtual worlds may appear to be little more than highly sophisticated computer games. Whilst they undoubtedly permit a form of interaction between individuals hitherto not possible, that characteristic alone would not afford them much significance. They are self-contained environments which turn on its head traditional legal thinking.

That the law must, and indeed does, govern in-world actions is also not in question in the book. While the Internet's reach is long the law's grasp is more than equal. However, what is reviewed is how the law applies to virtual worlds. How do we direct the laws of privacy, Intellectual Property, Contract and Consumer regulation to in-world conduct? What is it in the various elements of in-world architecture which permit us to say they fall within the ambit of particular legal treatment.

If one chooses to participate in any of the virtual landscapes there are thus legal and regulatory challenges to address. The law does not prevent participation in virtual worlds but it does drag physical world concerns into the fantasy realm.

It is clear that the Internet's evolution at each phase of development is always far in advance of the market of potential adopters. This pattern has been the career of the commercial Internet from the outset. In 2000, those who recognised the medium's perfect application to retail business were correct in their analysis but sadly too far ahead of the actual consumer market to yield proper commercial return. Most failed but had they been introduced three to four years later they would undoubtedly have succeeded.

Next, the development of the medium for distributing media content. First music. Then film and television. The Internet is developing broadcast property away from television screens but once again, the ability to render digital music and movies online existed long before the disruptive transition was appreciated by rights holders and the media industry. However, once established, music and film downloads changed the consumption of media content for all time.

Most recently has come Web 2.0, the next generation of the Internet which provides enhanced levels of interaction for the user. Social networking websites are one manifestation and have taken even the most passionate of Internet evangelists by surprise by the sheer scale and speed of their adoption. They are now a permanent feature of the wired world.

Bebo, *MySpace* and *Facebook* collectively have more than 301 million users globally.

Instead of users simply consuming media content they can for the first time create their own online environment. The Internet is no longer merely a collection of website destinations. It is participative. It is a fully interactive medium which engages with a plethora of apparatus such as the Apple iPhone and Blackberry. It is this capacity on the part of users of the Internet to participate and the corresponding ability to create user generated content which is making social networks and now virtual worlds so interesting.

Virtual worlds are then the latest manifestation of the Internet's inexorable appetite for development.

Virtual worlds call for the creation of a fantasy environment or virtual self. They are the natural extension of the popularity of social networks, a three dimensional (3D) manifestation of a social life. Whether they will be regarded as the ultimate in escapism and merely futile societies, or hugely beneficial tools for corporate development and innovation has yet to be determined.

These environments are, however, poised to make the leap from the plaything of Internet enthusiasts to the conservative and exceedingly grounded life of business managers.

The concept of such online environments is hard to grasp and certainly difficult to comprehend in terms of a meaningful tool for social and business dialogue. This difficulty is, in part, explained by the initial application of virtual worlds as predominantly a form of sophisticated online games. However so called Massive Multiplayer Online Role Playing Games have forged virtual worlds in which real world businesses are rapidly building digital presences. The 3D web has arrived with major brands such as Adidas, MTV and Sky News having virtual world presence. It is a chaotic environment harnessing business opportunities and brand engagement and blurring the distinction between social networking and role play. Hilary Clinton launched her 2008 presidential campaign through a virtual world. David Milliband, as Foreign Secretary became the first senior politician in the UK to create his own avatar. Virtual worlds are not just a remarkable means of communication, they are also a territory. Sweden has opened an Embassy in one such environment.

Understanding virtual worlds requires an understanding of the user's relationship to their technology. For many people, the virtual world they inhabit is connected to their identity in the same way as the clothes they wear or the cars they drive.

The most famous of all virtual worlds is the Second Life platform. Second Life proclaims itself as 'vast digital content'. It is a privately owned San Francisco based company called Linden Labs. It was founded by Philip Rosedale, the former Chief Technology Officer of RealNetworks. Second Life was launched to the public in 2003 and in 2009 has 17 million registered users. It is free to casual users but a small monthly payment is required for land ownership. Created by Linden Lab, Second Life is more like real world and there is no game which is the key driver. It is purely about living and socialising in an alternative reality. Communication between avatars is via instant messaging, proximity-based chat and also voice. The world has a virtual currency called Linden dollars which can be purchased with real currency or earned through undertaking a virtual job or manufacturing items to sell in the virtual world. One can practice almost any occupation in-world and then the earned Linden dollars may be exchanged for real money on Second Life's currency exchange, the LindeX, at fluctuating exchange rates.

Virtual forums draw on the basic human desire to belong and express oneself. They connect people and enable a dialogue between companies and their customers.

The interesting feature about virtual worlds is that they are not restricted to being merely sophisticated social networks. Companies such as Cisco Systems and IBM are using them to engage with employees as well as existing and potential customers. Cisco Systems owns several islands in Second Life and offers public classes. Virtual worlds are not merely fantasy lands, they are areas where people can have a different kind of interaction. Cisco believes the medium offers exciting new ways to educate both employees and customers about their services by delivering information in a more interactive format.

Advertising agencies have won pitches within the virtual world and even run advertising campaigns for cars in-world ahead of their first appearance on television.

Virtual worlds offer us the opportunity to see the world not as it is but as we would like it to be. They have a significance far beyond the transient conversations they facilitate.

The law as it relates to virtual worlds is complex. Whilst there has been a great deal of new law introduced since e-commerce became a meaningful it cannot govern all issues which may present themselves in the in-world sphere. So, where no specific law applies to virtual worlds this book seeks to apply accepted legal principles to various aspects of the virtual world experience.

This approach to an understanding of how the environments will be treated under the law will prevail for some time. Such is the process of legal development that legislation must be interpreted by the courts to establish how it impacts on specific facts. This is the preserve of case law. Given the short time since the introduction of virtual worlds and indeed Internet social networks in general there is very little case law precedent.

However, there is no doubt that virtual worlds will find themselves grounded firmly in the precincts of the courts. It is only a matter of time. The law will therefore develop in the coming years.

So this book is written for anyone interested in virtual worlds and social networks whether commercially because they want to explore the possibilities such environments present, or simply for academic curiosity. Similarly, it is for anyone who wishes to participate in virtual worlds and who simply wish to venture into a new domain unlike anything the real world offers.

It is hoped that this book explains the law in as straightforward a manner as a review of such abstract environments permits. It is applied throughout in an in-world context. In this way it is hoped the reader will gain a good understanding of the legal issues which govern the expanding and fascinating environments that are virtual worlds.

Andrew Sparrow
June 2009

CHAPTER 2 Entering into the Virtual World and v-commerce Contract Formation

2.1 The Geneology of Virtual Worlds and Social Networks

In this chapter we will examine the issue of how legally binding contracts are made within virtual environments and Internet social networks. The generic term for business conducted within virtual worlds is virtual commerce or v-commerce. We will use these terms throughout the book.

To understand virtual worlds requires an appreciation of their geneology, an examination of how they operate and what features they possess.

The Internet has evolved as a universal interconnected network of audio, video and electronic text communications that blur the distinction between interpersonal and mass communication, and between public and private communication. It allows forms of communication, that were previously separate, to overlap and interconnect. The latest indications are that whilst people are spending more time online they are visiting fewer websites. People often access the same websites so many Internet websites are seldom visited and remain unknown.

Virtual worlds are the perfect manifestation of this evolution. They become destination environments for Internet users and hence fit the trend of more focussed Internet access and, above all, they are participative.

Social network websites enable their inhabitants to connect to friends and colleagues, send emails and instant messages, blog and post personal information profiles. These profiles can include photographs, videos, images and audio. Some social networks are dedicated to particular topics or groups.

Virtual world content is created in an online game like 3D digital environment. Typically they provide inhabitants with a scripting language and development environment which enables them to build new objects.

Social networks are varied but typically share certain characteristics.[1] Many social networks allow users to create a profile of themselves and 'friend' (connect with) other users. Examples include *Facebook* and *MySpace*. Users grant access to their profile to other people through 'friending'. These profiles allow people to share photographs, comments and news of events. Users can also create groups to signal through association their values or ideals. Other networks focus on specific forms of expression. For example, *Twitter* is a social network tool based around 'microblogging', and features small dispatches that are

---

1 Demos Report: *Network Citizens – Power and Responsibility at Work.*

akin to short 'status' updates – where someone is, something they have seen or a brief thought. Websites like *Flickr* focus on photos, videos or music. These have been augmented by platforms that facilitate the exchange of ideas and that help collaborative working. One of the most important features of social network technologies is that they allow inhabitants to create, map, visualise and define ideas, connections and relationships.

How are virtual worlds defined? There are doubtless many descriptions and indeed those will vary according to the precise characteristic of the particular world.

Individuals are represented within the world typically as 'avatars'. This is the inhabitant's virtual representation of himself in a computer game.

Philip Rosedale, the creator of Second Life has said virtual worlds are what we always expected the Internet to be. Cyberspace was always supposed to be full of other people, but when you are on a website, in fact there is nobody else there. A virtual world is a changeable 3D world that everybody collectively owns and which you can alter. That is what makes virtual worlds so different and what makes the experience of being there so different. Virtual worlds contextualise social encounters in a way that social networking cannot do. Without places it is hard to have activities. Rosedale says that the bowling alley or alcohol does not matter as much as the people but if you do not have the bowling alley or the alcohol it is just an empty room and no-one comes. Virtual worlds are social networks with a purpose. Games have always been a platform for engagement between people.

It is estimated that the combined value of the major virtual world economies now exceeds the Gross Domestic Product of many nation states. That value is built around the creation, acquisition and trading of virtual property and possessions. Each can be bought and sold in-world and may even be auctioned online. There is an increasing array of virtual worlds. In addition, the manner in which one participates is becoming more diverse. Most worlds are active worlds wherein participants interact with a variety of avatars both individual and corporate. However, more recently a series of private worlds have developed. These environments can be branded to an organisation's particular brand. They are in essence 'white labelled' worlds with customised orientation areas. The attraction of such environments includes the ability of a company to wholly control the fixtures and participants in-world. They can, for example, exclude competitor companies from the environment. They can configure the world so that the entire experience is the brand. By contrast, active worlds have an element of chaos because of the lack of direct influence.

Virtual worlds offer the user a much richer experience than a website. There is, of course, the ability to see each others avatars and then communicate by text. In addition, virtual worlds allow the operator to see who is looking at what part of the virtual environment – rather like being able to see which web pages are being viewed.

There are many potential business applications for virtual worlds. It is useful to briefly consider some of these before we turn to a review of how contracts can be formed in-world. For example, one can own land in-world. Indeed most virtual worlds operate on the basis of land ownership within the environment. This allows inhabitants to build, display, and store their virtual creations, as well as host events and businesses. Users can purchase land and develop their own piece of the virtual world. Typically, this is by payment of a monthly fee plus a land use fee proportional to the amount of land the user owns.

Collaborative design also lends itself perfectly to the virtual environment. Customers and partners in disparate locations can co-create a real life product or service in real time. The environment software usually provides flexible building tools to allow manipulation of geometric primitives in a simple interface. These can be stretched into new shapes, their textures and physical qualities altered. One can create objects of all kinds and sizes. It is possible to import into the environment jpegs and other standard graphic files to texture the objects one creates. Technology also enables the objects to respond to gravity, inertia, propulsion, and wind from in-world weather systems. Objects cast shadows and can appear to be illuminated by the sun.

Simulation of real life environments can be done at low cost, enabling anonymous feedback. Companies have used the virtual environment to demonstrate how it can be used to design the real world customer experience of a real world building. This included the layout of the building, systems and user interaction with corporate personnel using role play. A synthetic modelling environment can be built to test real world physical environments before building them. At the touch of a button a variety of designs can be accessed. Such collaborative design can address health and safety issues. Uses have included the design of petrol stations. The forecourt can be made transparent by the click of the mouse revealing the intricacies of pipes, pumps and tanks that the driver needs to be aware of when reversing the petrol tanker into the petrol station. Airport terminal building prototypes can be used to simulate the customer check-in procedure, role playing emergency procedures when a suspect package is found.

Marketing opportunities exist. In Chapter 6 we will consider marketing as it applies to virtual worlds in detail. Businesses can run marketing campaigns to test a real world campaign. Virtual focus groups can be set up. Product placement can be undertaken in-world as can brand positioning.

Virtual conferring and meetings are yet another feature of virtual worlds. Using the multiple communication streams of audio and video media gives inhabitants a rich experience and an environment in which to be innovative.

Learning and training within the corporate organisation can be delivered by peer to peer group communication of complex information using the 3D spatial element within virtual worlds. It is possible to train customers and employees in an immersive environment using realistic role playing scenarios to practice business processes. It is interesting to note the opinion of Sir Tim Berners-Lee, recognised as the creator of the first website and the World Wide Web who said;[2] 'What's exciting is that people are building new social systems, new systems of review, new systems of governance. My hope is that those will produce ... new ways of working together effectively and fairly which we can use globally to manage ourselves as a planet.'

Berners-Lee sees virtual worlds as credible tools and the continuance of this process of development which underpins the Internet.

It is clear whether the virtual world is active or customised for a company, there is still the ability to form legally binding contracts in-world.

The manner in which contractual relations can be forged is itself fascinating. It is possible to sell virtual world's assets purely in-world or into the real world. For example, Domino's Pizzas who are represented in Second Life, may take your pizza order in-world and deliver the actual pizza in the real world. These contracts may be between the virtual

2 Sir Tim Berners-Lee talking to BBC Online in March 2008.

world operator and its users, or between users themselves – avatar to avatar. Finally contracts may be formed between users and the outside world.

It is also possible to sell virtual world assets, for example on eBay – itself a phenomenon of modern society. One can also buy Linden Dollars on eBay. In fact, the whole process of contractual formation in the digital environment is at once easy to accomplish, and easy to bring about significant and sometimes unintended consequences.

One often thinks of contracts as weighty legal agreements signed in the physical world by the instrument of the pen. Of course the concept of contractual relations has evolved with every technological innovation from the telephone to the fax machine. Binding legal relations can be created by exchange of email, SMS text message and over the Internet by interacting with an e-commerce website.

Clearly there are many in-world interactions which do not constitute meaningful legal relations. They are not intended by the principals who direct their avatars to be anything more than a forum for fascinating exchange between individuals whose interests coincide on a virtual island. Even where the environment is populated by well-known retailers often this presence is simply to promote the brand in an otherwise baron setting.

However, well-known brands such as Dell Computers also have representation in virtual worlds. Their presence is fascinating because they are depicted as physical shops with all the associated corporate branding and product display. One's avatar moves about within the environment freely. The environment lends itself to a form of community with other avatars. One can talk to other users through their avatars about the products. Dell, for their part, can see who is looking at which of their products and in what part of the virtual shop.

Payment for products can be made in-world using Linden Dollars, for example, in the case of Second Life, or in that forum, 'round world' via a transactional website from a Second Life hyperlink generally in US Dollars. Linden Dollars are exchangeable for US Dollars.

As business, in particular, comes to adopt these most unique networks then the potential for enforceable contractual relations becomes manifest.

However, it is also clear that the very nature of virtual worlds presents a raft of new legal problems. At what point would a contract come into existence? To understand how a participant, whether business or virtual consumer, can operate safely in such worlds, it is necessary to consider how English law approaches the matter of contract formation generally. This is because these long established legal principles will doubtless apply to v-commerce and shape the way which virtual environments must be configured.

In this section we will examine these contract law considerations and see how a contract can be made in-world.

The assertion by Bill Gates in his book *The Road Ahead* that the Internet 'will carry us into a new world of low friction, low overhead capitalism, in which market information will be plentiful and transaction costs low' has proved correct. However, it is likely that not even Gates had in mind the advent of the avatar.

Virtual worlds represent a triumph of technology over the bonds which hitherto prevented instantaneous communication on a truly global scale.

Since these worlds fit within an established legal framework, so it is necessary to understand the process of contract formation.

Such an appreciation is vital to in-world business as the sheer openness of the environments can cause problems.

2.2 Creating an Avatar and Navigating the Virtual World

It is worth considering briefly how an inhabitant of a virtual world enters the environment and begins to navigate within the world.

The user must first design their in-world profile and form their avatar. Virtual worlds are essentially about personal expression and one's avatar is the most personal expression of all. The avatar is your persona in the virtual world. Despite offering almost infinite possibilities, the tool to personalise the avatar is very simple to use. An inhabitant may compile physical characteristics which usually mirror their own physical appearance. This includes choosing body shape, skin tone, hair and eye colour. They will then clothe the avatar and may select garments from a menu. Most virtual worlds employ tools to guide the user and these consist of the map which allows users to find other inhabitants and view upcoming events' information.

A search menu then permits the user to learn more about a particular event seen on the in-world map. The user may then search for it, and read its description. If it appears to be an aspect of the virtual world they find of interest they can move (or 'teleport') there.

Once the user arrives, they may find out about the other inhabitants in that section by right-clicking on anybody's avatar and choosing the 'View Profile' option to learn about them. The user can then move about the environment and this travel is graphically depicted so that points of perspective in the environment may be viewed by the user.

Typically, within a short period of time other inhabitants will approach the new users' avatar and introduce themselves.

Within this dynamic society of people, the idea is to find people with similar interests to the user. Once the user meets people they have an affinity with, it is easy to communicate and maintain contact with them.

At any time there are many events where the user inhabitant can socialise, for example, party at nightclubs, attend fashion shows and art openings or just play games. Inhabitants may also form groups ranging from neighbourhood associations to fans of science fiction movies.

The ability also exists to move between virtual world environments so that one can take on avatar and seamlessly cross multiple virtual worlds. In this way it is possible to build a cross-worlds community of users and stimulate cross-worlds interactions.

2.3 How Contract Law enters Virtual Worlds and Social Networks

So, we have seen how an inhabitant enters a virtual environment and engages others by way of an avatar. The question then arises whether contracts can be made through that identity with others?

English law requires a number of things to happen before a legally binding contract can be said to have been formed. A contract is founded on agreement. In its purest form agreement arises from offer and acceptance. One person makes an offer, another person accepts that offer. For present purposes those people may be operating through avatars but if the substance of their interaction satisfies the legal tests for formulation of viable contracts then, with certain other necessities being achieved, they can form binding relations. Every avatar, of course, has a human being sitting at a computer directing their avatar's actions.

This of course is conceptually difficult to imagine and, in fact, the practical experience in-world may still preclude the effective enforcement of a contract even though the constituent parts which are usually required may exist. For example, one of the attractions of an avatar existence is simply that one can relate in-world but never disclose one's true identity. This makes contract enforcement problematic. In addition, it might be that the avatar is directed by someone who lacks the legal capacity to form contractual relations – such as a child.

However, our review must focus on what the law demands for contract formation. There are four elements to constitute a legally enforceable contract. They are:

1. Offer.
2. Acceptance.
3. Consideration (usually payment).
4. An intention to create legal relations.

2.3.1 OFFER

An offer is a proposition put by one person (or persons) to another person (or persons) coupled by an intimation that he is willing to be bound to that proposition. The Offeror, that is, the person who makes the offer, may make his offer to a particular person, or to a group of persons or, as in the context of the Internet, the entire world. Offers made in the virtual world environment are most likely made by businesses in-world to other participants in that world, or similarly by individuals through their avatars to other individuals acting through their own avatars.

This offer may be made in writing, in the case of the virtual world this will be by in-world email, or in spoken words, or even by conduct. The first two can be grasped immediately. Often in the real world the written contract takes the form of an elaborate document with numerous clauses and sub clauses. In the virtual world however such written contracts might simply be an exchange between avatars whereby one communicates to the other by email,

'I'm selling my motorcycle for £1,000, would you like to buy it?' The response also made by email text 'Yes I would' followed by other messages culminating in an agreement to transfer ownership of the motorcycle in the real world could amount to an enforceable contract in law.

How can conduct create an offer? Well, an every day act of conduct which constitutes an offer can be found in a bus driver pulling up at a bus stop.

The intimation that the Offeror is willing to be bound need not be stated in words be they written or spoken. It may be, and frequently is, inferred from the nature of the Offeror's proposition or from the circumstances from which the proposition is made.

When you make an offer, you are expressing a desire to enter into a contract based on specified terms and conditions on the understanding that if the other party accepts, the agreement will be legally binding.

Offers can be made using almost any form of communication. Over the years, as new means of communication developed, the courts had to establish how contracts were to be formed by the use of developing mediums. From simple letter post, to the advent of the telephone, fax machine, more recently by email, SMS text, the Internet and of course through virtual world environments. In virtual worlds an inhabitant does not necessarily talk – you and your avatar type.

It is vital to consider in the context of virtual worlds, this legal explanation of what constitutes an 'offer'. English law states that if a reasonable person would interpret a particular action or communication as an offer (a readiness to bind oneself), it is an offer whether the party intended it or not.

It is therefore the appearance of an offer which is more important than actual intent. It can be seen that this is where the danger to virtual world presence exists. Careless in-world statements or poorly designed in-world representations could amount to a business making unintentional offers to other participants in the virtual world which could result in unwanted binding legal contracts once consumers (via their avatars) accept.

Offers can be of goods or services. It is an interesting question in the context of virtual worlds, what is the legal nature of 'assets' sold in-world? Aside from physical goods sold via the virtual world into the real world, virtual assets are unlikely to be characterised as 'goods'. Under English law those virtual assets are most likely to be classed as 'services'.

This distinction is significant because there is differing treatment under the law between contracts for the supply of goods and contracts for the supply of services.

If we consider the transfer of in-world assets only as between inhabitants those are unlikely to be classed as a sale of goods. They might constitute a supply of services. If one considers the actual form of what would be happening it can be seen that a digital asset within the virtual world is simply a piece of software code which enables the virtual representation of the particular asset. When a software code is usually supplied to a user, its use is granted by way of licence to use that software. For example, most of us are familiar with Microsoft products and will know that when those products are used they are being used under a standard software licence issued by Microsoft. Thus, given that in-world experiences are founded on computer programs, it follows that any transfer of digital assets must be regarded as a transfer of software code. The proper manner in which software code is made available for use is by software licence.

Now, in the case of the Microsoft or other software supplier licences, one is presented with a licence agreement which is accepted online by the user clicking on the 'I Accept' command upon installation of the software. In the case of the transfer of a digital asset in-world, whilst we have seen that it must be regarded as a software licence, there will be no in-world command which makes it clear that the transferee is being granted a licence to use the digital asset. The transfer will most likely just occur seamlessly.

Whilst the property featured in virtual worlds may be just that – virtual, it has not prevented real world money being made by individuals from transacting such property. The most notorious at the time of writing is Ailin Graef, a German woman who became a millionaire through the development of 'land' in Second Life. In the US there has been litigation in the courts in the form of a case by a Pennsylvanian lawyer, Marc Bragg, over his purchase of a large amount of online real estate which was condemned as improper by Second Life and confiscated.

2.3.2 V-COMMERCE OFFERS DISTINGUISHED FROM INVITATIONS TO TREAT.

There is a concept in English Contract law which might appear strange at first hearing but which is founded on sound reasoning and very necessary in any sales environment. In-world retailing is no exception.

It is necessary to distinguish a true offer from an 'invitation to treat' The importance of the distinction is that if a true offer is made and is then accepted the person making the offer is bound by it. Conversely, if what the person making the offer said or did is not a true offer, but merely an invitation to treat, the other person cannot, by saying 'I accept', bind the offeror and thus create a contract. Important though this distinction is, it is not always easy to make.

The contrast between the two principles can best be illustrated by the use of examples common to commercial life.

First, the tender situation. Here, the distinction between an offer and an invitation to treat is reasonably clearly seen. If a company asks a number of suppliers to put in tenders for supplying it with some particular goods or services, the company is not, thereby, making an offer to those suppliers.

Consequently, the company is not bound to accept the lowest or any other tender. It is not the company which makes the offer, the offer comes from the supplier in the form of a tender or estimate.

The next example of an invitation to treat is the display of articles on shelves in a shop. The offer is not made by the shop owner. They are only making an invitation to treat. The offer is in fact made by the customer taking the item or items to the cash desk and tendering money to purchase. That offer by the customer can then be accepted or refused by the shop. The courts take the same view of goods displayed in a shop window.

If we pursue this legal analysis into the virtual world or social network environment we may conclude that the display for example of virtual assets in-world by a virtual commerce retailer would not in itself constitute an offer for sale of those assets to inhabitants visiting the retailers island. The island site would amount to an invitation to treat. The inhabitant makes the offer to purchase the assets by approaching the island and initiating the purchase process. The in-world retailer would be free at that stage to decide whether to continue with the sale of the virtual assets, or indeed physical goods where the inhabitant is afforded the ability to teleport from the in-world environment to the in-world retailers' e-commerce website.

The same rule applies to an in-world advertisement. The general rule is that an advertisement is not an offer, merely an invitation to treat. We consider advertisements in the context of virtual worlds and social networks in Chapter 6.

For the virtual commerce business to protect itself from making unintentional offers, it therefore needs to observe the fine distinction between an offer and an invitation.

The Internet of course uses modern digital technology. It is not a closed system like telex and it offers much more through its interconnecting networks. Anyone with a PC or suitably enabled mobile phone, a modem, suitable programs and a paid up subscription to one of the Internet Service Providers (ISPs) or telecommunication companies, can gain access to the system. The user can obtain information from websites, send messages through email, and order merchandise and services.

There is a distinction however between the Internet at large and the kind of environments which are the subject of this book. Virtual worlds and Internet social networks are in many respects closed environments though they each rely on the open system which is the Internet. They are based on communities which inherently introduce a degree of restriction albeit that the numbers of participants to such environments may be millions.

The point to appreciate is that a contract need not be a detailed formal document. It is possible to form a legally binding contract by the simple exchange of email or in-world text as between avatars or between users of a social network. Whilst this is true in reality there might be arguments over the uncertainty of the precise terms in such a situation. The court may refuse to confirm an in-world contract if there are so many aspects of the purported agreement so unclear as to make the contract void for uncertainty. Nonetheless, simple in-world email or text exchange can create legal relations so care must be taken.

2.3.3 THE VIRTUAL WORLD OR SOCIAL NETWORK WEBSITE

A Website operated by a virtual world provider or social network provider is primarily a forum for interaction between inhabitants of the environments. However, if there are opportunities for business transaction – v-commerce in the case of virtual worlds, such websites also become the electronic equivalent of a shop window.

It is important the virtual world or social network operator makes it clear that its website does not constitute an irrevocable offer for sale of the various merchandise or services made available through the website.

If one contemplates the issue, if that part of the content available for sale in a virtual world or social network constitutes an offer at law then the in-world business will have no control over to whom it becomes legally bound. This would be a commercially intolerable scenario, applying to both operators of such environments and to the v-commerce retailers who occupy an island presence or are situated within a social network

By the inclusion of an appropriate disclaimer, each will ensure that it has the ability to select inhabitants and manage its supply of content, merchandise or services.

There are many practical reasons why operators of virtual worlds or social networks and the in-world retailers they host may not wish to deal with all inhabitants of their environments. For example, those inhabitants might be from several jurisdictions around the world. The social network or virtual world website may be targeted to specific audiences and it is common for companies to operate various websites if the company is international, perhaps with one site covering Europe, and another governing the US market. Thus, it is important for the operator of the environment to retain the power to accept or refuse. In this way it can decline inhabitants without the fear of being in breach of contract.

This issue of jurisdiction is important and if, for example, a v-commerce retailer only ever intends to accept in-world orders from inhabitants based in the UK it must, in its e-commerce website to which the inhabitant teleports, place a notice on that website stating that the contents of its website are for UK customers only.

2.3.4 V-COMMERCE EXCLUSION CLAUSES

Most people are familiar with clauses in contracts which seek to restrict or limit a company's legal liability in certain situations. Such devices are called Disclaimers or Exclusion Clauses. They are terms in a contract which seek to exempt one of the parties from liability in certain events. The same principles apply to what are called Limitation Clauses. These are clauses which attempt to limit, rather than wholly exclude, a party's liability. An example is a clause which states that complaints must be made within a certain period of time.

Exclusion clauses are a perfectly legitimate device in contracts between parties of equal bargaining power. In general, the courts will regard two businesses which wish to enter into a contract, as having equal bargaining power. Clearly, there are in reality, significant differences in commercial strength between businesses and many commercial dealings are entered into on terms favourable to the stronger party. That is simple commercial reality. Broadly though, the law treats both businesses as having a greater understanding of commercial transactions than say the individual consumer. The same can be said in the context of v-commerce business dealings. If an in-world company strikes a poor commercial deal with another in-world company, the courts are not likely to intervene for that reason alone.

However, there are circumstances where the courts will intervene and which actually have great relevance to v-commerce transactions. This is where the parties are unequal. Here, exclusion clauses may be unfair. The law will regard a business and a consumer as unequal parties – the business treated as the dominant party. In essence, the law says that businesses are more likely to be savvy when it comes to striking deals than the average consumer. The relative positions therefore mean that the consumer is in a potentially vulnerable capacity. For this reason in the UK, as indeed throughout the EU, consumers are afforded considerable protection when dealing with businesses. It is that policy which dictates much of the law relating to online sales to consumers and which we consider in this book in the context of virtual worlds and social networks. It is of clear application to v-commerce transactions because it is very likely the individual who controls the avatar in the virtual environment, or indeed the person who participates in an Internet social network, will be a private consumer rather than a business. Moreover, both these environments attract younger people, frequently teenagers, and so the inhabitants are also likely to be inexperienced in commercial dealings.

Online consumer trade, of course, has seen huge growth in recent years, particularly for items such as flight bookings, hotel bookings, books, CD and DVD purchases. It has fulfilled even the most ambitious expectations for e-commerce although the journey has been long and many early commercial entrants to online retailing failed along the way.

As stated, the law assumes that consumers deserve greater legal protection. It is therefore essential the v-commerce retailer appreciates who its in-world presence is targeted towards as this will determine the nature and extent of the virtual world legal terms and conditions it will operate. The same restraint also applies to the operators of virtual worlds and social networks. In Chapter 3 we consider some examples of virtual world legal terms and conditions.

Virtual worlds do not operate in a vacuum. Over many years the law has evolved. There are a number of Acts of Parliament and European Regulations which are designed to give the consumer high levels of protection when dealing with businesses. It is useful to consider these briefly. These laws are not written for v-commerce trade alone but have particular relevance to it.

2.3.4.1 The Unfair Contract Terms Act 1977

The first significant statutory attempt to regulate unfair contract terms is now more than thirty years old but still governs today. The Unfair Contract Terms Act 1977 (as amended) (UCTA) is the Act which dominates exclusion and limitation clauses and how they are to be regarded at law. The Act undoubtedly applies to v-commerce legal terms imposed on consumers and to in-world sales of goods or services.

It is first necessary to study two definitions in the Act. First, 'Business Liability' and second, 'Deals as Consumer'. Most of the Act applies only to business liability and the consumer has a specially favoured status under the legislation.

'Business Liability' is liability arising from things done by a person in the course of business or from the occupation of business premises. The latter element is of interest in the context of virtual worlds. Could a virtual island presence of a retailer be regarded as occupation of business premises?

Clearly, when this legislation was framed virtual worlds had not been conceived. The question may fall for determination in future case law but it is submitted that the better view is that the courts would not regard a virtual island on which a retailer resides, as occupation of business premises within the meaning of the Act. In any event, the first element of the definition, 'in the course of business' is more likely to bring an in-world retailer within the ambit of the Act. Clearly, even though it may be configured for trade virtually, an in-world retailer is still acting as a business.

A person 'Deals as Consumer' if he does not make the contract in the course of a business and the other party does make the contract in the course of a business. Thus, an inhabitant of a virtual world acting via their avatar may well deal as a consumer even though they do so in the realm of virtual reality.

If the v-commerce contract is for the supply of goods, there is an additional point, namely that the goods must be of a type ordinarily supplied for private use or consumption.

The Act provides various safeguards for consumers. In the case of loss or damage, an in-world retailer company cannot exclude or restrict its business liability for negligence except insofar as the terms or notice satisfies the requirement of reasonableness.

This requirement of reasonableness would operate in the context of v-commerce as follows. The term in the v-commerce contract must be a fair and reasonable one to be included in the contract having regard to all the circumstances which were, or ought to have been, known to or in the contemplation of the parties when the contract was made.

The Act lays down guidelines for the application of the reasonableness test. So, for example, when one party deals as an in-world consumer or on the in-world retailers standard written terms of business that retailer cannot:

- If it is in breach of contract exclude or restrict its business liability in respect of the breach.
- Claim to be entitled to render a contractual performance substantially different from that which was reasonably expected of it.

- Claim to be entitled to render no performance at all, except in all three cases, subject to the requirement of reasonableness.

2.3.4.2 The Unfair Terms in Consumer Contracts Regulations 1994

Further protection for consumers is contained in The Unfair Terms in Consumer Contracts Regulations 1994.These Regulations came into force on 1 July 1995.

Once again, in common with many other laws considered in this book, they have application throughout the EU as they give effect to a European Community Directive (93/13/EEC). This Directive exists to promote harmonisation of the laws of member states so as to ensure that contracts with consumers do not include terms which are unfair to the consumer. They apply to standard contracts entered into between the sellers or suppliers of goods or services to consumers and will have application to v-commerce transactions between in-world retailers and consumers acting by their avatar. Similarly, they apply to online contracts conducted between businesses and consumers within Internet social networks. The Regulations introduce a general concept of 'unfairness' in contract terms.

V-commerce contract terms are subject to a test of fairness. If they are regarded as unfair they will be of no legal effect. Regulation 5(1) states that if such terms are unfair 'they shall not be binding on the consumer'. The definition of a consumer under the Regulations is quite wide. Regulation 2(1) defines a consumer as a 'natural person who, in making a contract to which these Regulations apply, is acting for purposes which are outside his business'. This definition includes small business persons for activities which are incidental to their business. It can be seen that the Regulations will apply to v-commerce transactions. Although an individual may act through the medium of an avatar whilst in the environment, that individual is still a natural person.

2.3.4.3 The Consumer Protection from Unfair Trading Regulations 2008

The protection which consumers have under the general law within the UK and the EU extends further with the introduction of new Regulations which again have their source in the European Commission. These laws, written with the interests of consumers in the physical world in mind, nonetheless have application to the activity of in-world retailers and so we shall briefly consider their ambit.

The Consumer Protection from Unfair Trading Regulations 2008 came into force on 26 May 2008.

The Regulations state that unfair commercial practices are prohibited. If we apply their provisions in the context of Internet virtual worlds or social networks, a commercial practice is unfair if:

a) it contravenes the requirements of professional diligence; and
b) it materially distorts or is likely to materially distort the economic behaviour of the average consumer with regard to the product.

A commercial practice is also unfair if:

a) it is a misleading action;
b) it is a misleading omission;

c) it is aggressive.

The Regulations also recite what constitutes misleading actions. An in-world commercial practice is a misleading action:

a) if it contains false information and is therefore untruthful or its overall presentation in any way deceives or is likely to deceive the average consumer, even if the information is factually correct; and
b) it causes or is likely to cause the average consumer to take a transactional decision he would not have taken otherwise.

An in-world commercial practice satisfies the conditions of this paragraph if:

a) it concerns any marketing of a product (including comparative advertising) which creates confusion with any products, trademarks, trade names or other distinguishing marks of a competitor; or
b) it concerns any failure by an in-world trader to comply with a commitment contained in a code of conduct which the virtual trader has undertaken to comply with, if:

    i) the in-world trader indicates in a commercial practice that he is bound by that code of conduct, and
    ii) the commitment is firm and capable of being verified and is not aspirational, and it causes or is likely to cause the average consumer inhabiting the virtual world or social network to take a transactional decision he would not have taken otherwise, taking account of its factual context and of all its features and circumstances.

The matters referred to above include:

a) the existence or nature of the product;
b) the main characteristics of the product;
c) the extent of the in-world trader's commitments;
d) the motives for the commercial practice;
e) the nature of the sales process;
f) any statement or symbol relating to direct or indirect sponsorship or approval of the trader or the product;
g) the price or the manner in which the price is calculated;
h) the existence of a specific price advantage;
i) the need for a service, part, replacement or repair;
j) the nature, attributes and rights of the in-world trader;
k) the consumer's rights or the risks he may face.

The Regulations state that the 'main characteristics of the product' include several issues and it is worth reciting these here:

a) availability of the product;
b) benefits of the product;
c) risks of the product;

d) execution of the product;
e) composition of the product;
f) accessories of the product;
g) after-sale customer assistance concerning the product;
h) the handling of complaints about the product;
i) the method and date of manufacture of the product;
j) the method and date of provision of the product;
k) delivery of the product;
l) fitness for purpose of the product;
m) usage of the product;
n) quantity of the product;
o) specification of the product;
p) geographical or commercial origin of the product – this of course has special relevance in the context of virtual world commerce; and
q) results to be expected from use of the product.

The Regulations also define the 'nature, attributes and rights' as far as concern the in-world trader and these include the virtual trader's:

a) identity;
b) assets;
c) qualifications;
d) status;
e) approval;
f) affiliations or connections;
g) ownership of industrial, commercial or intellectual property rights; and
h) awards and distinctions.

2.3.4.3.1 Misleading v-commerce Practices

The Regulations make clear that an (in-world) commercial practice is a misleading omission if, in its factual context, the (in-world) commercial practice omits material information, or perhaps the (in-world) commercial practice hides material information, or provides material information in a manner which is unclear, unintelligible, ambiguous or untimely, or fails to identify its commercial intent, unless this is already apparent. If any of these things causes or is likely to cause the average consumer inhabitant of a virtual world to take a transactional decision he would not have taken otherwise.

The matters referred to above are:

a) all the features and circumstances of the commercial practice;
b) the limitations of the medium used to communicate the commercial practice (including limitations of space or time). This has particular application to virtual world or social network environments because by their very nature they may have inherent limitations whether in terms of graphical depiction or constraints on text.

Finally, where the medium used to communicate the commercial practice imposes limitations of space or time, any measures taken by the virtual trader to make the information available to consumer inhabitants by other means. So, perhaps the virtual retailer might also communicate information by providing a hyperlink to its full e-commerce website from the virtual world. Alternatively, it might (by obtaining and abiding by the Data Protection requirements explained in Chapter 7) send the inhabitant relevant information to the inhabitant's physical home address.

The Regulations confirm that 'material information' means:

a) the information which the average consumer needs, according to the context, to take an informed transactional decision; and
b) any information requirement which applies in relation to a commercial communication as a result of other legal obligation which apply within the EU – such as Data Protection (Chapter 7) or the E-commerce Regulations which we examine in Chapter 4.

Where a commercial practice is an invitation to purchase, the following information will be material if not already apparent from the context in addition to any other information which is material information:

a) the main characteristics of the in-world product, to the extent appropriate to the medium by which the invitation to purchase is communicated;
b) the identity of the virtual trader, such as his trading name, and the identity of any other trader on whose behalf the trader is acting;
c) the geographical address of the virtual trader and the geographical address of any other trader on whose behalf the trader is acting;
d) either:

    i) the price, including any taxes; or
    ii) where the nature of the in-world product is such that the price cannot reasonably be calculated in advance, the manner in which the price is calculated.

e) where appropriate, either:

    i) all additional freight, delivery or postal charges; or
    ii) where such charges cannot reasonably be calculated in advance, the fact that such charges may be payable;

In addition, the following matters:

a) arrangements for payment;
b) arrangements for delivery;
c) arrangements for performance;
d) complaint handling policy;
e) for products and transactions involving a right of withdrawal or cancellation, the existence of such a right.

2.3.4.3.2 Aggressive v-commerce Practices

A commercial practice is aggressive if, in its factual context, taking account of all of its features and circumstances:

a) it significantly impairs or is likely significantly to impair the average consumer inhabitant's freedom of choice or conduct in relation to the product concerned through the use of harassment, coercion or undue influence; and
b) it thereby causes or is likely to cause him to take a transactional decision he would not have taken otherwise.

In determining whether an in-world commercial practice uses harassment, coercion or undue influence account shall be taken of for example:

a) its timing, location, nature or persistence;
b) the use of threatening or abusive language or behaviour;
c) any onerous or disproportionate non-contractual barrier imposed by the trader where a consumer wishes to exercise rights under the contract, including rights to terminate a contract or to switch to another product or another trader; and
d) any threat to take any action which cannot legally be taken.

'Undue influence' means exploiting a position of power in relation to the consumer inhabitant so as to apply pressure in a way which significantly limits the consumer inhabitant's ability to make an informed decision.

It must be stated that an operator of a virtual world or social network should and most likely would feature in its in-world legal terms and conditions, and generally clear guidelines for its in-world retailers to meet these legal obligations.

An in-world retailer is guilty of an offence if:

a) he knowingly or recklessly engages in a commercial practice which contravenes the requirements of professional diligence; and
b) the practice materially distorts or is likely to materially distort the economic behaviour of the average consumer with regard to the product under regulation.

An in-world retailer who engages in a commercial practice without regard to whether the practice contravenes the requirements of professional diligence shall be deemed recklessly to engage in the practice, whether or not the virtual retailer has reason for believing that the practice might contravene those requirements.

An in-world retailer guilty of an offence under the Regulations is liable:

a) on summary conviction, to a fine not exceeding the statutory maximum; or
b) on conviction on indictment, to a fine or imprisonment for a term not exceeding two years or both.

Where an offence under the Regulations committed by a virtual retailer company is proved:

a) to have been committed with the consent or connivance of an officer of the company; or
b) to be attributable to any neglect on his part, the officer as well as the virtual retailer company is guilty of the offence and liable to be proceeded against.

Reference to an officer of a virtual retailer company includes reference to:

a) a director, manager, secretary or other similar officer; and
b) a person purporting to act as a director, manager, secretary or other similar officer.

It is a defence for an in-world retailer to prove:

a) that the commission of the offence was due to:

    i) a mistake;
    ii) reliance on information supplied to him by another person;
    iii) the act or default of another person;
    iv) an accident; or
    v) another cause beyond his control; and

b) that he took all reasonable precautions and exercised all due diligence to avoid the commission of such an offence by himself or any person under his control.

2.4 Capacity

Online games and virtual worlds are not just the preserve of adults. Young children are embracing the genre through websites such as webkinz.com where children can play online games and look after virtual pets. Most of the child focussed worlds are free to join, making their money from advertising (see Chapter 6) and by selling accessories for the pet or avatar. Large media companies have identified the potential for this pre-teenage market by adopting the tactic of controlling and exploiting the gaming environment through acquisition and ownership. In 2005 Viacom acquired Neopets, a virtual world for children for £150m. Disney's own Virtual Magic Kingdom is one of the most popular sites in terms of global web traffic. Club Penguin is another virtual world targeted at the very young.

It is clear therefore that these worlds are growing and the temptation for their owners is to market and promote their own products or those of others in-world to the children who participate.

There are, however, contextual issues to appreciate. Virtual worlds are addictive environments, rather like computer games. The question of age restrictions features large.

How does the law address this question of contracting with children in virtual worlds?

Under the English law of contract, people below the age of majority, which is eighteen, are called minors (children). The law is founded on two principles. The first, is that the law must protect the child against his or her inexperience, which may enable an adult to take unfair advantage of him or to induce him to enter into an improvident contract. This principle is on the basis of the general rule that a child is not bound by his contracts, except for the supply of 'necessaries' not likely to apply in the virtual world.

The second principle is that the law should not cause unnecessary hardship to adults who deal fairly with children. Under this principle certain contracts with children are valid.

Whilst it is beyond the scope of this book to examine the various situations where v-commerce contracts can be upheld against children, suffice it to say that the law in this sphere has equal application to virtual worlds and social networks.

CHAPTER **3**

Legal Terms and Conditions Governing Participation in Virtual Worlds

Virtual worlds and Internet social networks are highly complex environments both from the technical software perspective and as regards legal governance. In this section we will consider some of the issues which will be covered by the legal terms and conditions which seek to control participation in these worlds. The legal terms need to regulate some sophisticated concepts which we will examine below but also more routine though equally important issues. Before turning to a review of the legal terms and conditions, it is useful to describe how a typical environment will direct the new user. The virtual world or social network website will typically display details which will include a description of the environment and service. How one may participate in-world and instructions for downloading the service. Any user computer system requirements will be highlighted. The website will then set out some of the salient features of the service which may include drawing attention to its various in-world policies and guidelines. If an in-world currency is made available, a description of how that currency operates will be provided including how it may be bought and sold, trading limits and any fees which attach to its trading. Any special features of the service will be described such as for example sections of the environment which contain music, arts and culture, fashion or in-world tutorials. One of the principal attractions of a virtual world experience is the ability to own virtual land. How an inhabitant purchases that land, its pricing and fees and how virtual land auctions may be conducted will be explained. Another feature inherent in online networks of this kind is the ability to participate. There will be in-world forums and events which inhabitants may take part in and these will be explained generally.

As virtual and social network environments are complex, usually the operator of the service will provide support services and these will be described on the website together with any knowledge base which the world maintains. Other information one might expect to see will include how a new inhabitant may find a technical solution provider who will build the user's world within the environment. We will examine later the concept of virtual islands and assets which the inhabitant may own. These may in part be produced by the inhabitant themselves attendant to joining the service using the tools made available by the operator of the environment. However, more substantial in-world presence may need the services of an external software developer to design and build the assets. Finally, details of how to contact the operator of the service and its management personnel and other corporate details should be set out. We will consider elsewhere in this book the laws which impact on the information which must be provided to users.

Having described detail of the kind above, the website will then contain a section containing the legal terms and conditions.

3.1 How to Ensure Legal Terms Govern the In-world Experience

In this section we will review the principal terms and conditions which should operate to govern the participation by those who engage in a virtual world. This might include the sale of promotional material. As throughout this book, we will refer to the term avatar though, of course, that character fiction is in fact the virtual manifestation of an individual who controls its actions. For convenience of explanation we will simply use this generic term.

In Chapter 6 we examine the development of marketing products and services in-world. The brands want to reach out to these eclectic environments and find new audiences.

The manner in which merchandise must be made available to in-world visitors is prescribed by a variety of laws which many companies may not appreciate.

In the UK there are many legislative requirements which govern the information which websites must display. The full extent of these depends upon the range of services the website provides. Given that virtual worlds are complex forums with links to the e-commerce website of in-world retailers, the extent of legal control will be significant. The virtual world operator would want to gather information from its users, and it is highly likely that the website will utilise and display the intellectual property of the operator and third parties. For a website of reasonable sophistication, providing a good range of content for users, there may well be at least nine separate pieces of legislation which must be complied with before the website can meet its full legal responsibilities. These include obligations under the E-Commerce Regulations 2002, (Chapter 4); Data Protection Act 1998, (Chapter 7); The Privacy and Electronic Communications Regulations 2002, (Chapter 6); The Consumer Protection (Contracts Concluded by Means of Distance Communication) Regulations 2000 (Chapter 8); The Unfair Contract Terms Act 1977; (Chapter 2); Unfair Terms In Consumer Contracts Regulations 1999; Sale of Goods Act 1979; The Supply of Goods and Services Act 1982, and the Disability Discrimination Act 1995 (Chapter 12). In addition to these pieces of legislation there is also case law which interprets particular statutory provisions. There will be an ever increasing bank of case law decisions turning on virtual world experience over the coming years as individual and commercial use of such forums grows.

3.2 Example Clauses for a Virtual World Service

When one participates in a virtual world environment a contract comes into existence between the provider of the service and the user. This is because as we have seen, the operation of a commercial website brings with it certain legal requirements. Since virtual worlds are a form of Internet environment so to they must be governed by law. Many aspects of the service will be controlled by those legal necessities but there will be some very compelling reasons why a provider would want to draw limits to its duties in the provision of the service. The provider will want to set out clearly the basis on which the environment is offered. It will thus need to define the extent of both its legal and commercial obligations.

The manner in which this is achieved is the use of legal terms and conditions which will appear in the virtual world environment and which, if properly displayed, will be incorporated into the experience and govern the relations between provider and participant.

Different virtual worlds have a varied approached to the inhabitant's core 'rights'. For example, in terms of minimum information required of the user Disney's *Club Penguin* calls for email address and birthdate. So too Disney's *Toontown Online*, and MTV's *Virtual Worlds*. Habbo Hotel requires the same information. IMVU.com asks for email address, birth date, first and last name and country of residence. Second Life requires the inhabitant's first and last name, gender, country, birthday, email address, credit card information and/or *Paypal* account name for premium accounts.

As discussed earlier, the virtual world terms and conditions must be brought to the attention of the user before the agreement to provide access to the virtual environment is concluded in order for those terms to be validly incorporated into the contract. Under English law the most effective way this can be achieved is to require the user to click through the terms before being able to proceed further into the virtual environment. This is known as a 'click wrap' contract. The proper place for the display of the terms is at the point prior to the completion of the subscription to the service. Most virtual world websites will feature a section to be completed by the user when they first register as participants to the service. This process is now likely to be familiar to all web users. The terms can also govern access if reasonable steps have been taken to bring them to the attention of the online user before the contract is entered into. It is unclear just how that might occur but it is not safe to simply build a hyperlink on the website to the legal terms where that hyperlink appears at the bottom of a webpage requiring the user to scroll down to the page in order to even see the terms.

There is some uncertainty in the context of mobile access to virtual world websites. For example, if the virtual world operator wishes to market to a consumer base via their mobile telephones, there are clear rules it must follow. We consider at Chapter 6 how the operator must go about targeting and notifying those phone subscribers. If the promotional content produced by the operator contains an offer, for example, to buy products from virtual retailers featured in-world at discounted rates the limitation in screen size of the mobile apparatus will almost certainly prevent the display on the page of full terms and conditions. Therefore the operator might refer to the full terms in a prominent part of the webpage used by mobile phone visitors. Those terms might then be displayed on a website and the URL for that site listed in the mobile invitation. Whilst this is the only practical way to address the problem of notification of terms one can see the difficulties it presents.

The opening paragraphs of the virtual world legal terms and conditions should request that the user carefully read the terms and that by clicking the 'I Accept' button, usually appearing at the bottom of the terms, the visitor agrees to be bound by the terms. The steps necessary for the visitor to conclude the contract must be set out as required by the E-Commerce Regulations which we consider at Chapter 4.

Essentially, the terms and conditions are designed to limit or exclude so far as is possible, the legal exposure of the operator of the virtual world. It is then useful to examine the kind of issues which the operator will want to address in its virtual world terms. Certain of the terms will cover issues which are easy to grasp, others will address issues which are very important but perhaps not so obvious. We are talking here of a company which has decided to develop its own virtual world environment and offer it to general Internet users, some of them being consumers and some, perhaps, other business participants.

It is important to bear in mind that although the operator of a virtual world will wish to limit or exclude as much legal liability as possible in delivery of the service, if it is based in the UK it will be subject to extensive consumer protection legislation which afford consumers in the UK extensive implied rights. The degree to which limitation and exclusion clauses have legal efficacy depends largely on the reasonableness of such clauses. The following review of suggested clauses contains such limitations but when drafting similar restrictions it is important to have in mind this issue of reasonableness because the courts will not give legal effect to exclusions which are obviously unfair to a consumer in the overall context of the service being provided.

The terms will commence by specifying how they come to govern the use of the virtual environment. For the purposes of illustration we will call our environment 'virtualcommerce.org.uk' and this will be used throughout the description. They will state that the following terms (the 'Terms') describe the basis on which the company (the 'Provider') makes available access to its services. That making available will be conditional upon the inhabitant's (the 'User') agreement to all of the terms and conditions contained in the Terms. In addition, the User will agree to comply with any related policies which the Provider requires acceptance. Typically this will include a Privacy Policy (See Chapter 7) linked to (by way of the provided URLs) the Terms. This use of hypertext links to enable easy cross referencing of important information is quite common and perfectly acceptable from a legal perspective. Remember, we have seen that legal terms must be brought to the attention of the user, or a reasonable opportunity to see those terms afforded to the user, before a contract is concluded. The use of hypertext links achieves this satisfactorily.

The Terms will state that by using virtualcommerce.org.uk, the User agrees to these Terms. If the User does not so agree, the Terms will state that the User is prohibited from accessing or using virtualcommerce.org.uk, which may amend the Terms at any time in its sole discretion, effective upon posting the amended Terms at the domain or subdomains of its website or by communicating these changes through any written contact method it has established with the User, such as email.

It will be stated that virtualcommerce.org.uk is the multi-user online service offered by the Provider. As the service will use software to support its availability it will be made clear that, this software, together with the website and the messaging and protocols that simulate the virtualcommerce.org.uk environment, together constitute the service (the 'Service').

Virtual worlds rely for their very functioning upon the interaction of users within the environment. The essential infrastructure – the various virtual assets and islands will feature as pre-programmed features but it is the movement and participation of avatars acting under the direction of their principals which make full control over the environment impossible. Therefore, the service provider of the environment will want to make it clear in the terms and conditions that they do not control various aspects of the Service.

The terms will state that the user will be required to acknowledge that virtualcommerce.org.uk allows participants to interact online regarding topics and content chosen by users of the service, and that users can alter the service environment on a real-time basis. Usually the service provider would not regulate the content of communications between users or users' interactions with its service. The terms will state that virtualcommerce.org.uk has very limited control over the quality, morality, legality, truthfulness or accuracy of various aspects of the service.

Again, given the nature of virtual environments consisting of content provided both by the service provider and content from other participants, the intellectual property rights of each must be set clear. There will be graphics, sound effects, video, music, audio, computer programs, animation, text and other creative features of the environment which will be provided by independent content providers, and they will be provided under a licence to use the same. In addition, there will be contributions from other users of virtualcommerce.org.uk

These participants will have rights in their respective content under copyright and other applicable laws. The terms will state that such rights are not licensed or otherwise transferred by mere use of the service.

The user will be asked to acknowledge that their creation of content is not in any way based upon any expectation of compensation from virtualcommerce.org.uk. The creation of such content is only to engage in an effective way in the environment. It is not to be undertaken with a view to being paid by the service provider.

Virtual worlds usually permit a form of trading in-world. This may be between participant avatars, between the operators and the avatar, or between third party companies which advertise goods and services in the environment. Typically there will be links to that company's e-commerce website where the participant can complete an online transaction instigated in-world. In such a case, the payment method will be by the usual means of credit or debit card. However, if virtual currencies are adopted then the terms and conditions need to address how that currency is to be regarded.

The currency will usually be expressed as a limited license right available for purchase or free distribution at virtualcommerce.org.uk's discretion, and is not redeemable for monetary value from virtualcommerce.org.uk

The inhabitant will acknowledge that the service includes a component of in-world fictional currency which constitutes a limited license right to use a feature of the virtual world as permitted by Virtual Commerce. The terms will state that Virtual Commerce may charge fees for the right to use their currency, or may distribute it without charge, in its sole discretion.

The user will be required to agree that virtualcommerce.org.uk has the absolute right to manage, regulate, modify or eliminate its currency as it sees fit in its sole discretion, in any general or specific case. virtualcommerce.org.uk will make clear it will have no liability to the user based on its exercise of such right.

In the context of this virtual currency, many worlds also offer an exchange service which permits the transfer of license rights to use that virtual currency.

For the purpose of illustration we will call the exchange Virtual Commerce Exchange (VCE). VCE will administer transactions among users for the purchase and sale of the licensed right to use the virtual currency.

This kind of service, is of course by its nature complex in its execution and also in defining its basis. The terms and conditions will need to specify how VCE operates clearly.

In the context of a currency transfer the term 'sell' should be defined. For example, it might state that sell means to transfer for consideration to another participant the licensed right to use the virtual currency in accordance with the terms and conditions. The term 'buy' may be defined as to receive for consideration from another participant the licensed right to use the virtual currency in accordance with the terms and conditions.

Continuing the definitions of the constituent parts of VCE the term 'sell order' will be stated to mean a request from a participant in virtualcommerce.org.uk to list the virtual currency for sale on VCE at a requested sale price, and the term 'buy order' stated to mean a request from a participant in virtualcommerce.org.uk to match open sale listings with a requested purchase price and facilitate completion of the sale of the virtual currency.

The terms and conditions will make clear that virtualcommerce.org.uk may deny any sell order or buy order individually or with respect to general volume or price limitations set by virtualcommerce.org.uk for any reason. Similarly, virtualcommerce.org.uk may limit sellers or buyers to any group of users at any time. In addition, they may halt, suspend, discontinue, or reverse any currency exchange transaction. Such action may apply whether the transaction is merely proposed, pending or even past in cases of actual or suspected fraud, infringement of other laws, or deliberate disruptions to or interference with virtualcommerce.org.uk's service.

Virtual world environments are highly sophisticated platforms requiring significant maintenance on the part of the operating company. It will be necessary for the operator to periodically conduct scheduled maintenance. There will inevitably be instances where interruption to the service will be unscheduled.

The terms and conditions must cover this liklihood by stating that virtualcommerce.org.uk reserves the right to interrupt its service with or without prior notice for any reason or no reason. Further, it will state that no liability will arise on its part for any interruption of the service, delay or its failure to perform. The user will be required to acknowledge that it shall not be entitled to any refunds of fees for interruption of service or failure to perform. virtualcommerce.org.uk will also reserve the right at any time and for any reason to change or eliminate any aspect of the virtual world service as it sees fit in its sole discretion.

It will be necessary for the user to open an account with virtualcommerce.org.uk in order to participate in the virtual world and interact with other avatars and businesses. Thus, the terms and conditions will address this registration requirement. The user must provide true, accurate, current and complete information about themselves when they complete the registration form which will appear as part of the registration process before entering the environment.

virtualcommerce.org.uk will wish to have the right to make any inquiries it considers necessary to validate that registration data. Clearly, any company which operates a virtual world will want to protect itself and other users from fraudulent activity and so this question of the accuracy of data provided by users is very important. virtualcommerce.org.uk will want to reserve all rights to pursue legal action against any person who misrepresents personal information or is otherwise untruthful about their identity. In addition, the right to suspend or cancel user accounts registered with inaccurate or incomplete information should be reserved. Although as stated, virtualcommerce.org.uk will demand accurate data to protect its other users it will still state in its terms and conditions that it cannot guarantee the accuracy of any information submitted by any user of the service, nor any identity information about any user.

In Chapter 2 we examined the question of how age is a critical element of contractual formation and the obvious need for the law to protect children in matters of contractual relations. Virtual worlds are highly innovative and the latest manifestation of the Internet's continuing evolvement.

It is young people in general who are likely to embrace such environments more quickly not least because they are wholly familiar with the technology and are not daunted by what might appear quite complicated technical functions. Given this potential audience, the operators of virtual worlds must address the question of age profile. The terms and conditions will state that users must be over a specified age to participate in the service. There are certain virtual worlds which are only intended to be used by children, and there are others which have separate areas in the environment which are for the exclusive use of children. In each case there is a critical need to ensure that those child environments are not violated by adults misrepresenting their status. The terms and conditions will state that the user must be at least perhaps 13 years of age to participate in the service. Users under the age of 18 are prohibited from accessing the service other than in the area designated by virtualcommerce.org.uk for use by users from 13 to 17 years of age (the 'CV Minor'). Users age 18 and older are prohibited from accessing CV Minor. The terms should state that any user age 18 and older who gains unauthorised access to CV Minor will face immediate termination of any or all accounts held by such user for any area of the service.

As the Internet and hence any virtual world service is global and can (unless effective geo-filtering technologies are applied to its design) from anywhere in the world, the matter of the age of majority needs to be considered so that the terms will state that if the inhabitant resides in a jurisdiction where the age of majority is greater than 18 years old they are prohibited from accessing virtualcommerce.org.uk until they have reached such age of majority.

The terms will say that by accepting them when opening an account outside CV Minor, the user represents that they are an adult 18 years of age or older. Similarly, by accepting the terms in connection with an account for use in CV Minor, they represent that:

a) they are at least 13 years of age and less than 18 years of age;
b) they have read and accept the terms;
c) their parent or legal guardian has consented to them having an account for the use of CV Minor and participating in the service, and to providing personal information for their account;
d) finally, that their parent or legal guardian has read and accepted the terms and conditions.

It should be made clear in the terms that virtualcommerce.org.uk cannot control whether adults gain access to CV Minor and makes no representation that users inside CV Minor are not adults.

All websites which seek to offer security to their users, adopt the password system whereby the user gains access to their personal account by the use of their chosen password. The same is true of virtual worlds, virtualcommerce.org.uk will state that its users must choose an account name to identify themselves. That password however will also serve as the name for the graphical representation of the users body in-world (their 'Avatar'). The rules concerning how passwords are arrived at and utilised will be set clear in the terms. Typically, the user will be told they may not select as their account name the name of another person to the extent that could cause deception or confusion. Nor should they use a name which violates any trademark right, copyright, or other proprietary right, or one which may mislead other users, or a name which virtualcommerce.org.uk deems in its discretion to be vulgar or otherwise offensive. virtualcommerce.org.uk will wish to reserve the right to delete or change any account name for any reason it sees fit. The user will be informed they are fully responsible for all activities conducted through their account or under their account name.

The terms will state that when the inhabitant's account is opened, they must select a password and the user is responsible for maintaining the confidentiality of that password and is responsible for any harm resulting from its disclosure, or authorising the disclosure of their password, or from use by anybody else of their password to gain access to their account or account name. The disclosure of the inhabitant's password to any other person will be stated to be entirely at their own risk.

To achieve the necessary degree of security the user will be required to submit an indication of unique identity in the account registration process. This might be a credit card or other payment information, or SMS message code. When an account is created, the information given for the account must match the address, phone number, and/or other unique identifier information associated with the identification method.

Usually the inhabitant will be told they may not transfer their account to any third party without the prior written consent of virtualcommerce.org.uk.

The question of how accounts may be cancelled should be addressed in the terms and conditions. Typically it would be stated that accounts may be cancelled by the user at any time and upon election to cancel, the account will be cancelled within 24 hours. However, if the user has paid for a period in advance they will be allowed to use the remaining time.

virtualcommerce.org.uk should reserve the right at any time for any reason to suspend or terminate the inhabitant's account, terminate the agreement with the user and/or refuse any or all current or future use of the service without notice or liability to the Inhabitant. The consequences (or rather absence thereof) to virtualcommerce.org.uk of such summary termination should be stated. The user will be informed they shall receive no refund or exchange for any unused time on a subscription, any license or subscription fees, any content or data associated with their account, or for anything else.

Clearly, participation in the virtual world requires Internet access and the inhabitant will be reminded that they are responsible for all fees associated with their own Internet connection.

Next, the terms and conditions of use need to address the issue of the legal basis upon which the inhabitant of the world accesses the service. In Chapter 5 we examine how operators of virtual worlds retain value in the intellectual property rights they possess both generally and those rights connected with the software and technical configuration of the virtual environment. We consider there the applicability of the software licence to govern the use of that intellectual property. Thus, in the terms and conditions virtualcommerce.org.uk will make clear how its service is to be regarded and the terms will reflect this characteristic of a licence. The terms will say that virtualcommerce.org.uk grants the user a non-exclusive, limited, fully revocable license to use the software which virtualcommerce.org.uk has developed (or has had developed for it by a software developer) (the Software) and the service generally during the time the user is in full compliance with the terms and conditions.

Virtual worlds permit the creation of content in a variety of forms including animation, music and text. virtualcommerce.org.uk would typically acknowledge that the inhabitant will retain any and all applicable copyright and other intellectual property rights with respect to any content the inhabitant creates using the service, to the extent the inhabitant has such rights under applicable law.

However, there needs to be a legal mechanism which allows for the use of such content within the virtual environment and that mechanism is a licence granted by the inhabitant to virtualcommerce.org.uk. The terms and conditions will state that the user agrees that by submitting their content to any area of the service, they automatically grant (and they represent and warrant that they have the right to grant) to virtualcommerce.org.uk, a royalty-free, worldwide, fully paid-up, perpetual, irrevocable, non-exclusive right and license to:

a) use, reproduce and distribute the inhabitant's content within the virtual world as permitted by the inhabitant; and
b) use and reproduce (and to authorise third parties to use and reproduce) any of the inhabitant's content in any or all media for marketing and/or promotional purposes in connection with the virtual world.

The inhabitant will be able to terminate this licence, usually by notice stating their request to discontinue the distribution of their content.

Whilst the inhabitant will own the intellectual property rights in their content featured in-world, virtualcommerce.org.uk will want to have proprietary rights in the method of access to its virtual environment. The inhabitant will be informed that they do not own the account used to access the environment, nor do they own any data virtualcommerce.org.uk stores on its servers including any data representing or embodying any or all of the inhabitant's content. The inhabitant's intellectual property rights do not confer any rights to data stored by or on behalf of virtualcommerce.org.uk

Next, the manner in which the textures and environment content developed by virtualcommerce.org.uk and which represent the presentational display of the virtual world are utilised by the inhabitant, must be addressed. The terms will confirm that during any period in which the inhabitants account is active, virtualcommerce.org.uk grants them permission to create still and/or moving media, for use only within the virtual world environment, which use includes the 'textures' and/or 'environmental content' that are both created or owned by virtualcommerce.org.uk and displayed by it in-world.

In addition to the terms and conditions which virtualcommerce.org.uk operates, it will also adopt certain standards and rules which govern the user's participation and conduct in the virtual world. These rules will be posted on the website and referenced by the terms and conditions.

In addition to abiding at all times by those rules, the inhabitant will confirm they will not take any action or upload, post, email or otherwise transmit content that infringes or violates any third party rights. Next, they will not impersonate any person or company without their consent or falsely state or otherwise misrepresent affiliation with a person or company. The rules will state they must not take any action or upload, post, email or otherwise transmit content which is determined by virtualcommerce.org.uk at its sole discretion to be harmful, threatening, abusive, harassing, defamatory, vulgar, obscene, or which breaches another's privacy, is hateful, or racially, ethnically or otherwise objectionable.

As the virtual world is a software system, the preservation of its functional integrity is vital. It is a fact of computer use that viruses can be introduced via the Internet and a number of these achieve global significance if they are sufficiently disruptive. Therefore the inhabitant will be informed they must not take any action or upload, post, email or otherwise transmit content that contains any viruses, Trojan horses, worms, spyware, time bombs, cancelbots or other computer damaging programming routines intended to detrimentally interfere with, surreptitiously intercept or expropriate any system, data or personal information.

Other activity which will almost certainly disrupt the proper functioning of the virtual world service and which will be highlighted as barred by virtualcommerce.org.uk will include the inhabitant uploading, posting, emailing or otherwise transmitting any content that would infringe any right or duty under any law or under contractual or fiduciary relationship. Such content might include inside information, proprietary and confidential information learned or disclosed by the inhabitant as part of an employment relationship or under a nondisclosure agreement.

In addition, the uploading, posting, emailing or other transmission of any unsolicited or unauthorised advertising, or promotional materials, that are in the nature of junk mail, spam, chain letters, pyramid schemes, or any other form of solicitation that virtualcommerce.org.uk considers in its sole discretion to be of similar nature, will be forbidden.

Any activity which interferes with or disrupts the virtual world or servers or networks connected to it, or any attempt to gain access to any other inhabitant's account or password will be stated in the terms as reason for termination of the inhabitant's account. So will abusing or attempting to abuse, or otherwise harassing another user.

The use of the virtual world by the inhabitant will necessarily require that user to access the software provided by virtualcommerce.org.uk. The terms will confirm that the inhabitant must not introduce independent software into the environment and that the inhabitant must not create or provide any server emulators or other means that provide access to or use of the servers without the written consent of virtualcommerce.org.uk

In any software licence the licensee will be required to agree not to interfere with the software in any way or copy it. As the virtual world environment is a software application, use of which is granted by a limited licence to the user, the same requirement pertains. Thus, virtualcommerce.org.uk will require the user to confirm that they will not modify, adapt, reverse engineer, decompile or attempt to discover the source code of the virtualcommerce.org.uk software. In addition, they must not create any derivative works of that software or copy or distribute any of the written materials associated with the virtual world service. There will also be a restriction on the user charging any third party for using the software to access and/or use the virtual world service.

The whole purpose of virtual world environments is to make possible communication between inhabitants in a unique manner. Such environments are not intended to be a forum for invective. However, it is conceivable that disagreements can arise between users of the service. Given the nature of the service virtualcommerce.org.uk will not be able to monitor all in-world communications between users. It will not wish to become involved with such disputes and the terms will state that as a condition of access to the service, the user releases virtualcommerce.org.uk from all claims, demands and damages arising out of or in any way connected with any dispute the user has or claims to have with one or more other users of the service. virtualcommerce.org.uk might reserve the right, but not the obligation, to resolve in good faith disputes between inhabitants relating to the service but will not make judgments regarding legal issues or claims and any attempted resolution will have no bearing on any real-world legal disputes in which inhabitants of the service may become involved. The inhabitant will be asked to confirm that they will indemnify virtualcommerce.org.uk from any liability or claims which may arise as a result of its attempt at a resolution relating to the service.

As we have noted, one of the attractions of virtual worlds is the fact that an inhabitant can move seamlessly online between the virtual world environment and external websites perhaps operated by in-world commercial participants. So, for example, the virtual world may be occupied by a retail brand and the inhabitant may be able to walk into and through the virtual store and select goods which appear in the display. In order to complete a purchase of the goods the inhabitant may transact in-world using the currency provided by the operator of the world, or, if physical goods are to be transacted the inhabitant will exit the environment and move to the e-commerce website operated by the retailer.

virtualcommerce.org.uk will wish to exclude liability for the content of those independent websites linked to its environment. The terms will state that it is not responsible for any software used with or in connection with virtualcommerce.org.uk and that it does not control and is not responsible for any information the inhabitant provides to parties other than it. Further, virtualcommerce.org.uk is not a party to the inhabitant's agreement with any party that provides software, products or services to in connection with the virtual environment.

Clearly, the operator of a virtual world will want to be able to provide an uninterrupted service to its inhabitants. However, technical difficulties will inevitably give rise to periods when the service will be unavailable. Therefore in the terms and conditions it will be stated that virtualcommerce.org.uk does not ensure continuous, error-free, secure or virus-free operation of its service, its software or the inhabitants account. The inhabitant will acknowledge that no refunds for fees based on such a failure will be made.

As we have noted, virtual worlds are populated not simply by individuals but by businesses which take up property in the environment. These may be retailers, professional service firms or a host of other business types. Whenever a business exposes itself to the marketplace and particularly via an intermediary it will want to seek comfort on the level of financial damages it might secure in the event it suffers some loss as a result of some action on the part of an intermediary. The virtual world provider will conversely wish to avoid financial exposure as far as possible. This is because it will understand that its business inhabitants could potentially claim thousands if not millions of pounds if its virtual presence is interrupted or its reputation damaged. This is likely where the business can claim for consequential losses. These are losses which arise as a consequence of the original breach by the virtual world operator and may include lost business or damage to commercial reputation. In short, damages which may not have been foreseeable by the operator but which might have arisen because of its failure.

The terms will thus address this very important issue. They will state that virtualcommerce.org.uk will not be liable for any consequential, special, incidental, punitive or exemplary damages including without limitation, any damages for lost profits however arising out of or in connection with the service, the software, termination of the service, or suspension or termination of a users account. Usually the terms will specify a financial limit on the liability which is typically a nominal sum.

The exclusion will go further and seek to indemnify and hold harmless virtualcommerce.org.uk and, for example, its shareholders, directors, subsidiaries, employees, licensees, distributors, and independent content providers, from all damages, liabilities, claims and expenses.

We will consider in Chapter 7 the law relating to data protection as it applies to virtual worlds. The issue of data protection must be addressed in the terms and conditions by way of a privacy policy.

The extent to which the operator of a virtual world may wish to utilise the personal information of its inhabitants will depend on the commercial model it intends to operate. Whatever it intends to do, it must make that use absolutely clear in the terms. For example, it may simply keep the data for its own purposes in which case the terms will state that the personal information the inhabitant provides to virtualcommerce.org.uk during registration is used for virtualcommerce.org.uk's internal purposes only.

If it wishes to use the information for other purposes it must state that clearly and specify for what purposes. For example, the terms may say that virtualcommerce.org.uk will not give any of the inhabitant's personal information to any third party without the inhabitant's express approval except; as reasonably necessary to fulfil the users service request, for customer support, billing and credit verification services, to comply with tax and other applicable laws or as otherwise authorised by the inhabitant, to law enforcement or other appropriate third parties in connection with criminal investigations and other investigations of fraud. In the UK for example, under the Regulation of Investigatory Powers Act 2000, law enforcement and other government agencies have extensive powers when investigating illegal activity such as suspected fraud which enable the authorities against a warrant to monitor Internet communications.

Typically, virtualcommerce.org.uk will want to have the ability to track, record, observe or follow any and all of an inhabitant's interactions within the virtual world. It may share general, demographic, or aggregated information with third parties about its user base and virtual world usage. However, that information will not include or be linked to any personal information without the inhabitant's consent. In other words, it will not be biographical data, merely statistical detail.

The issue of disputes which may arise must also be addressed in the terms. Clearly, the formal legal process may apply by way of court action. The governing law should be stated as English Law with the English courts having jurisdiction. However, it is common for operators of a service to offer an alternative dispute resolution or arbitration process should a dispute, arise with a user of the service. The reasons for this are to avoid the cost of court proceedings. In most cases a dispute whilst unwelcome and frustrating from a user perspective, may not involve very significant sums of money which makes legal proceedings disproportionately expensive.

If arbitration is offered then the process needs to be set out in the terms. There are many providers of commercial mediation services in the UK with considerable experience in resolving disputes. The terms will state that a party electing arbitration shall initiate it through an established alternative dispute resolution provider mutually agreed upon by the parties. That provider and the parties must comply with rules along the following lines:

a) the arbitration shall be conducted, at the option of the party seeking relief, by telephone, online, or based solely on written submissions;
b) the arbitration shall not involve any personal appearance by the parties or witnesses unless otherwise mutually agreed by the parties. This is based purely on practical considerations since the parties may well be located far apart and only interact in-world where geography has no significance. Finally, the terms would usually state that any judgment on the award rendered by the arbitrator may be entered in any court of competent jurisdiction.

The terms will make clear that the virtual world service is operated by virtualcommerce.org.uk from the UK and it makes no representation that any aspect of the service is appropriate or available for use in jurisdictions outside the UK. Inhabitants who choose to access the service from other locations are responsible for compliance with applicable local laws

The terms will state that they contain the entire understanding and agreement between virtualcommerce.org.uk and the inhabitant. It is usual to specify that if any provision of the terms shall be held by a court of competent jurisdiction to be unlawful, void, or for any reason unenforceable, then that provision shall be deemed severable from the terms and shall not affect the validity and enforceability of the remaining provisions.

3.3 Legal Terms and Conditions Governing Third Party Virtual Retailers Featured In-world

We have considered, above, the ambit of matters most likely to be featured in the legal terms and conditions which will govern the access to a virtual world service by an inhabitant. As has been noted in that review and elsewhere in this book, virtual environments are also populated by retail brands. The degree to which such retailers are present will vary. Some brands will have very prominent island virtual stores in-world where the inhabitant may select and purchase goods both virtual and real world from that store. Others may similarly operate a virtual store presence but due to the nature of their products, may wish to require the inhabitant to migrate seamlessly from the virtual world to the retailers own e-commerce website where the actual purchase process may take place.

The manner in which the in-world retailer operates its store will determine how the legal terms and conditions will feature. The most likely and practical solution would be the transfer in-world to the e-commerce website as described above. This is because it would be difficult and certainly disruptive to the inhabitant's virtual experience if they had to navigate through legal terms in-world. It is better for that process to occur in an online environment designed to address the process. In either case, however, the inhabitant's purchase of the goods or services must not be concluded before the terms have been presented adequately.

The following review is intended to guide the reader through some of the more important legal issues which are likely to relate to an in-world retailer's terms and conditions. For this purpose we will assume that the inhabitant has been directed by hyperlink to the retailer's e-commerce website extraneous to the virtual world. We will further assume that the retailer provides physical merchandise such as the sale of DVDs and other physical matter. We will refer to the in-world retailer for descriptive purposes as Vretail.

The terms will contain the same preliminary detail as featured in the terms reviewed previously in Section 3.2. Thus, issues surrounding the importance for the inhabitant to be directed to read the terms will be common.

One issue the in-world retailer might want to consider is the supply of alternative merchandise if the product ordered by the in-world inhabitant is not available. This will depend on the type of product to be supplied and it is really a matter of how Vretail wishes to meet customer expectations. If it does want this flexibility then it should insert a clause in its Terms to allow for supply of alternative products.

We consider in Chapter 8 the requirements of the Consumer Protection (Contracts Concluded by Means of Distance Communication) Regulations 2000. It will be noted that the online customer must be told their rights under those Regulations. The place to do this and to set out comprehensively the Vretail's returns policy is in the legal terms on its website.

Vretail should state that the in-world consumer has seven days in which to return any merchandise they have purchased and this includes if the inhabitant simply changes their mind.[1] The inhabitant must be instructed to notify Vretail in writing (which of course includes email) within those seven days. Vretail must then refund the in-world inhabitant as soon as possible. However, it is open to Vretail to require the inhabitant to be responsible for the costs of return post and packaging. If this is to be the case then it must be specified in the terms – it will not be implied by the courts. Clearly, the inhabitant is under an obligation to keep the merchandise in good condition within the meantime and this must be pointed out to them.

It is useful at this juncture to remember that this consumer right to return goods without question only applies to internet sales in the EU, and there are a number of exclusions. If for example, the in-world retailer offered deals such as hotel accommodation and theatre ticket sales, in other words, where the services are to be supplied on a particular date or specific period, then the Regulations will not apply. The reason being it would clearly be unfair for an in-world inhabitant to accept such deals, and then later cancel. In such cases the inhabitant does not have the right to a cancellation period of seven days. The other exception is the making available by an in-world retailer of downloaded content such as music or film files against payment. In this instance the inhabitant cannot demand a refund or cancel the contract since the benefit has already been obtained.

It can be seen that an in-world retailer's website may be difficult to place properly in the legal environment which governs online sales. Some products available from the linked website allow the inhabitant return rights. Other items may not. It is important to take advice from a new media lawyer with an understanding of Internet issues to ensure that whatever terms the in-world retailer wishes to incorporate in its website are properly drafted. This advice should be taken early as in reality it will impact on the overall virtual world strategy to be adopted by the virtual retailer.

---

1 Consumer Protection (Distance Selling) DS Regulations 2000 (SI 2000/2334).

The other aspect in relation to returns brings into play long established consumer legislation. English law implies certain warranties into consumer contracts whether they be for the sale of goods or for the provision of services. So, for example, the goods supplied must match their description. One can immediately appreciate here how this particular matter could present problems. For example, the virtual depiction of goods in-world using computer generated graphics may well not be an accurate representation of the goods in the real world.[2] The goods must be of satisfactory quality.[3] This includes their state and condition, their fitness for purpose, appearance and finish, safety, durability and freedom from minor defects. In addition, the law implies a warranty that the goods are fit for a particular purpose, if the in-world retailer knows that purpose, except where the circumstances show that the virtual world buyer did not rely, or it was unreasonable for him acting via his avatar, to rely on the skill or judgement of the retailer.[4] All these matters are implied by law into virtual world sales of goods supplied by in-world retailers to consumer inhabitants of the service. They cannot be excluded to any extent under the *Unfair Contract Terms Act 1977*. Even if the provisions were not included in the legal terms governing the sale, the virtual world inhabitant would benefit from their effect as the terms are implied by law. Clearly, it is desirable for Vretail to address the implied warranties in the terms since as we can see, a variety of other legal requirements need to be incorporated.

However, if Vretail were supplying goods or services to another business which might be a participant in the virtual world service, the position differs. The Unfair Contract Terms Act 1977 allows for the foregoing implied warranties to be limited or indeed excluded but this is subject to the test of reasonableness. It is quite possible for an in-world retailer to target both virtual environment consumers and other businesses. This might depend upon the nature of the service being provided but, if this is the case, careful thought needs to be given to the website terms. It will always depend on the actual nature of the retailer's website and what it provides but, as a rule, two sets of legal terms would have to be drawn. Each would be accessed by a clearly worded guide notifying the virtual world inhabitant who has automatically migrated from the virtual world, which terms they must read. The inhabitant must then be forced through by way of the click wrap contract explained above. Once again advice should be taken on this issue. There is a balance to be struck between proper legal compliance and populating the virtual presence and even the linked website with an over abundance of legal terms.

We have focussed on the supply of merchandise via a linked website. The law though affords similar implied protection for in-world consumer inhabitants where the virtual retailer is supplying a service. This time the governing legislation is the *Supply of Goods and Services Act 1982*. The requirement of this legislation is simple enough to grasp, though harder to test. It is that the virtual world supplier will carry out the services with reasonable care and skill.[5] Also, where the time for the services to be carried out is not specified in the terms, but determined by a course of dealing between the parties, or

2 Sale of Goods Act 1979 Section 13(1).

3 Sale of Goods Act 1979 Section 14(2).

4 Sale of Goods Act 1979 Section 14(3).

5 Supply of Goods and Services Act 1982 Section 13.

left to be fixed in a manner agreed by the terms, the in-world supplier will carry out the service within a reasonable time.[6]

The same principle applies to the payment to be made for the services. Where the consideration for the services to be carried out is not specified in the website terms but determined by a course of dealing, or to be agreed by the parties, the in-world recipient of the services will pay a reasonable charge.[7] In view of the implied requirement, it is always better for the virtual retailer to fix the price of any services provided via its virtual world-linked website.

It is useful to note here our constant reference to consideration as opposed to money particularly in the context of virtual worlds. English law refers to a valid contract having 'consideration' as a vital constituent part of its ingredients. Without consideration there can be no contract. In the real world this is why some contracts contain a nominal sum of say £1 by way of price. This may not be the true value of the transaction but is inserted merely to satisfy the legal requirement that there be some consideration. Consideration can be money or monies' worth. It might be that a virtual world inhabitant can claim products or the benefit of services in the virtual world environment but the inhabitant must do something in return, not necessarily pay a sum of money. A contract can therefore be valid and satisfy the need for consideration in a number of forms.

Pragmatically, the most effective policy is for the in-world retailer to have a satisfactory quality management and returns policy in place as a matter of commercial good sense. The use of legal terms, particularly those which seek to limit liability, offer further control over commercial exposure which, in the context of virtual world sales, is attractive. However, to ensure the continued goodwill of those participating in the virtual world environment, first class service should always prevail.

At Chapter 7 we consider the vitally important issue of personal privacy laws in virtual worlds. We now turn to the matter of in-world data collection and how it should be specified in the legal terms by a virtual retailer. Virtual environments in common with the Internet in general have made possible the capture of data to a degree hitherto not possible. This might appear at first confusing to the reader since, in many respects, virtual worlds offer the ultimate in subterfuge. An inhabitant operating through their personal avatar can move easily around the environment and interact with other inhabitants similarly functioning without ever revealing who they are. However, as we have seen, an inhabitant must register with the virtual world operator to gain access to the service in the first place. That personal information must not be easily made available to third parties such as in-world retailers unless the inhabitant has consented to such transfer. In addition, if the inhabitant wishes to purchase goods or services from linked websites operated by in-world retailers then they will need to reveal significant personal information such as name, real world address and credit card details.

The data does not just include biographical personal information in the form of an in-world participant's name and address. Software tracking devices provide virtual world operators and retailers the ability to streamline the supply of goods and services to the inhabitant based on that inhabitant's previous buying behaviour. Recommendations as to other related purchases can be brought to the inhabitant's attention and thus, greater sales achieved by this clever deployment of technology. Indeed, this ability to gather highly

6 Supply of Goods and Services Act 1982 Section 14(1).

7 Supply of Goods and Services Act 1982 Section 14(1).

targeted information about in-world consumers may be one of the principal attractions to the in-world retailer making its content available in the environment. Virtual world markets are revealing that people have interests in subjects and items which the mass audience might find curious. However, enough inhabitants may share the interest to make in-world distribution of content to them commercially viable if the content owner can find them. Social networking websites such as *MySpace* for example have already proved hugely useful conduits for this targeted activity

As we will see in Chapter 7 in our review of the Data Protection regime, there are, however, strict controls as to the use of personally identifiable information in the EU. Those controls have huge significance to virtual world business and the in-world retailer must be cognisant of its legal obligations. The place where compliance with those Data Protection legal obligations must be achieved, is the linked website Terms.

CHAPTER **4**

The Minimum Content the Law Requires for Virtual World and Social Network Websites

4.1 The Electronic Commerce (EC Directive) Regulations 2002

There is now a plethora of virtual world environments and many of these are becoming trusted brands with high standards of customer care. However, with the growth in sophistication of online use, many other virtual world services will become available by a range of companies.

In 2002, in response to a growing concern that consumers might become unwitting victims of virtual businesses which operate only online and who cannot be traced if they do not honour their obligations, the European Union (EU) introduced a set of Regulations. These are designed to provide consumers throughout the 27 member states more comfort when buying goods or services over the Internet. This protection only applies to consumers who visit commercial websites but the requirements which the Regulations set down clearly dictate how any business website must operate including virtual world environments.

In the UK the Regulations are called the *Electronic Commerce (EC Directive Regulations 2002 (FI2002No2013))*. They transpose the main requirements of the EU *E-Commerce Directive (2000/31/EC)* into UK Law.

4.2 Overview

Every company which operates a virtual world website must comply with the Regulations if that virtual world offers merchandise or services. So too must any e-commerce websites which may be linked to the virtual world. Failure to comply can lead to prosecution by the relevant authorities.

The E-Commerce Regulations (the Regulations) were introduced to encourage greater use of E-Commerce by removing barriers across Europe and enhance consumer confidence by clarifying the rights and obligations of business and consumers when dealing online.

The Regulations also seek to promote the single market in Europe by ensuring the free movement of 'information society services' across the European Economic Area. That area, of course, includes the 27 member states of the EU together with Iceland, Norway and Liechstenstein. The term, 'information society services' is defined in the Regulations as covering 'any service normally provided for remuneration, at a distance, by means of electronic equipment for the processing (including digital compression) and storage of data, and at the individual request of a recipient of a service'. Essentially it means all commercial on-line services. Virtual world services and Internet social networks, although not envisaged when the Regulations were framed, will fall within their ambit since most virtual environments possess, as we have seen elsewhere in this book, a commercial dimension. In this chapter we will replace the term 'information society services' with virtual world and social networks as the same may be said to be interchangeable. It is submitted that although at the time of writing virtual world forums have not directly fallen for review under the terms of the Regulations, they are nonetheless subject to their provisions.

The Regulations have particular relevance to a virtual world if it advertises goods or services on-line. This includes:

- via the Internet;
- on interactive television; and
- by mobile telephones.

The Internet and mobile phones are the primary means of access to virtual forums.

The Regulations cover a number of aspects of electronic trade including provisions for the national law that will apply to online services

Also, they clarify the information a virtual world service provider must give to its online users. These details include discounts and offers which might feature in-world and which are offered by the service provider, and how to conclude contracts on its website.

The Regulations also set out limitations on a virtual world service providers' liability for unlawful information it unwittingly carries or stores in the environment.

If a virtual world operator wishes to sell merchandise or render some service via its website it must meet its legal obligations enshrined in the Regulations. Non-compliance has consequences. For example, an inhabitant of the service who purchased goods from the virtual world may cancel their order. They may seek a Court Order against the service provider. They may also sue the service provider for breach of statutory duty if they can demonstrate that they have suffered loss because of its failure to comply with the Regulations.

If a virtual world service provider operates a website which does not comply with the Regulations there are penalties which, in addition to the financial consequences, would also cause considerable damage to goodwill. Allied to the Regulations are the *Stop Now Orders (EC Directive) Regulations 2001*. These permit The Director Generals of Fair Trading and Trading Standards Departments in the UK to apply to the Court for a *Stop Now Order* if the service providers failure to comply with the Regulations 'harms the collective interest of consumers'. The Stop Now Order requires the service provider to immediately cease operation of its virtual world and take it off line. When one considers that the website is the only means by which a virtual world can exist it can be seen that a Stop Now Order is a very severe penalty. The virtual world must remain offline until the corrective work has been completed. Given the significant financial loss that could ensue from the enforced shut down it is obviously important for the service provider to ensure its virtual environment complies with the Regulations at all times.

The Courts also have the power to order the publication of corrective statements with a view to eliminating the continuing effects of past infringements. Failure by a virtual world service provider to comply with a Stop Now Order could result in its being held in contempt of court. The consequence of that might be a fine and/or imprisonment of its principal officers or Directors.

There are a number of organisations in the UK which can enforce the Regulations. Examples include Trading Standards Departments, the Office of Fair Trading and the Independent Committee for the Supervision of Standards of Telephone Information Services (ICSTIS). It is important to appreciate that the risk of being identified as being in breach of the Regulations is high. Any inhabitant who might visit the virtual world can report the service provider to the appropriate body with a view to, for example, the Trading Standards Department then taking action against the virtual world service provider.

The E-Commerce Regulations also impact the question of whose law will apply to in-world cross border commercial activity. The Regulations liberalise the provision of virtual world services in two key ways. First, they require a UK established virtual world service provider to comply with UK laws even if it is providing the service in another member state. In other words, the UK established virtual world service provider will have to comply with UK law even if it is providing its services to, for example, German inhabitants.

The Regulations also prevent the UK from restricting the provision of virtual world services from another member state in the EU. In essence, there is nothing to stop, for example, a French virtual world operator based in Paris from providing virtual world services available in the UK and targeted towards UK inhabitants of virtual environments.

However, these rules are subject to a number of qualifications and exclusions. We examine later the importance of specifying which country's law will govern the operation of a virtual world service. The Regulations also include the freedom to choose the law which applies to a virtual world service and specify certain contractual obligations with regard to contracts made via virtual environments.

The Regulations do not however deal with the jurisdiction of the Courts, that is, which Court will hear a cross border dispute between, for example, a virtual world operator based in the UK and an in-world retailer company based in Spain.

4.3 The Regulations in Detail

The Regulations specify certain minimum information requirements and these may be divided into three categories.

4.3.1 MINIMUM INFORMATION REQUIREMENTS IMPOSED ON VIRTUAL WORLDS

One still sees commercial websites operated by companies in the UK which provide only a mobile phone number or email address as the contact information of the operator. This limited data contravenes the E-Commerce Regulations.

Regulation 6 requires the general information to be provided by a person providing an information society service. It states that a person providing a virtual world or social network shall make available to inhabitants of the service and any relevant enforcement authority, in a form and manner which is easily, directly and permanently accessible, the following information:

a) the name of the provider of the virtual world or social network;
b) the geographic address at which the provider is established;
c) the details of the provider, including its electronic mail address, which make it possible to contact it rapidly and communicate with it in a direct and effective manner;
d) where the provider is registered in a trade or similar register available to the public, details of the register in which the provider is entered and his registration number, or equivalent means of identification in that register;
e) where the provision of the service is subject to an authorisation scheme, the particulars of the relevant supervisory authority;
f) where the provider exercises a regulated profession:

    i) the details of any professional body or similar institution with which the provider is registered;
    ii) its professional title and the member state where that title has been granted;
    iii) a reference to the professional rules applicable to the provider in the member state of establishment and the means to access them; and

g) If the virtual world is making available merchandise or services via its environment to inhabitants, it will almost certainly fall within the VAT threshold. If so its VAT Registration number must be published on the website.

(2) Where the provider of a social network or virtual world refers to prices, these shall be indicated clearly and unambiguously and, in particular, shall indicate whether they are inclusive of tax and delivery costs. This requirement only applies where the operator itself makes available such merchandise or service. If its various in-world retailers are the only organisations which do so, then it is they who must comply with the E-Commerce Regulations.

4.3.2 COMMERCIAL COMMUNICATIONS PROMOTING THE VIRTUAL WORLD

The Regulations impose an obligation on the operator of a virtual world or social network to provide clear information in any electronic communications which are designed to promote (directly or indirectly) its service or image. The Regulations define 'commercial communication' as a 'means a communication, in any form, designed to promote, directly or indirectly, the goods, services or image of any person pursuing a commercial, industrial or craft activity or exercising a regulated profession, other than a communication:

a) consisting only of information allowing direct access to the activity of that person including a geographic address, a domain name or an electronic mail address; or
b) relating to the goods, services or image of that person provided that the communication has been prepared independently of the person making it (and for this purpose, a communication prepared without financial consideration is to be taken to have been prepared independently unless the contrary is shown)'

Examples of such electronic communications would include emails advertising the virtual world or social network environment. In Chapter 6 we examine the broader requirements the virtual world operator must adhere to in terms of its online advertising and promotion. The E-Commerce Regulations build on those.

Regulation 7 states that the provider of a virtual world or social network shall ensure that any commercial communication provided by it and which constitutes or forms part of its service shall:

a) be clearly identifiable as a commercial communication;
b) clearly identify the person on whose behalf the commercial communication is made;
c) clearly identify as such any promotional offer (including any discount, premium or gift) and ensure that any conditions which must be met to qualify for it are easily accessible, and presented clearly and unambiguously; and
d) clearly identify as such any promotional competition or game and ensure that any conditions for participation are easily accessible and presented clearly and unambiguously.

Regulation 8 goes on to say that the provider of a virtual world or social network shall ensure that any unsolicited commercial communication sent by it by electronic mail is clearly and unambiguously identifiable as such as soon as it is received.

So, the operator must provide clear identification of the person on whose behalf the communication is sent. For example, the email header might read *'Unsolicited Commercial Communication sent on behalf of* virtualcommerce.org.uk *Ltd'*

4.3.3 IN-WORLD ELECTRONIC CONTRACTS

We noted in Chapter 2 in relation to the formation of online contracts that the method by which a contract must be created over the Internet is subject to a number of requirements. The E-Commerce Regulations add to those more general stipulations. Whilst we refer here to the operator being under a duty, that only applies if the operator itself is entering into the contract with its inhabitants once in-world. If, as is also likely, it is an in-world retailer entering into the contract then it is that retailer which must comply. The essential information which a virtual world operator or in-world retailer must provide to the inhabitants of the environment is described below.

Regulation 9 sets forth the information to be provided where contracts are concluded by electronic means. It states that, unless parties who are not consumers have agreed otherwise, where a contract is to be concluded by electronic means a service provider shall, prior to an order being placed by the recipient of a service, provide to that recipient in a clear, comprehensible and unambiguous manner the following information:

a) the different technical steps to follow to conclude the contract;
b) whether or not the concluded contract will be filed by the service provider and whether it will be accessible;
c) the technical means for identifying and correcting input errors prior to the placing of the order; and

d) the languages offered for the conclusion of the contract. It is likely that the virtual world provider operates the environment across many jurisdictions or targets certain features of the service to particular countries. If this is the case an indication of the languages which are offered by the provider to conclude the contract must be displayed.

In addition, unless parties who are not consumers have agreed otherwise, a service provider shall indicate which relevant codes of conduct he subscribes to and give information on how those codes can be consulted electronically.

The Regulations also say that, where the service provider provides terms and conditions applicable to the contract to the inhabitant, the service provider shall make them available to him in a way that allows him to store and reproduce them. In effect, print them.

It can be seen that in-world commerce will be subject to the provisions of the Electronic Commerce Regulations. They will govern commercial transactions between in-world retailers and inhabitants of the environment who are consumers. They will cover commercial transactions between the operator of the virtual world and the inhabitant or operator of a social network and its subscribers where those user or subscribers are consumers.

In other words, there must be clear guidance in-world as to how the contract to purchase, for example, a laptop from a computer retailer is completed. We have seen in Chapter 3 how in-world legal terms and conditions govern relations between provider and consumer inhabitant and how such terms must be clicked through before the inhabitant can conclude the purchase. The Regulations state that the point at which they will be legally bound must be made clear to the inhabitant. There can be no ambiguity. Further, the in-world retailer or operator must provide confirmation of whether the contract will be filed by the company and whether it can be accessed by the inhabitant.

Even today, the method which consumers, whether in virtual worlds or simply online in general, must adopt to purchase goods or services is quite cumbersome. The purchaser must physically type their name, address, credit card details and other necessary data. Whilst most websites automatically remember this detail when the inhabitant returns to make further purchases, it is a process which can give rise to input errors. Therefore, the Regulations require that a clear identification of the technical means to enable its online customers to correct any inputting errors must be shown.

However, there is an exception to the above requirements for full information to be provided in relation to a contract. The Regulations state that those requirements shall not apply to contracts concluded exclusively by exchange of electronic mail or by equivalent individual communications. In the context of a virtual world, it may be that individual inhabitants acting via their avatars agree to transact and enter into a contract. That exchange may well be by text exchange in-world. In this scenario, it would appear that the Regulations will not apply. Neither would the email exchange between consumer subscribers to a social network.

There are other requirements imposed by the Regulations and which will apply to in-world commercial transactions and contracts concluded within social networks.

Regulation 11 deals with the placing of the order. It states that unless parties who are not consumers have agreed otherwise, where the recipient of the service places his order through technological means, a service provider shall:

a) acknowledge receipt of the order to the recipient of the service without undue delay and by electronic means; and

  i) the order and the acknowledgement of receipt will be deemed to be received when the parties to whom they are addressed are able to access them; and
  ii) the acknowledgement of receipt may take the form of the provision of the service paid for where that service is an information society service.

b) make available to the recipient of the service appropriate, effective and accessible technical means allowing him to identify and correct input errors prior to the placing of the order.

So, for example, when the virtual world subscriber enters into an online subscription with the operator it is necessary for the operator to acknowledge receipt of the subscription request without undue delay and by electronic means. Similarly, where any contract is entered into in-world between the operator and an inhabitant, or an in-world retailer and inhabitant, or between a retailer within a social network and a subscriber to that network, each such transaction must be acknowledged in the above form.

We examined in our review of online contracts generally in Chapter 2 the distinction between an offer and an invitation to treat and the dangers of sending an automatic electronic bounce back message to enquirers. It is therefore very important when adopting the form of electronic acknowledgement required by the Regulations that the text of that acknowledgement makes it clear that the acknowledgement is not a formal Acceptance of the approach made by the would be subscriber.

Once again however, this obligation does not apply to contracts concluded exclusively by exchange of electronic mail or by equivalent individual communications. Thus, the in-world text exchange between avatars will not be caught by the provision, nor would the email exchange between consumer subscribers to a social network.

Regulation 13 sets out the liability of the service provider which fails to adhere to the requirements outlined above. The provisions shall be enforceable, at the suit of any recipient of a service, by an action against the service provider for damages for breach of statutory duty.

If an in-world retailer or operator of the environment or indeed a retailer within a social network fails to comply with the requirements about acknowledging an order then the consumer inhabitant or subscriber to the social network has the right to rescind the contract.

Regulation 15 provides where a person:

a) has entered into a contract to which these Regulations apply; and
b) the service provider has not made available means of allowing him to identify and correct input errors in compliance with regulation 11(1)(b), he shall be entitled to rescind the contract unless any court having jurisdiction in relation to the contract in question orders otherwise on the application of the service provider.

It is important to remember that all these requirements embodied in the Regulations relating to in-world electronic contracting apply to any virtual world operator which advertises its service via the Internet, mobile phone or interactive television.

4.3.4 THE OBLIGATIONS ON A VIRTUAL WORLD OPERATOR UNDER THE E-COMMERCE REGULATIONS.

There are technological constraints which the Regulations recognise, in delivering the information which a user of a virtual world must receive. For example the 160 character limit on a mobile text message, may mean that the virtual world operator may not be able to provide all the information required by the Regulations. As the use of sophisticated 3G mobile phone services increases there are likely to be more tie ins between operators of virtual worlds and the mobile phone networks. Virtual environment promotion on 3G phones is an effective marketing strategy. Commercial experience to date suggests that phone subscribers are happy to access social networks on their phones. However, to expect detailed legal terms to be available on the screen of the mobile phone is unrealistic. Therefore the information requirements outlined above will be met if the information is accessible by other means.

If the potential inhabitant decides to subscribe to the virtual service via their mobile phone, the virtual world operator should be able to satisfy its requirements if it places the relevant information on its principal website.

Given that virtual worlds are Internet based environments they inevitably are prone to the disruption which can on occasion affect networks. Temporary interruptions to online services do arise from time to time. We saw in our review of the virtual world operator's service terms and conditions why it is important for the company to exclude liability for occasional transient disruption to its virtual service. The Regulations also appreciate that temporary interruptions to the availability of information are essential, for example for maintenance purposes, or unavoidable, for example if the computer system crashes because of a virus. Such interruptions will not place the operator of the virtual service automatically in breach of its legal obligations.

That said, the need for a robust Internet service is going to be of prime importance to the operator. Any unforeseen downtime or interruption to the online environment is going to cause annoyance to its inhabitants who are likely to be unforgiving when it comes to poor in-world functionality, or no functionality at all. Virtual world inhabitants which are hard to secure can be easily lost as a result of downtime. This means that the relationship between the virtual world operator and its hosting company is key. Usually, the penalty levied against a hosting provider for downtime is by way of service level credits. These are financial penalties which trigger upon the hosting service being unavailable for any length of time. They are usually measured in terms of minutes against prescribed time frames with fixed cost consequences. This issue is addressed in Chapter 3.

It will be clear to the reader that virtual world services are grounded firmly in real world legal constraints. The information requirements summarised above are in addition to other legal controls. These include the *Consumer Protection (Contracts Concluded at a Distance) Regulations 2000*. Those Regulations, among other things, require the virtual world operator to provide a description of its service, details of any guarantees offered and full details of its inhabitant's rights to cancel a subscription.

The website terms and conditions applicable to the virtual world operator's online service must be made available in a way which allows the inhabitant to store and reproduce them. It is considered that this requirement will be satisfied if inhabitants are able to save the terms and conditions onto their computer and subsequently print them out.

One important legal protection afforded to ISPs is enshrined in the Regulations. It is an issue which has presented itself time and again since the commercial Internet became a reality. The E-Commerce Regulations limit the liability of ISPs who unwittingly carry or store unlawful content provided by others in certain circumstances. If a virtual world operator wishes to strike a deal with one of the ISPs for making available the environment via the ISP, the ISP will almost certainly include a confirmatory clause in the Agreement excluding their liability for certain content. The question is, however, could the operator of a virtual world service themselves be regarded as Internet Service Providers (ISPs)?

In many respects they are similar. They merely provide the environment for inhabitants to operate. The sheer wealth of content and in-world relations and transactions means that meaningful control on a minute by minute basis by the operator is impossible. Therefore, is it reasonable to hold operators of virtual worlds liable for matters which might occur in-world over which they have no influence? If virtual world operators are considered to be ISPs then they can claim exemption for such liability (subject to certain requirements such as a refusal to remove unlawful content once notified it exists in-world). If they are not to be regarded as ISPs they cannot claim this exemption. It is submitted that the better view is that virtual world operators are akin to ISPs and therefore they should be afforded the same umbrella protection. This does not mean however that they can claim complete immunity. They will still be under a duty to take down or bar access to inhabitants who are conducting unlawful activity in-world if notified of the same. Obvious examples include criminal actions by inhabitants but a likely activity will be defamatory statements made in-world by inhabitants. This subject is considered fully in Chapter 12.

4.3.5 LIABILITY OF INTERNET SERVICE PROVIDERS FOR CONTENT TRANSMITTED OVER THEIR NETWORKS

Internet Service Providers face an array of potential legal liabilities simply because their role makes them vulnerable to being victim of unlawful activity at the hands of a person or persons who use their service. One major area of difficulty is that of defamation and this issue is very important in the context of Internet social networks and virtual worlds. The Electronic Commerce Regulations cover this form of liability but also govern a much wider ambit of liability. In Chapter 12 we examine how the Regulations operate with regard to defamatory content which sits within a social network or virtual world. However, in this chapter we are only concerned with a review of the Electronic Commerce Regulations in their totality and so we will consider here what they say on the issue of liability of information service providers.

The Regulations implement for the UK the Directive on Electronic Commerce, issued on 8 June 2000: Directive 2000/311EC of the European Parliament and Council. It was made clear in the recitals that one of the objectives was to remove: 'existing and emerging disparities in Member States' legislation and case law concerning liability of service providers acting as intermediaries'.

This was necessary in order to avoid them preventing the smooth functioning of the internal market – in particular by impairing the development of cross-border services and producing distortions of competition. There is recognition that service providers may be obliged on occasion to act in order to prevent or stop unlawful activities. It was clearly thought desirable that the position should be made as clear as possible. The definition in regulation 2(1) which incorporates article 2(a) of the Directive states that an 'information society service' connotes: 'any service normally provided for remuneration, at a distance, by electronic means and at the individual request of a recipient of services'.

Regulation 17 is very important in the context of liability generally of those who provide Internet services such as ISPs. The regulation forms the bedrock of the legal treatment of ISPs. It deals with the concept of 'mere conduit'. The section states that where an information society service is provided which consists of the transmission in a communication network of information provided by a recipient of the service or the provision of access to a communication network, the service provider (if he otherwise would) shall not be liable for damages or for any other pecuniary remedy or for any criminal sanction as a result of that transmission where the service provider:

a) did not initiate the transmission;
b) did not select the receiver of the transmission; and
c) did not select or modify the information contained in the transmission.

The acts of transmission and of provision of access referred to in the first paragraph include the automatic, intermediate and transient storage of the information transmitted where:

a) this takes place for the sole purpose of carrying out the transmission in the communication network; and
b) the information is not stored for any period longer than is reasonably necessary for the transmission.

Thus, ISPs, for example, are not liable for the content which resides on their network. The basis of this principle is that the sheer volume of information which passes across networks means that those who operate the networks cannot possibly know what that information might comprise. Thus, if the information is unlawful for any reason, the provider of the service is not automatically liable.

The next principle which the Electronic Commerce Regulations capture is the process of Caching. Regulation 18 states where an information society service is provided which consists of the transmission in a communication network of information provided by a recipient of the service, the service provider (if he otherwise would) shall not be liable for damages or for any other pecuniary remedy or for any criminal sanction as a result of that transmission where:

a) the information is the subject of automatic, intermediate and temporary storage where that storage is for the sole purpose of making more efficient onward transmission of the information to other recipients of the service upon their request, and
b) the service provider:

    i) does not modify the information;
    ii) complies with conditions on access to the information;
    iii) complies with any rules regarding the updating of the information, specified in a manner widely recognised and used by industry;

iv) does not interfere with the lawful use of technology, widely recognised and used by industry, to obtain data on the use of the information; and
v) acts expeditiously to remove or to disable access to the information he has stored upon obtaining actual knowledge of the fact that the information at the initial source of the transmission has been removed from the network, or access to it has been disabled, or that a court or an administrative authority has ordered such removal or disablement.

A further issue dealt with by the Electronic Commerce Regulations is that of Hosting. This of course is a concept familiar to most people in the context of the Internet. Regulation 19 states that where an information society service is provided which consists of the storage of information provided by a recipient of the service, the service provider (if he otherwise would) shall not be liable for damages or for any other pecuniary remedy or for any criminal sanction as a result of that storage where:

a) the service provider:

   i) does not have actual knowledge of unlawful activity or information and, where a claim for damages is made, is not aware of facts or circumstances from which it would have been apparent to the service provider that the activity or information was unlawful; or
   ii) upon obtaining such knowledge or awareness, acts expeditiously to remove or to disable access to the information; and:

b) the recipient of the service was not acting under the authority or the control of the service provider.

It can be seen that the law does provide a high level of protection for those providing Internet social network or virtual world services if such services are regarded as constituting 'information society services'.

We examine whether this might be the case later in Chapter 12.

However, because virtual worlds and social networks are relatively recent online manifestations coming into existence after the Electronic Commerce Regulations were drawn, there are questions of how they ought to be treated at law.

In Chapter 3 we examined the typical contract terms and conditions which users of Internet social networks and virtual worlds will be asked to accept when they join the service. Those terms cover a variety of issues but as seen, deal with the question of legal liability of the operator of the social network or virtual world in a number of circumstances. The Electronic Commerce Regulations approach such terms and conditions as follows.

Regulation 20 sets out the position in a provision entitled 'Protection of rights'. It states that there is nothing to:

a) prevent a person agreeing different contractual terms; or
b) affect the rights of any party to apply to a court for relief to prevent or stop infringement of any rights.

So, the Regulations do allow for the operator of a virtual world or social network to incorporate its own terms and conditions as it sees fit. Those terms and conditions will however always be subject to the provisions of the Unfair Contract Terms Act 1977 and other legislation dealing with the requirements of reasonableness.

In this book we focus on the civil laws which impact on the operation of virtual worlds and social networks rather than the criminal law. However, one item within the Electronic Commerce Regulations which is of relevance in the current review is Regulation 21. This provides a defence in criminal legal proceedings against an Internet Service Provider and sets out the burden of proof. It applies where a service provider charged with an offence in criminal proceedings arising out of any transmission, provision of access or storage falling within Regulation 17, 18 or 19, relies on a defence under any of Regulations 17, 18 and 19. Where evidence is produced which is sufficient to raise an issue with respect to that defence, the court or jury shall assume that the defence is satisfied unless the prosecution proves beyond reasonable doubt that it is not.

We have noted the need for notice to be provided to the operator of a virtual world or social network where it is alleged that unlawful content is featured in-world or within the network.

Regulation 22 deals with the question of Notice for the purposes of actual knowledge. It states that in determining whether a virtual world or social network service provider has actual knowledge for the purposes of regulations 18(b)(v) and 19(a)(i), a court shall take into account all matters which appear to it in the particular circumstances to be relevant and, among other things, shall have regard to:

a) whether the service provider has received a notice through a means of contact made available in accordance with regulation 6(1)(c); and
b) the extent to which any notice includes:

    i) the full name and address of the sender of the notice;
    ii) details of the location of the information in question; and
    iii) details of the unlawful nature of the activity or information in question.

We examine in Chapter 12 how the courts have interpreted these Regulations and approached the general issue of liability of ISPs for content transmitted over their networks.

CHAPTER 5 Protecting and Exploiting Intellectual Property Rights in Virtual Worlds and Social Networks

5.1 Background

Virtual worlds are fascinating. A significant element of their legal status is that of the Intellectual Property Rights they embody. This is a complex area of law and in many respects virtual worlds have not been fully examined by lawmakers in connection with the treatment of such rights. So, in this chapter we will look at the issue from a variety of perspectives and much of that analysis will be predicated on a review of current legislation and case law which, whilst not framed specifically for virtual world environments, nonetheless has clear application.

Intellectual Property Rights which protect the value of creative ideas, are more vital than ever. Knowledge capital, more than physical capital drives the success of the economy.

The legal regime which protects Intellectual Property must strike a balance between creating incentives for innovation, without limiting access for follow-on innovators. At the same time, there still needs to be proper enforcement of rights against infringers. In the digital world these requirements are not easily accomplished.

Virtual worlds carry a variety of exposure to intellectual property not simply as software applications but also in the content which appears within the environment. For example, one use of the environments is in the entertainment sphere. A number of television production companies are exploring virtual worlds to deliver their content since they are all about entertainment and storytelling. Virtual worlds highlight how the way they can deliver their content is changing. Virtual worlds are an interface which allows content providers to render an intuitive environment which permits interaction between inhabitants of that three dimensional (3D) environment.

In this chapter we will examine how the concept of intellectual property, which is often difficult to grasp, sits within the even more complicated environment that is a virtual world.

This is a complex area of law but one of great significance. There will undoubtedly be cases in the future which turn on how a virtual world platform is to be regarded in terms of intellectual property assets. In addition, as the technology and its commercial potential and adoption increases, there will be ever more variants of virtual worlds, and issues of alleged copyright infringement will arise more frequently. For example, one developer may argue that another has infringed the copyright in his virtual world asset. The other may refute the claim. The way which the parties' lawyers will argue their case and which any court will determine the issue, will be to strip the overall works into component parts. The claimant developer will seek to demonstrate that the virtual world image comprises various elements which each attract copyright protection in their own right. They will attempt to claim as many facets of protection as possible in order to strengthen their overall argument. The defendant will need to reject each strand of argument. Thus, in this section we will take some time to review all angles which relate to a virtual world as a piece of copyright work. It must be stated that at the time of writing, there is no reported English case law on the issues to be discussed here. That is simply a feature of how new the concept of virtual environments is, and the modest use of it by business at this time. Litigation is beyond the means of most individuals when it comes to issues of ownership of intellectual property rights. It is business which usually places commercial value on intellectual property rights, so, as business begins to adopt virtual environments, the likelihood is that claims will increase and case law precedent will be forged.

It is therefore important to assess the known legal landscape in which virtual worlds sit because that will enable us to judge with some confidence how a court might approach the question of intellectual property rights in virtual environments.

Virtual worlds lend themselves to creativity. In theory, one can imagine something one moment and bring it to life the next. Almost everything in the virtual world is inhabitant-created. In addition, one can usually see what other in-world inhabitants are building in real time, and also browse the items for sale on the community websites linked to the virtual world.

One tends to think of computer games as relatively recent technology. However, the earliest computer games were created in the 1950s for the purposes of playing on industrial mainframe computers. The very first of these called, *Tennis for Two,* which possessed mass entertainment potential, was invented by American physicist William Higginbotham. The game allowed players to move a dot on an oscilloscope screen backwards and forwards. It was developed for Open Day visitors to the US nuclear research laboratory at Upton, New York with the intention of amusing them.

The development of modern telecommunications technology made possible what is now known as Massively Multiplayer Online Role-Playing Game (MMORPG). Although in the 1980s it was feasible for some games to be played by multiple computer users connected by a data line, the high costs associated with the technology ensured these games never achieved mass market penetration. It took modems and network cards to become standard features of personal computers for multi user environments to become practical.[1]

New media offers a range of ever more sophisticated platforms on which a company may make available its products or services. From television on mobile phones and portable games players, videos for iPods, broadcast mobile television and WiFi TV, the plethora of delivery methods each afford a particular opportunity using the respective technology to best effect. They are all forms of digital content – which means any form of content that is capable of being recorded in a computer readable form (that is, a series of ones and zeros). Digital technology is used for recording, reproducing and distributing information. As a result of the superior reproductive quality of digital formats and fast

1 Paul Gottlich, Institute of European Media Law, Saarbrucken, Brussels).

and cheap methods of delivering or accessing digital files such as broadband Internet access and 3G mobile telephony networks, digital content will replace analogue systems such as broadcast television, radio and video.

Why should virtual worlds be immune from the affairs of business? If it were, it would fly in the face of all other Internet experience. The early phase of the Internet was not characterised by e-commerce but it was only when that potential was realised did the Internet become a mainstream channel for business and consumers. Mobile phones did not start life as apparatus to access products. However, their development came to answer the needs of business. Blackberry devices enable near comprehensive ability to take business data such as email, diary and database information wherever the user travels. 3G services allow for the consumption of video and advertising media.

Whilst the concept of a virtual environment probably excluded business as a feature of the experience, it is business in its various forms which will bring the greatest advances and adoption of virtual worlds.

In each of the platforms described the need to protect the intellectual property rights of the company which makes its products or services available is paramount.

5.2 Copyright in Virtual Worlds

At the centre of all questions about rights in digital content is copyright. This is the right directed at the protection of creative endeavour. It also happens to be the most suitable intellectual property right for the fast moving environment of the online and on-demand world. It is low on bureaucracy and cost simply because the right arises automatically in qualifying works and requires no registration process. Copyright is based on a readily understandable concept which is if you have not copied, you have not infringed. Further, copyright is fairly international in its application.

The law in the UK is framed by statute and regulations and so in this chapter we will review the principal statute and regulation which governs copyright. However, law is also contained in the cases which so often interpret particular statutory provisions. It is thus case law which augments statute and such cases serve as precedents for other parties faced with similar circumstances.

The first question which arises is, in a virtual what is a virtual asset?

At its core a virtual asset is really a collection of ones and zeros. It is a digital image and its depiction in a computer graphical form is not 'goods' as such. If an in-world inhabitant uses *copyright* in connection with a virtual asset which the inhabitant has produced, is that inhabitant infringing the *copyright*?

The virtual asset may certainly be conceptually similar but one can begin to see the problem in law.

It is therefore important to review some of the cases which have been determined recently in the sphere of copyright in so far as it relates to computer programs and also books. Such a review will give the reader a good understanding of how the courts approach often complex issues of this kind. In addition, by considering these cases we can relate them to the virtual world concept and thus gain a reliable indicator as to how the courts are likely to approach copyright in virtual worlds over and above the legal treatment which exists in copyright legislation.

Copyright does not protect ideas themselves but rather their expression.

For example, if a company, or the virtual world development company engaged by it, devised a concept for that company's staging in a virtual world which was unique at the time as an idea, the mere idea itself could not be something which that company could protect by copyright. Perhaps the idea involves the ability for an avatar to move seamlessly between a variety of virtual world environments and for those worlds to be capable of viewing each other from a certain vantage point within those worlds just as one can view neighbouring office blocks from the window of one's own business. It might be that another company has the same idea in the context of a virtual world presence. Neither company could claim copyright in the idea of pan virtual world visibility.

However, how each company brings about the reality of their idea by technical configuration or design of their virtual world is what may attract copyright protection. Inevitably ideas must be given expression and it is to that expression that the law affords copyright.

If the computer code by which the idea for the virtual environment is converted into a functioning presence therein has been developed as an original piece of work it could gain copyright protection. It might even be capable of Patent protection if it is sufficiently unique.

There is often a difficulty for the courts in determining where a mere idea ends and where the expression of that idea begins.

Another potential problem and one which could easily fit the production of a virtual world environment is where a series of ideas taken together can amount to a substantial part of a copyright work. In the example above, the seamless transition from one virtual world to another is an idea. The ability to view other worlds from the confines of a virtual environment is another idea. Independently, they cannot gain copyright protection. Together, they just might.

Another concept which has come before the courts and which has particular relevance to our subject is the matter of 'look and feel'. This is a nebulous concept and one which can be explained by reference to a website.

A website is a combination of computer code, design and the text, images and other content which it incorporates, all being brought alive by the functionality of the website.

It is clear law that copyright exists in the text featured on the website and in the images such as photographs which appear on the website. Indeed, it is not uncommon for websites to use high quality photographs which are library pictures, the copyright for which is maintained by a photo agency such as Getty Images. Such agencies have vast libraries of photographs over which they have proprietary rights and which they seek to licence to users. These pictures might be of business men and women, for example, sitting in a board room. They are typically used by companies for their own marketing purposes, perhaps in brochures or other corporate material and often on their websites. On occasion, these photographs are used without the consent or licence of Getty Images on websites and quite often innocently. The Internet makes possible the easy transfer and transmission of photographs even if unauthorised. Getty have copyright in the photographs and can seek damages from those who use them even if the infringement is innocent.

The look and feel concept is however much more difficult to substantiate and even define but it is increasing in importance.

Perhaps the general functionality of the website taken in conjunction with the particular approach to graphical depiction might amount to a particular look and feel. Whilst virtual worlds will undoubtedly all share certain common features such as the use of avatars, it is possible a virtual world design could contain this feature of look and feel.

There are many new challenges to traditional legal treatment of copyright with the advent of virtual worlds. For example, just what responsibility carrier services should bear for ensuring that content does not infringe rights is the subject of a continuing debate between the content owners and service providers. In general, Internet Service Providers (ISPs) and telecommunication companies are protected by an exemption from liability for infringement if they only provide the facilities through which such content is distributed but do not themselves play a role in choosing, editing and displaying that content. There is a compelling policy rationale to this. If the providers were held liable it is unlikely the world wide web would have evolved to its current vital role as it would have been stifled by legal claims in the courts. The opposing argument is that if their commercial success is in some part reliant on the availability of unauthorised content via their services, they should bear some liability too.

Another challenge to copyright enforcement is finding and preventing those who take advantage of a copyright holders content without paying for it. For example, the uploaders of large volumes of music. It is often difficult in practice to trace such people although in the UK it is possible to obtain a court order to determine an Internet Protocol (IP) address of an infringer in order to trace their identity in the case of unlawful activity. The fact remains that many of these people may be based in territories where the law is weaker or more difficult to enforce.

In the context of virtual worlds another problem exists with established legal approach to copyright. Over the years terms such 'reasonable', 'non-commercial' and 'substantial' have been adopted by the courts although these expressions are not embodied in any legislation, rather having been built up in case law. Given that virtual worlds are environments in which inhabitants may move about and use copyrighted material to varying degrees of a variety of kinds such terms become interesting to test. Suppose an avatar wears an Yves St Laurent shirt to aid recognition by other participants. Imagine if an in-world island used by an inhabitant as a base in the environment plays a well known piece of music as visitors enter the domain, or displays an excerpt from a film on screens in that domain. Such uses may enhance the experience of other inhabitants but in fact will be infringements of copyright. In these instances questions such as the reasonableness of the use, whether it is purely non-commercial or constitutes a substantial infringement will be matters of fact in each case. The point to appreciate is that in the virtual world there may be an argument that greater latitude should be employed by the courts in defining these terms because virtual lands demand rich multi media content in order to function. Without the combination of music, moving images, sophisticated computer graphics which might themselves be depictions of well known brands, the user experience is poorer.

Consider also the ability to receive and immediately re-transmit to other inhabitants of a virtual world, a digital radio broadcast. This could, for example, involve a UK radio show being received by users based in New York. Can such an activity be properly described as copying? It certainly still represents an infringing act because it is using content in an unauthorised manner.

A virtual world operated by a business will contain many elements, each of which will attract copyright protection. In-world text, graphics, moving images, character depiction, advertisements, and data – all possess the ability to be safeguarded by the law. The fact that they might exist in a virtual sphere does not render their importance any less significant.

For example, in some virtual worlds one can view digital screens which come pre-loaded with videos. The question might be whether those in-world displayed videos are properly licensed for such display?

Star Wars producer George Lucas has significant interests in online gaming. In some virtual worlds one can buy Star Wars digital assets such as cruisers featured in the movies. Such images and graphical depiction ought, it follows, to be protected by copyright laws which would then restrict the use of valuable image portrayal.

Other examples include sporting merchandise such as football team shirts which of course carry great value as marketable commodities. The use of images or virtual graphics featuring Rolex watches would not be immune from legal protection.

Thus, the suggestion that there is no such thing as copyright on the Internet is clearly misplaced.

Copyright is a negative right. It is a right to restrain others from exploiting work without the owner's consent.

Copyright is governed by the *Copyright, Designs and Patents Act 1988* which came into effect in 1989. Section 1(1) of that Act states that copyright may subsist in the following types of work:

a) original literary, dramatic, musical or artistic works;
b) sound recordings, films, broadcasts or cable programmes; and
c) the typographical arrangement of published editions.

For a literary, dramatic, musical or artistic work to qualify for protection it must be original. The work needs to be novel or unique, it only has to originate from the writer. This means it must not be copied from any other work and it must embody a minimal degree of skill, judgement and labour.

Section 5A(1) states that sound recording copyright can subsist regardless of the medium on which the recording is made or the method by which the sounds are reproduced or produced.

To gain the protection of the Act one must be a 'qualified person'. There are three ways in which to be so qualified.

First, one must be a British citizen or domiciled here or, if a company, incorporated in England and Wales.

Alternatively the work must be first published in the UK. Here lies a problem with the Internet. It is not easy to be clear as to which country a work is said to be first published.

The third route is where the work is a broadcast or cable programme and is made or sent from the UK. Here again, problems can arise with the Internet.

However, it is rare for a work in the UK not to attract copyright protection because it has not met the above tests for qualification.

The 'author' is the person who creates the work, for example, the developer of the virtual world. The author though is not always the 'owner' of the work. Ownership may be assigned to, for example, the business which has engaged the developer to design the virtual world.

The matter of how long a copyright work lasts is now dealt with in the Copyright and Related Rights Regulations 2003 which are considered in detail below.

5.3 The Convergence of Media and Technology and How that Impacts Copyright in Virtual Worlds

In this book there is frequent reference to the convergence of media and technology and this is the issue which, in many instances, is causing the law difficulty. The convergence of traditional broadcasting and digital media is forcing the worlds of the Television, the PC and the mobile phone together. There are significant challenges and opportunities for any company making available, and licensing, material across these new media channels.

In a very short period of time people are learning to use mobile devices to watch television, play games and listen to music. Laptops can be turned into televisions via services which stream content from cable or satellite boxes over the Internet. Indeed new laptops are really media centres. They have high definition screens enabling the user to watch film and television programmes with little diminution of quality. The mobile phone industry is starting to deliver television channels over its wireless networks.

As virtual worlds grow more sophisticated and the design of game worlds more realistic, the more comparable they become to other forms of realistic audiovisual representation, such as film and television. The greater the similarity between a game and a film involving interactivity, the greater the possibility that the game could be protected as a film work.

The question might then be, what would such a work consist of and how might the copyright be held?

The issue of convergence presents difficulties in legal treatment. This is because comparable services, such as virtual worlds and interactive audio visual services, would be subject to comparable laws one might think. But they are not. The Audiovisual Services Directive for example contains provisions for all such services. However, it also stipulates that online games are excluded from its scope. Do, therefore, the core characteristics of virtual worlds differ from other types of audiovisual services? Certainly, virtual worlds stem from the world of software development and, therefore, when considering their place in the legal landscape, one typically approaches them from a perspective of software development and licensing. Indeed much of the legal protection afforded to virtual worlds as featured in the terms and conditions adopted by operators of those environments are heavily slanted toward this form of treatment (see Chapter 3).

Whilst this approach has, as its core, a sensible direction, a wholly unambiguous legal framework for virtual worlds is yet to be established. There are arguments for protecting virtual worlds not merely as works of software but also as audiovisual works. This is because virtual worlds may qualify as audiovisual media services on grounds not just of presentation but also of their inherent characteristics.

This legal treatment is important because it shapes the new business models which virtual worlds offer. The computer program could be protected either as software or as a film.

5.3.1 THE SOFTWARE DIRECTIVE AND THE COPYRIGHT DIRECTIVE

There are two European directives which have direct impact on how virtual worlds might be treated as works of intellectual property. Directive 91/250/EEC on the legal protection of computer programs is known as The Software Directive.

Directive 2001/29/EC on the harmonisation of certain aspects of copyright and related rights in the information society, known as the Copyright Directive, each give the European Union Member States a legally binding duty to provide protection to computer programs. The Software Directive sets the standard in this regard and the Copyright Directive complements it.

The Copyright Directive is enshrined in English law as The Copyright and Related Rights Regulations 2003 and we consider its provisions later in this chapter.

We will first test virtual worlds against the Software Directive in particular to see how the law approaches virtual environments.

5.3.2 THE PROTECTION OF VIRTUAL WORLDS AS COMPUTER SOFTWARE [2]

A virtual world consists of a computer program, the underlying concept of the environment, the design of the world, the characters in it and its multimedia representation in the form of graphics and sound. A computer program is an item of software and its various elements can secure copyright protection.

Internationally, the concept of protection for software is reflected in the World Intellectual Property Organisation Copyright Treaty (WIPO Copyright Treaty – WCT) in association with the Berne Convention for the Protection of Literary and Artistic Works as revised on 14 July 1967 ('the Berne Convention') and the Agreement on Trade-Related Aspects of Intellectual Property Rights (TRIPS).

The Berne Convention does not expressly identify computer programs as works but they are nonetheless protected as works of language by the non-exclusive nature of the list contained in Article 2(1). Computer programs enjoy protection under Article 5(1) of the Berne Convention.

Directives 91/250/EEC on the legal protection of computer programs (the 'Software Directive') and 2001/29/EC on the harmonisation of certain aspects of copyright and related rights in the information society (the 'Copyright Directive') give the Member States of the European Union a legally binding duty to afford protection to computer programs – the Software Directive setting the standard in this regard and the Copyright Directive complementing it.

The term 'computer program' as used in the Software Directive implies protection for computer programs in every form. The Directive affords program authors the right of permanent or temporary reproduction and the rights of translation, adaptation and reproduction of the programs results, as well as the right of distribution to the public of the original computer program or copies of it.

The Software Directive does not contain a definition of 'computer program'. When the Directive was drawn up it was decided to omit a definition in order not to restrict new developments. Thus, virtual worlds, which are a relatively recent software development,

---

2 Online Games from the Standpoint of Media and Copyright Law, by Paul Gottlich October 2007, *Legal Observations of the European Audiovisual Observatory*, Issue 2007–10.

will come within the ambit of the Directive. Therefore virtual worlds, inasmuch as they comprise data, printed matter or preparatory design materials or source codes enjoy protection from identical copying.

Another issue is whether the Software Directive covers a program's internal structural characteristics from imitation. Article 1(2) suggests a distinction between content and form by stipulating that protection will not extend to the ideas and principles underlying a program. In the context of virtual worlds this means that specific elements of content, for example the virtual environment's concept, its graphical layout and its methods of use, all of which influence the program code, are not protected. This might even extend to the 'virtual world engine', which is developed from the virtual world concept and substantially determines the program structure, which might also lie beyond the scope of copyright protection.

Because the definition of software in the Directive is so wide, it might mean that the Directive provides protection to the audiovisual form in which a virtual world is produced insofar as it regards the audiovisual elements and the program collectively as a work.

Article 1(2) states that protection is given to the expression of a computer program in any form. This could mean that the audiovisual representation of the program as it appears on the computer screen and is heard through the speakers, is included as a form of expression of the program.

The Directive does not afford protection to the interfaces. Interfaces are the components of a computer program that enable interaction between the software and the hardware and between the software and the user. For example, the virtual world environment will almost certainly have a command menu which controls sound, graphics and music. That menu constitutes the interface and it thus does not therefore attract copyright.

However, it would not be safe to rely upon a broad interpretation of the Directive to permit us to say that the audiovisual representation of a virtual world enjoys protection. This is because the Directive requires computer programs to be classed as literary works within the meaning of the Berne Convention so that the program enjoys protection as a work of language. That is, in the form of source code – language being the means of expression. Therefore, extending the protection to the program's audiovisual representation, would conflict with the logic of copyright law.

5.3.2.1 Case Law on the Protection of Virtual Worlds as Computer Software [3]

It is useful to consider some cases under English law. The first cases *Nova Productions Ltd v Mazooma Games Ltd* and *Nova Productions Ltd v Bell Fruit Games Ltd* involved copyright infringement in computer programs and in particular video games based on the theme of the table game of pool. The argument of look and feel was raised in the case which was difficult to mount given the perceived similarities between the visual outputs of the works concerned.

Nova Productions Ltd made an arcade game called *'Pocket Money'* which was based on the game of pool. Mazooma Games Ltd was the maker of a rival video game called *'Jackpot Pool'*. A third party, Bell Fruit Games Ltd made a video game called *'Trick Shot'*.

3 Online Games from the Standpoint of Media and Copyright Law, by Paul Gottlich October 2007, *Legal Observations of the European Audiovisual Observatory*, Issue 2007–10.

Nova contended there was an infringement of copyright and in its argument made the following points:

First, infringement of its artistic copyright, based on the visual appearance of the output, which meant the graphics displayed to the user.

Second, infringement of its literary copyright based on the computer program which meant the software code and preparatory design material for the software code.

Finally, infringement of its dramatic copyright as its computer game could be considered a dramatic work.

In essence, Nova were saying that whilst the defendant companies had not directly copied the software code of *'Pocket Money'* that code had nevertheless been infringed because of the alleged similarity between the visual appearance of each game.

When the case first went to court the Judge held that most of the features in Mazooma's games had not come from Nova's game and that none of them had been copied in the way they had been implemented in Nova's game.

With regard to the artistic works the Judge said that, although the individual frames were artistic works, each game actually looked and played differently. The similarities only existed in that each game featured a pool table, balls and a cue. The Judge held that although certain aspects of Mazooma's games were derived from *'Pocket Money'* the copying that had taken place was not sufficient to be classed as copyright infringement. There had simply been a combination of general ideas and principles which underlie a computer program but which were not protected by copyright law. It was held that although there could be no substantial infringement based on the individual frames, separate copyright protection could still be given to the series of still frames which demonstrated the in-time movement of the cue and power meter.

As far as the dramatic works argument, it was first held that there was sufficient unity within the game for it to be capable of performance, as the sequence of images differed each time the game is not capable of performance before an audience, therefore it could not amount to a dramatic work.

Nova's argument in respect of infringement of its literary copyright concerning the non-textual copying, that is, the look and feel element, also failed initially. It was decided that the similarities in the outputs of the programs did not mean there were similarities in the software.

Nova appealed the court's decision to the Court of Appeal in relation to the artistic and literary works only. In respect of artistic works, Nova argued that copyright existed not only in the individual frames of the graphics but also in the series of frames. The court, however, rejected this and held that a series of still images was not anything more than a series of frames, so each would have its own copyright and nothing more. This was on the basis that a series of stills was just that. Further, a series of graphic works is a series of graphic works, not a single graphic work in itself. Thus, the argument on artistic works failed as the approach argued was outside the Copyright, Designs and Patents Act 1988. It was held that copyright attached to an individual image and there was no additional copyright in a series of those images.

An interesting example in the context of our current review of virtual world implications was given in the case. Cartoon frames showed Felix the cat running over a cliff, looking down and falling. This would not be infringed by a cartoon by Donald Duck doing the same thing. It was also stated that copyright in moving images is protected by copyright in films. If Nova's argument was correct then the series of still images which provides the illusion of movement would itself create a further kind of copyright work protecting moving images. This, it was held, was far beyond what the legislation intended. Finally, it was held by the Court of Appeal that even if Nova had succeeded on the first point of their argument they would have failed at the second stage as there was not reproduction of a substantial part.

Nova also failed on its argument about literary copyright infringement. The reason they failed was as follows. It was held that protection was being sought for ideas and not their expression. Nova had relied on an earlier case where the Judge held that a copyright work may express certain ideas which are not protected because they have no connection with the literary, dramatic, musical or artistic nature of the work. The other proposition is that certain ideas expressed by copyright work may not be protected because, although they are ideas of a literary, dramatic or artistic nature, they are not original.

Nova argued that the ideas which were copied did have a connection with the nature of the work and should therefore be considered but this was not accepted by the Court of Appeal. It was stated that idea of what a computer program should do was insufficiently related to the nature of the program and was not part of the skill and effort protected by this type of copyright.

The court said that not all of the skill which goes into a copyright work is protected and clarified that an idea consisting of a combination of ideas is still just an idea, and not an expression of ideas and that which had inspired the defendant's game was too general to be regarded as a substantial part of Nova's game. Finally, the literary argument on copyright failed on the ground that what was found to have inspired some aspects of the defendant's game is just too general to amount to a substantial part of it. It said that there are ideas which have little to do with the skill and effort expended by the programmer and do not constitute the form of expression of the literary works they relied upon.

Previous court decisions had determined that, where an idea is sufficiently general, then even if an original work embodies it, the mere taking of that idea will not infringe. But if the idea is detailed, then there may be an infringement. It is a question of degree.[4] The argument based on literary copyright infringement raised by Nova also failed on the basis of the nature of copyright in computer programs. Making a computer program that emulates the functions, business logic and intended results of another, but which does not involve the copying of the program source code is not an infringement.

In another case *(Navitaire v Easyjet)* the court stated that two completely different computer programs can produce an identical result, not a result identical at any level of abstraction. This is so even if the author of one has no access at all to the other but only to its results. Thus, there can be no copyright infringement in a computer code based on any similarity in the visual output from that code.

This principle has particular application to a virtual world animation. It may be that what is depicted in the environment in terms of graphical representation of items, buildings and other assets, is similar to other virtual environment treatment. However, provided the underlying software code which has produced the two similar worlds is different, there will be no copyright infringement. Mere emulation of the virtual world is not sufficient to amount to a copying.

Another argument used by Nova in its claim was that if they failed in their action there would be no effective protection for games against copying where a party copies

4 *Ibos Computers v Barclays Mercantile.*

the rules of a game but not its graphics. The consequence of such a stance, Nova claimed, would amount to a stifling of copyright. However, it was contended by Mazooma that not all things are covered by copyright, that most if not every work is, to some extent, influenced or derived from other works. So it is very important that copyright is not allowed to intervene to stifle the creation of works that are actually very different, as the individual games were in that particular case.

It can be seen that an application of the principles set down in the Nova case affords a high level of latitude in the creation of virtual worlds. The courts are unlikely to become involved where two or more virtual worlds appear very similar whether that similarity is based on their graphical appearance, or even the concept upon which they might be based.

In our example of the idea for functionality of a virtual world connected with the ability to transfer from one world to another seamlessly, or the capacity to view other worlds from the point of orientation in one world, might be treated as follows in the courts. If two developers of virtual environments each have the same goal for achieving the functionality as described, the latter version of the two in terms of production, will not be regarded as having copied the first. The same may be said even if the second version to be launched contains similar graphical appearance to the first.

The only manner in which the second world could incur the hostile treatment of the courts would be if the second world had utilised the software source code upon which the first was constructed.

It is said by the courts whenever asked to determine cases of this kind that if protection for such general ideas were given by the law, copyright would become an instrument of oppression rather than an incentive for creation which it is intended to be.

The Novas case highlights how hard it is to bring a case against a defendant based on copying of the 'look and feel' of a virtual world.

The court decisions referred to above also make clear that it will be necessary to identify specific well defined and low level features of the work that have been copied and, in turn, prove that these features are not in fact commonplace in the industry concerned.

Thus, there are undoubtedly going to be features of any virtual world representation which will be common to most, if not all, such environments. At its most basic level, the use of avatars in each world is such a common application. Perhaps even the way the avatars appear to move within the world on the computer screen is another area which would be regarded as so common a feature as not to attract copyright protection.

The interesting thing about our review of the court cases above is that even if a software developer devised a very clever way in which avatars could be seen to communicate with each other, perhaps actually using accurate lip movements mirroring those of their human principals, that in itself would not give the developer copyright protection. It may well provide them with a market advantage in commercial terms for as long as they possessed the unique capacity to create such movement. However, if another developer then produced the same representation of communication for avatars in-world, that other developer will not have infringed the work of the first.

Another issue to consider is the true 'author' of a software program. Which means the physical person who created it, that is, the programmer. If a computer program is created by an employee under the terms of his or her employment and in the absence of any agreement to the contrary, all rights in the program automatically transfer to the employer under a principle called as cession legis. However, under a pure contractual relationship, the author's rights do not transfer automatically. The principle of cession legis, does not extend to contractual as well as employer – employee relationships.

In the environment which is a virtual world, it is possible inhabitants could acquire joint copyright in the actual computer program. This might be because, by virtue of the tools made available in the environment, the inhabitant has the ability to create wholly new individual environments, objects and characters. This is an interesting issue because, whilst the inhabitant will not be able to show a 'cost' to himself for the development, what cannot be denied is that the actual program code is generated through his creative input. Indeed, the creative processes which are deployed are exactly the same as normal programming which uses a set of design tools. It is the way the tools are applied that effects the transition into a game. The inhabitant using the tools establishes the audiovisual sequences of events and the ultimate program code. So, do the inhabitants of a virtual world, using the tools, become co-authors of the virtual world program?

There might be two scenarios which relate here. In the first, the inhabitant has made his or her own creative contribution except that the contribution of the virtual world engine, in the form of the tools used, is still recognisable. The inhabitant might acquire copyright in the adaptation of the program. In the second case, the inhabitant has drawn upon the multiple potential of the tools to create something that the programmer could not have anticipated. In this scenario, the inhabitant would acquire his or her own copyright.

The most likely view is that the inhabitants of a virtual world are creating only small sections of an in-world program – not the virtual environment itself. However, it is likely that cases will turn on their own facts and the possibility of joint authorship being held to apply in certain circumstances cannot be ruled out.

5.3.3 THE PROTECTION OF VIRTUAL WORLDS AS FILMS

If a virtual world can be classed as a film or audiovisual work, it might be eligible for wider ranging protection which extends to its audiovisual representation. Clearly, it is understood that copyright protection relates to film works. The question whether a virtual environment might be protected as a film depends on how the concept of 'film' is defined. A 'film' is a cinematographic or audiovisual work or moving images, whether or not accompanied by sound.

The Audiovisual Services Directive had its origins in 1989 and was then called the Television Without Frontiers Directive. The reasons for it were that the term 'film' tended to be understood in a traditional sense associated with existing circuits of exploitation. Almost every film was shown initially in cinemas and only subsequently could television rights be exercised. It was to extend this narrow conception and embrace other types of work that the term 'audiovisual work' was used. The original Directive thus recognised a non-exclusive definition of audiovisual work as including everything from feature films and films made for television to series and documentaries.

It is helpful to review the definition of audiovisual work and examine whether a computer game can be protected as a cinematographic work or as moving pictures. A cinematographic work is not merely a compilation of the works necessary for its production, that is, a screenplay, storyboard, music and original work of literature. It is a type of work in its own right, for which individual creativity is required. When one seeks to protect such a work, one is not viewing it as separate components, such as the music and images. One is looking at it in terms of the actual film in totality.

In the case of a computer game, the creativity lies in the translation of the game idea into a playable audiovisual form. The manner in which a cinematographic work comes into being, typically a sequence of 25 images per second, is not relevant to its protection as a film. The defining factor is the impression created of a moving image. Therefore, the protection extends to films created on computer. Most computer games today comprise moving images and so on this basis, a computer game attracts protection as an 'audiovisual work'.

If we now look at virtual world environments the same analysis may be undertaken. Whilst it may be the case that the imagery featured in-world may not be as sophisticated as that in a computer game (at least in terms of a basic avatar depiction) the environment still consists of moving images. Thus, on the face of it, a virtual world could secure protection as an audiovisual work.

However, the issue may not rest there. Could a further distinction be brought to bear between film and virtual worlds?

A traditional film constitutes a closed system. The various scenes such as action and dramatic development can not be altered to any significant degree. In contrast, a virtual world allows for an entirely dynamic operation. Individuals, acting through their avatars, may move freely about the virtual geography. They can determine where they go, who they encounter and thus, participation is highly interactive. The question might then arise whether protection of cinematographic works extends only to unalterable sequences of images?

One view is that a virtual world is not film because it offers the potential to generate different sequences of images. To counter this argument, it could be said that to assert that because an in-world inhabitant determined the order of the action and thus produced his or her own film is tenuous. This is because inhabitants cannot select individual sound and image sequences and combine them at will. All they can do, through their decisions in the course of the environment, is to influence the output of individual variants already determined by the virtual world's software creator.

The only artistic creation is that of the creators and not the inhabitant. The precise content of the in-world journey as experienced by the inhabitant as they traverse the geography is immaterial. Elements of the setting, such as landscape and standard avatars cannot be considered in isolation, the virtual world must be seen as a complete entity. The audiovisual manifestation of the game is based on predetermined possible sequences of images, which are called up in the process of directing the avatar through the virtual world. The image sequences are not therefore creatively determined by the inhabitant.

If we look at the issue of whether a virtual world can attract copyright in another way by analogy to film production we can assess further how the courts might approach the question.

In the case of films, the individual creative input such as determining the sequences of images comes from the director, the editors and actors all on the basis of a storyboard. The same detailed process applies to the formulation of a virtual environment. The in-world concept must be translated into a computer program. The environment, characters, various islands (other than those which are designed by in-world retailers for example) are created graphically. The operation of the environment in terms of its dynamic features and functionality have to be programmed. The virtual world designer in this case is the 'director' and the various characters in the form of avatars are the 'cast'. On this basis, a virtual world can be classed as a film and secure protection in that way.

There are other indicators of how the environment may be regarded by the courts on the issue of intellectual property rights. A film enjoys protection irrespective of the mechanisms which bring it to form. Modern computer animation features such as *Shrek* or *Finding Nemo* are created entirely on computer. If films depended only on the use of photographic technology, none of these productions would constitute a film. If, as is in fact the case, animated features are recognised as films, then the term 'audiovisual work' must be ascribed a broader meaning. The representation on a screen against a background of sound effects delivered on speakers falls within the accepted concept of an audiovisual work. Adopting this logic, a virtual world would also be covered by the notion of film within the meaning of the Audio Visual Directive.

It would be reasonable to assert, therefore, that a virtual world can attract dual protection both as a 'cinematographic work' and as software.

5.4 Copyright in the Creative Inspiration for Virtual Worlds

Since we are exploring how copyright law might serve to protect virtual world development it is perhaps useful also to review the case law on copyright as it has come to be developed in the sphere of books. The reason why this is a helpful exercise is because the very nature of virtual worlds is to present the best of the imaginings of their creators. The whole purpose of virtual environments is to produce a setting unlike anything the physical world can offer. Such a platform can then bring forth and inspire ideas and strategies which would not have been conceived without the existence of the virtual platform.

This propensity to create and to inspire lends itself then to the creative strengths of individuals rather than the brilliance of the software developer who designs the underlying code which allows the virtual world to function. It is a distinction which does not seek to diminish the value of either talent but one which is a legitimate one when reviewing the case law in the context of copyright and applying that law to the as yet untested sphere of virtual worlds.

These cases really focus on the issue of inspiration versus infringement.

5.4.1 CASE LAW ON COPYRIGHT IN CREATIVE INSPIRATION

The most famous case related to the novel *'The Da Vinci Code'* which was subsequently made into a major film. *Baigent and another v The Random House Group Ltd* saw the claimants allege that the novel which was published by the defendant company infringed the copyright in their book entitled *'The Holy Blood and the Holy Grail'.*

Baigent had spent five years researching his book, which described the theory that the bloodline of Jesus had not only survived in France but had merged with the Merovingian bloodline around the fifteenth century and carried on. Dan Brown and his wife had spent a year conducting research during the writing of *The Da Vinci Code*. His book was presented as a thriller work of fiction. Whilst it concerned the bloodline of Jesus it was also based in the present day and was set against the background of a fundamentalist Catholic society called Opus Dei. Dan Brown acknowledged that he had looked at Baigent's book before his own book was finished. Baigent also acknowledged that there was a good deal of material in Dan Brown's book that was not derived from his own work. However, Baigent contended that Brown had used the central theme of his book as the basis for *The Da Vinci Code* and had copied a substantial part of his book to produce an altered copy of 'colourable imitation'. In so doing there had been a non-textual infringement of the copyright of Baigent's book. Random House admitted that although Brown had admitted that he made use of Baigent's book in the writing of his own book he had not copied a substantial part of it nor had he copied the central theme.

Crucial to an understanding of the issue which the case addressed is this central theme. The claimants argued that Brown had taken it from Baigent's book which was broken down into 15 elements of the Holy Grail/bloodline thesis. The 15 elements include, for example, that Jesus was of royal blood with a legitimate claim to the throne of Palestine; that he would have been married and, as expected of any Jew at the time, he would have had children; that the Holy Grail consisted of Jesus' bloodline; that this bloodline had intermarried with that of the royal line of the Franks, and continues to this day.

When the case first came to court, the court acknowledged that copyright protection can extend to this selection, arrangement and compilation of research material, but that does not extend to information, facts, ideas, theories and themes. Copyright protection in this way could have enabled the claimants to monopolise historical research, knowledge, theories or arguments.

The questions the court was asked to determine were:

1. What relevant material was to be found in both works?
2. How much, if any, of that had been copied from *'The Holy Blood and the Holy Grail'*.
3. Whether what was copied was on the copyright side of the line between ideas and expression?
4. Whether any of the material that was copied and did qualify as expression, rather than ideas, amounted to a substantial part of *'The Holy Blood and the Holy Grail'*.

The court held that 11 of the 15 elements had been copied by Brown but that those elements did not form the central theme of Baigent's book. That central theme itself was not genuine but an artificial contrivance created for the purposes of asserting infringement. This, in fact, was admitted by the claimants in evidence. They had also failed to show any architecture or structure other than a chronological order of events which as too general.

The case was appealed to the Court of Appeal which upheld the original court's decision but also said the question was whether the central theme was a substantial part of Baigent's book.

Lord Justice Mummery gave invaluable guidance on what to check for when looking at copyright infringement cases by offering a checklist which, whilst not exhaustive, is still very useful.

1. What were the similarities between the alleged infringing work and the original copyright work?
2. What access, direct or indirect, did the author of the alleged infringing work have to the original copyright work?
3. Did the author of the alleged infringing work make some use in his work of material derived by him, directly or indirectly, from the original work?

4. If the defendant contends that no such use is made, what is his explanation for the similarities between the alleged infringing work and the original copyright work? Are they coincidental or similar sources?
5. If use was made of the original copyright work, did the use amount in all the circumstances to a substantial part of the original work?
6. What are the factors which justify evaluating the part copied in the alleged infringing work as a substantial part?

If we were to apply the above tests to a dispute surrounding virtual world development it makes clear how the courts are likely to approach the question if presented with such a dispute.

It can be seen that the constituent parts of the reasoning involves the degree of access the alleged infringer has to the original work. In the case of a virtual world this could be quite easily achieved by participating in the virtual environment itself for a period of time. If there are similarities between the two worlds the question might then be, did the second developer make use of material in the first world? This might be some characteristic of the first world unlike any other feature so it would not, for example, include the use of virtual shop windows already an in-world feature and used by many major brands. If the second developer states that he did not use any material he must explain why the similarities exist? If use was in fact made of the first world material, did the use amount to a substantial part of the first world? This would always be a question of fact in each case but if, for example, the first world used as a backdrop for the entire environment, a loosely based representation of a combination of various terminal buildings at London's Heathrow Airport, JFK Airport in New York and Washington Dulles Airport in the US. Suppose those assets were arranged in a particular orientation and then suppose that an in-world participant could only transfer between buildings by going through a virtual security screen which asked specific questions of the participant. That work might attract some copyright protection on the part of the first world developer. If that same representation was then embodied in the second world it would be a question of degree to establish copyright infringement. Would the absence only of the virtual security desk feature make the copying of the first two elements acceptable as not amounting to a substantial part?

The *Da Vinci* case does offer very helpful guidance on the issue of copyright claims. Lord Justice Mummery's checklist is a good starting point. The case itself did not suggest a lower level of protection for historical works. However this appears to be the result as architecture, character and themes will be harder to identify in historical as opposed to fictional works.

Whilst the defendant in the case did profit from the inspiration he had found in Baigent's book, inspiration will not be a sufficient basis for a copyright infringement claim because copyright promotes rather than stifles creativity.

However, authors and developers must be careful about the amount of inspiration the take from other copyright works because they may be seen to be infringing such works if they had taken a substantial part. It is still possible for copyright to be claimed where the work alleged to have been infringed is not based on the copying of actual text, that is, non-textual look and feel claims/theme claims. The original elements in the plot of a play or novel can be a substantial part of a work, so that copyright may be infringed by work that does not even reproduce a sentence of the original work.

Where there is no literal copying of text (non-textual and look and feel claims) to get copyright protection and to allege copyright infringement, the claimant's work has got to be sufficiently clear and developed to be identifiable from the defendants work. A key feature in *the Da Vinci Code* case was that the claimant's inability to show a genuine central theme and architecture connecting the actual elements of the theme. Thus, authors and developers of virtual worlds will need to fully particularise the precise elements of their work that they claim have been copied.

It is still a grey area as to what will be regarded as inspiration as opposed to infringement and it will always be a question of degree.

There are some useful practical tips for developers of virtual worlds who wish to preserve the status of their works which may be used in 'look and feel' claims.

They include preserving the preparatory materials as they may be able to protect the idea through literary copyright. Such material can include flow charts, diagrams and technical functionality guides and operating manuals.

Distinctive ideas will have better protection. In many ways, of course, this is the great attraction of virtual worlds and how they come to be devised and organised. There is a tremendous opportunity for skilled developers to produce environments which both achieve the technical needs of the company which engages them to develop the world, and provide creative expression.

Ensure that what is claimed to have been taken is a substantial part of the copyright work. This will always be a question for each case.

Concentrate on the similarities in the alleged copy but also be careful not to ignore the differences as this could give a false impression of copying. It is a natural tendency, when one identifies a degree of similarity between two works, perhaps one's own and another that follows, to look closely at the areas where the two reflect. However, this is a dangerous exercise because it may well be that vast elements of the second work in fact depart from the original work and then go on to offer enhanced functionality for example. Thus, the second work may only have drawn inspiration from the first and that is perfectly permissible in copyright law.

Given the nature of virtual world development it can be seen that the issues which we have focused on in this section have particular relevance. Copyright infringement is one of the most significant concerns a business should be alive to, when it embarks upon developing its own virtual world and engages a firm of software developers for this purpose.

It would be prudent for such a business to include a clause in its Agreement with the developer in which the developer provides a warranty that they have not infringed the copyright of others whilst developing the virtual world. It will often be a difficult question as we have seen but, at the very least, such a warranty should be sought with a view to minimising the legal exposure of the business. That said, if a successful claim were to be brought by another company against the business on the basis that the virtual world was held by a court to constitute infringement, the likely order of the court would be that the virtual world be taken down and designed afresh. Damages will also be a likely consequence, awarded against the business whose virtual world offends. Thus, there will still be considerable disruption to the business whilst that remedial work is undertaken. The business would also seek and indemnity from its software developer to meet such damages and attendant costs in the event of such a claim. However, on a practical level whilst such clauses are essential, if the developer has by then gone into insolvency, or otherwise does not have sufficient financial resource to meet any claim, the business will still be exposed financially. In addition, it may be difficult to negotiate a clause with places risk on the developer.

It is useful to note that Linden Labs have clear reference to the question of Intellectual Property Rights in their Second Life environment terms and conditions. Those terms state that all Intellectual Property produced by creators who feature in-world belongs to those creators. Thus, a company with a Second Life presence will bring to that environment several items of intellectual property. These will include its corporate trading style logo for example. Its various products or services may well in themselves attract copyright, trademark or patent protection. So, a company may operate safely in-world in that its intellectual property rights have just as much standing in a virtual environment as they do in the real world. However, Linden Lab also state in their terms and conditions that as operator of the system, they:

a) reserve rights to terminate accounts and hold onto assets without reimbursement; and
b) reserve rights to deny, block or reverse Linden Dollar transactions; and
c) take broad Intellectual Property rights in all content and code.

This latter provision is entirely consistent with the treatment of Intellectual Property in the context of any software application which is licensed by the developer to the user.

5.5 Copyright Liability in Virtual Worlds – Issues for Virtual World Service Providers

The question of copyright infringement is rarely solely whether a breach has occurred, but rather who is responsible for that breach occurring and thus liable for its consequences. The issue of whether ISPs should be responsible for the actions of their end-users is not new. There is legislation which addresses the matter in the form of the Electronic Commerce (EC Directive) Regulations 2002. Copyright infringement is likely to be one of the key areas in relation to ISP liability.

There are two European directives which assist with answering the question being the Copyright and Related Rights Regulations considered in this chapter, and the E-commerce Regulations reviewed more fully at Chapter 4. It is useful to consider the E-commerce Regulations in this section in the context of copyright infringement. The Regulations provide certain immunities for activities which are undertaken by what are described as 'information society service providers' (ISSPs).

5.5.1 THE TRANSMISSION IMMUNITY

Subject to certain conditions, ISPs will not be liable where the service consists of the transmission of information provided by a recipient of the service or the provision of access to a communications network. This is known as the transmission immunity. The service provider such as the operator of a virtual world, will not be liable for any financial remedy which would include damages, or criminal penalty where it did not initiate the transmission or it did not select the receiver of the transmission. It will also escape liability if it did not select or modify the information contained in the transmission.

5.5.2 THE CACHING IMMUNITY

The virtual world operator will not be liable where the relevant information is cached. That means, where it is the subject of automatic, intermediate and temporary storage for the sole purpose of ensuring efficient onward transmission to recipients on request. The exemption from liability will however depend on the following. The operator does not modify the information; it complies with conditions of access; it complies with any rules regarding updating of the information, specified in a manner widely recognised and used by industry. Further, it does not interfere with the lawful use of technology, widely recognised and used by industry to obtain data on the use of the information. In addition, the operator must act expeditiously to remove or disable access to the information on obtaining actual knowledge that the information has been removed from the network, or access to it has been disabled, or that a court has ordered such removal or disablement.

5.5.3 THE HOSTING IMMUNITY

In Chapter 9 we examine the issues which a virtual world operator must appreciate in terms of its hosting liability. Most virtual worlds and social networks store and stream content provided by end users being the inhabitants of the environment. Where the virtual world operator stores on its servers information provided by the service recipient, that recipient is not acting under the authority of the provider. The provider will not be liable if it does not have actual knowledge of unlawful activity and, where a claim for damages is made, is not aware of facts or circumstances from which it would have been apparent that the activity or information was unlawful. The E-commerce regulations do not define 'actual knowledge' and the courts will have discretion as to what this might constitute. It would seem that notice of the allegedly defamatory material will have to be specific to be effective. The provider will not be liable if, on obtaining knowledge or awareness, it then acts expeditiously to remove or to disable access to the information.

There also exists a general principle of 'no monitoring'. This means that EU member states must not impose a general obligation on virtual world operators to monitor the information which they transmit or store. Nor do they have an obligation to actively seek facts or circumstances indicating illegal activity.

5.5.4 CURRENT CONTROVERSIES SURROUNDING LIABILITY OF SERVICE PROVIDERS

It can be seen that there are several ways in which the operator of a virtual world can escape legal liability, certainly for copyright infringement for the content displayed in the environment. The approach taken by the legislators was in recognition of the fact that the sheer scale of information which passed on networks meant that any effective control by those who manage those networks was impossible.

The regulations indicate that the various immunities were aimed at 'intermediary service providers' whose activities are of a 'mere technical, automatic and passive nature'. However, those who believe that content rights holders should have more protection against the online distribution of their content argue that the actions of some online service providers are not purely passive or technical, and so go beyond the coverage intended by the regulations. In addition, it is likely that some types of services are not expressly covered by the 2002 regulations. While the implication is that they will be protected by the immunities, as they are also likely to be hosting or transmitting content, it is arguable that a service provider primarily providing a service not expressly covered may find itself without protection.

It is important to appreciate that even when the 2002 regulations were being framed much of what has become commonplace Internet services had not matured or did not exist. The regulations were designed to govern organisations such as the ISPs who allow you access to the Internet, for example; BT Broadband or Tiscali Broadband. In fact, as we see from this book, there are now services such as social networking websites and virtual words which may constitute information society service providers.

Copyright holders such as musicians, film producers, authors and others, argue that the purpose and activities of certain online services are not purely passive or technical, and so go beyond the coverage intended by the current legislation. *YouTube*, for example, indexes clips and puts them in order, allowing for comments and categorisation.

The defences outlined above only succeed if the ISP is not performing any active role aside from enabling the provider of material to provide it to the end user. In addition, the ISP must not be gaining any independent economic benefit beyond the provision of its basic service. Under the Electronic Commerce Regulations 2002, if ISPs do not know about offending material and they remove it when notified, they may escape liability.

There are as yet no reported English law cases on the issue but in a Belgian case of *Sabam (Belgian Society of Authors, Composers and Publishers) v Scarlett*, the courts at first instance decided to block people from sharing music peer to peer files over the Internet. It ordered the ISP to use software called Audible Magic to filter out offending material under threat of a fine of 2,500 euros per day.

It is always going to be a balance between the needs of ISP's and content owners.

5.6 Case Law on Distributing Media Content over the Internet Without Consent

It is useful to review how the courts have approached the development of distributing media content, specifically music over the Internet, without the copyright holder's consent. Virtual worlds and, of course, Internet social networks permit the presentation of media content, be it film extracts or audio clips within the environment. These works may be featured as part of a wider multimedia depiction. For example, an avatar may inhabit a virtual bar or restaurant. That location may have a television as a computer modelled asset upon which is shown a film or television programme. Alternatively, there might be music playing in the restaurant. The question thus arises how this media content is to be treated at law where its use within the virtual environment has not been authorised by the content owner.

A more dramatic example would be where media content of this kind is offered for distribution among inhabitants of the environment, perhaps by download.

It is probably easy to appreciate that the cases thus far determined by the courts have centred on music distribution. This is because the music industry was the first to face the challenges presented by the Internet .

In recent years a number of software programs became available which enabled the user to download music tracks via their PC either at home or at work. The music could be obtained free as it had been uploaded as a file by someone else. The power of the Internet as a superdistribution channel meant that those works could be accessed anywhere in the world. The form of these software programs has altered as has the manner in which music is accessed for free without the copyright holder's consent. It is important in determining the precise legal basis for objection.

A helpful starting point when reviewing whether merely providing the means to make illegal copies attracts legal liability is the 1984 'Sony' or Betamax' case. The United States Supreme Court had to decide whether or not the Betamax video machine was an illegal instrument of contributory copyright infringement. In *Sony v Universal City Studios 104 US 774 (1984)* the Court had to determine the legality of the Betamax machine which could both play pre recorded films and videos legally and also could be used to record illegally. The court held that the machine was not illegal. The UK case of *CBS Songs v Amstrad (1988) RPC 567* came to a similar conclusion. The House of Lords held that there was no infringement of copyright in the marketing of a twin cassette deck which could clearly be used for infringing purposes, that of copying music cassettes without permission. It has therefore been apparent for some time that the provision of a service or equipment to facilitate copying, where that service or equipment has other legitimate uses, may not be an infringement or illegal.

If one were to apply the reasoning of these aged court decisions to the virtual world environment one might conclude that the provision of film or musical media content in the environment might be regarded as incidental to the overall features of the virtual world. After all, the environment will undoubtedly contain many features including computer modelled assets and in-world services and perhaps retail presence.

The laws considered below introduced recently and designed to protect copyright in the Internet era clearly provide the means to protect against unlawful distribution of media content in virtual worlds or social networks. However, they do leave some anomalies. For example, one can acquire an unwanted music DVD free with a weekend newspaper yet be subject to a fine if one downloads the same film from the Internet. If someone spends a day listening to the radio and recording tracks for their MP3 player then that is, to all practical purposes, acceptable. However, if they download the same songs from the Internet into their iPod that is caught by the new Regulations.

Other commentators make the point that one consequence of the Internet is that thousands of movies might suddenly become available that would not physically fit on the shelves of those who acquire them. The question arises should film companies and other media owners have the right to extract royalties from titles that would not have seen the light of day but for the long tail of the Internet?

The essential fact is that for all the efforts of the media industry there is likely to be a degree to which they will always be helpless against the practical power of the Internet. In today's world as soon as something is recorded there is a real risk that it will find its way on to the Internet.

In attempting to combat illegal use of media content over the Internet the entertainment industries have turned their attention to the ISPs, telecommunications companies and software providers such as Verizon, Napster and Aimster.

The largest market for music distribution and Internet use is the United States and therefore it is of little surprise that the majority of the case law which has determined the issue is North American. Nonetheless, those cases serve as clear guidance as to how the UK has approached the problem both in terms of policy and legal argument.

In the US the equivalent body to the UK's British Phonographic Industry (BPI) is the Recording Industry Association of America (RIAA). The RIAA, faced with the explosion of Internet file swappers downloading music from the Internet for free, decided to take direct legal action. The RIAA on behalf of the record companies as well as some artists sought to sue Napster. The RIAA managed to obtain the subscriber and user details of those individuals who they considered were 'chronic' abusers of Internet download services. In 2000 the organisation sought legal action in *RIAA v Napster (2000)*. File sharing software was made available on a central server that enabled users to see which other users had music in MP3 compressed form that they would like to acquire. This two way link up to share music became known as peer to peer. Napster drew over sixty million users a day. The US District Court held that Napster file swapping service was illegal. Napster had raised a variety of defences to the action by the RIAA. These included the argument rehearsed in previous eras and noted above, that the service had non-infringing as well as infringing uses. This argument in principle might be one the operator of a virtual world may use in addition to other basis of defence such as those embodied in the Electronic Commerce Regulations 2002. In addition, its service had the effect of boosting record sales and that the plaintiffs themselves were in the business of facilitating file-swapping citing RIAA member Sony's manufacture of MP3 players.

The court rejected all these arguments and granted an interim injunction against the file swapping service. Napster was found to have facilitated illegal copying by individual users and were ordered to pay significant damages. The company could not survive the damages award and ceased operation. The company was declared bankrupt in 2002. The suspension of the Napster service drove users to other peer to peer websites.

The Napster case was followed by action which represented a major victory for copyright holders in the US. In *RIAA v Aimster (2002)* the record industry once again sought the assistance of the law in its fight against the unauthorised uploading and downloading of music. In 2001 Aimster had applied to the US District Court to have its service declared legal. The response from the RIAA representing copyright holders was to institute legal proceedings against Aimster alleging contributory and vicarious copyright infringements. The court accepted the RIAA arguments and determined that Aimster had clear knowledge of infringements taking place on its service. Further, Aimster had materially contributed to these infringements. In addition, Aimster could supervise the infringements if it so wanted and that Aimster had benefited financially from these infringements. It was stated that Aimster was a service whose very raison d'etre appears to be the facilitation of and contribution to copyright infringement on a massive scale. Aimster was ordered to prevent users from uploading and downloading copyright works or cease operations if it could not do so and to employ technical measures to prevent copyright infringement.

The next case resulted in the RIAA suffering a set back. In *MGM Studios and Others v Grokster & Streamcast Networks (2003)* the legal tide changed. In 2001 MGM had launched legal actions against KaZaA, Grokster and StreamCast Networks for contributory and vicarious copyright infringement. Given the need for urgent determination on the question, both sides to the dispute sought an expedited ruling on liability. The court decided in favour of StreamCast Networks and Grokster. The court was able to distinguish its decision from earlier cases on the following basis.

First, the software had non-infringing uses. Second, the defendants had no actual knowledge of specific infringements and could not supervise infringements. This latter point was important because unlike the Napster system, the Grokster facility had no centralised system. File sharers on the Internet could access each other's files without recourse to any list operated by the service provider.

Alongside the legal cases being brought with some rapidity against those organisations which operated music download facilities without the consent of the copyright holders, the RIAA went about taking legal action against serial users of such services. These, of course, included individuals in their homes who were taking advantage of the ability to obtain music for free via the Internet. The RIAA in this tactic were seeking to make examples of those people and to send a message out to other individuals tempted to do the same thing. This approach brought to the public attention the case of Brianna Lahara who then aged twelve years had a love of television theme music, the successful artist Christina Aguilera and the nursery song *If You're Happy and You Know It.* Her mother agreed to pay $2,000 in compensation. The RIAA issued a statement announcing the settlement and quoting the little girl as saying *'I am sorry for what I have done. I love music and don't want to hurt the artists I love.'*

This tactic of making examples of individuals who download music illegally was to be followed in the UK two years later. This approach was considered by some to be a high risk public relations strategy. Many questioned the wisdom of multi million pound companies suing individuals of modest means. However, the strategy of a sustained public relations campaign aimed at dissuading individuals from downloading music illegally and legal proceedings appears to have been highly effective.

In the UK the courts have also been asked to decide on legality of facilitating copyright infringement. In *Sony Music Entertainment (UK) Ltd v Easyinternetcafe Ltd (2003)* the High Court held that Easyinternetcafes were guilty of copyright infringement by allowing customers to download music without permission and to burn CD copies of these at Easyinternet's chain of cafes.

In June 2005 the US Supreme Court tried to balance the competing demands of copyright owners and technology developers in a ruling which serves as the best guide to how the US courts approach the issue. In *MGM v Grokster* (2005) the court held that the distributors of peer to peer software could be liable for infringements committed with their software. The court reached the conclusion by the use of the concept of active inducement from the US Patent Act. At the same time the court affirmed that the distributor of a product used to infringe will not incur liability by virtue of the act of distribution so long as the product is capable of a substantial non-infringing use. On the face of it the latest chapter in the Grokster saga appears to be a music industry victory. The Supreme Court reversed the United States Federal Court of Appeals Ninth Circuit decision which had found that Grokster had no case to answer with regard to the use of its file sharing software to transfer illegally copied files.

The Plaintiffs had argued what is known as 'active inducement'. Active Inducement concentrates on the defendant's conduct rather than his technology. The court found that one who distributes a device with the object of promoting its use to infringe copyright, as shown by clear expression or other affirmative steps taken to foster infringement, is liable for the resulting acts of infringement by third parties.

It is considered that the decision has powered the digital future of legitimate US online businesses including file sharing networks by making those who promote theft accountable. The concern on the part of technology innovators is that the case has created a new era of uncertainty for software innovation.

It is clear that a distributor's mere knowledge of infringing potential or actual infringement would not be enough to subject the distributor to liability. By analogy, it may be that the operator of a virtual world or social network may argue that their Internet services are similar in that they may well know media content is featured in-world but that would not of itself bring about legal liability on their part.

It is possible in light of these various cases to assess some of the tests which the courts might consider when reviewing software technology which has both infringing and non-infringing uses. This is useful for our purposes because there might be a software application developed for use in a virtual world or Internet Social Network which is innovative and designed to address a particular role but which also enables some form of media distribution. We consider later in this chapter the capacity of many Social Networks to allow their users to create software applications which may reside within the environment for use by other users of the service.

It can be seen that the potential for copyright infringement will continue as the technology continues to evolve.

First, are there substantial non-infringing uses and can the defendant, perhaps the virtual world operator or in-world application developer, prove this? This was the issue in the *Sony Betamax, MGM v Grokster*, and *RIAA v Aimster* cases.

Second, does the virtual world software developer have clear knowledge of infringing uses? Wilful blindness is no defence as was the decision in the *RIAA v Aimster, Grokster* and *Napster* cases.

Third, is the software developer or virtual world operator able to supervise infringement if it so wanted? This issue was considered in the Easyinternet case. We have considered that this may be quite possible in the context in particular of many virtual worlds.

Fourth, has the software developer or virtual world operator materially contributed to infringements. For example, does it provide any assistance to those individuals who infringe? It might be argued perhaps that the underlying software tools which enable a software application developed by an inhabitant for use by other inhabitants, might be said to so contribute. However, this will always be a question of fact and it may be difficult to establish a link between the mere tools provided by the virtual world operator and the finished software application developed by the inhabitant.

Finally, does the software developer or virtual world operator financially benefit from infringing uses even where the provider is not infringing itself?

5.7 The Copyright and Related Rights Regulations 2003 and Their Application to Virtual Worlds

5.7.1 SUMMARY OF NEW RIGHTS GRANTED BY THE REGULATIONS

How then has the law had to adapt to meet this new era? As we have noted, in English law, copyright is governed by the Copyright, Designs and Patents Act 1988. This legislation brought together under one statute a good deal of previous law in the sphere of copyright but in the twenty years since its introduction the world of media technology has wholly changed. It was clear that new provisions would have to be drafted to properly transpose the fundamental principles contained in the 1988 Act to address the digital age. The result of a lengthy and detailed consultation process is the *Copyright and Related Rights Regulations 2003* which came into effect in England and Wales on 31 October 2003.

In essence, the new Regulations attempt to clarify the rights of those who own copyright in literary, dramatic, musical or artistic work, or in a sound recording or broadcast when the media by which those works can be distributed are multifarious. The Regulations cover various aspects of copyright law. The main areas of change are:

- The introduction of new rights for authors and performers to control any 'communication to the public' of their work. The new rights cover for example, enabling Internet access including virtual world access, cable transmission and dissemination to mobile phones and other mobile devices. These rights permit rightholders such as the music and film industries to pursue unauthorised use of their works in digital form. In addition businesses that are very dependent on acquiring and granting rights of exploitation of works created by third parties such as publishing companies, record companies and information service providers.
- Amendment to the exceptions to copyright. The Regulations established one mandatory and many permissive exceptions to copyright. One area of change is that the exception of fair dealing for research and private study has been significantly cut back to make it clear that the exception only applies to copying for non-commercial purposes.
- Circumvention of technical protection. The Regulations enhance the protection available for works supplied in copy-protected form, for example, encrypted documents or data. It may be that certain content featured in a virtual world environment is so encrypted. Knowing circumvention of measures to protect works is of itself an unlawful act, regardless of whether any acts of copyright infringement are carried out in the process. Similarly, the provision or commercial possession of hacking or cracking tools designed to get around the virtual world security features, may involve not only civil wrongs but also criminal offences. Only limited exceptions are available, for example, research into cryptography not prejudicially affecting the rights of the copyright owner. Rightholders who use copy protection are encouraged to establish voluntary means for enabling lawful users of their works to carry out acts which are permitted exceptions to copyright such as private non-commercial study. This has been done by enabling users to complain to the Department for Business, Enterprise & Regulatory Reform (BERR) who has power to make appropriate directions if no voluntary means for access are provided.

- New remedies are available for the knowing removal or alteration of 'electronic rights management information'. This could include for example, copyright notices or numbering systems, such as the publishing industry's ISBN numbering system. Apart from the notice function served by a copyright notice, it is expected that certain types of rights management will increasingly be used to facilitate automated systems of payment of royalties to rightholders for the electronic exploitation of their works with the result that removal or alteration of this information will directly impact revenue flows. It may be that a virtual world environment contains access to music or film content files which the performer or content owner is entitled to remuneration if that content is consumed by the in-world participant. The protection thus reinforces the message that works in electronic form continue to be protected by copyright, and enables the development of automated payment schemes.
- The court has powers to grant injunctions against service providers, for example, ISPs, who have actual knowledge of use of their services to infringe copyright. It is the case that rightholders remain concerned that some service providers will not respond promptly to requests to prevent the use of their services to distribute infringing copies of copyrighted works such as new music, film recordings or computer games within virtual worlds, with the effect that sales of the product will be depressed because copies are freely available through the in-world service. This power to injunct builds on the protection in this area under the Electronic Commerce (EC Directive) Regulations 2002 (see chapter on e-commerce regulations).
- Copyright and related rights give the operator of a virtual world or other rightholder, for example the media owner of music or film content featured in-world, the exclusive right to do or authorise reproduction, that is, the copying, of their content. In addition to the right to distribute copies to in-world inhabitants, communication of their content to those inhabitants, for example by showing or playing a film in the virtual world environment. Infringement occurs when any of the above acts are carried out or authorised by a party without the consent or licence of the copyright owner or rightholder.

5.7.1.1 Provisions Relating to Broadcasts

The Regulations amend the definition of a broadcast and Section 4 states that; 'Broadcast' means an electronic transmission of visual images, sounds or other information which is transmitted for simultaneous reception by members of the public and is capable of being lawfully received by them, or is transmitted at a time determined solely by the person making the transmission for presentation to members of the public.

Broadcasting means wired or wireless. It is important to note that this definition does not include use of the Internet per se. So, the display of virtual world activity is not of itself classed as a 'Broadcast'. However, if the Internet transmission, and thus the virtual world activity accompanies another transmission by for example television it will be classed as a 'Broadcast' and caught by the Regulations.

The section says:

'Excepted from the definition of 'broadcast' is any Internet transmission unless it is:

a) a transmission taking place simultaneously on the Internet and by other means;

b) a concurrent transmission of a live event; or
c) a transmission of recorded moving images or sounds forming part of a programme service offered by the person responsible for making the transmission, being a service in which programmes are transmitted at scheduled times determined by that person.'

So, one can see that a virtual world computer animation, for example, which is simultaneously transmitted live on television would be included in the definition of Broadcast as far as the virtual world characterisation is concerned.

The Regulations go on to clarify which acts are restricted by copyright by Section 6 headed 'Infringement by communication to the public':

1. The communication to the public of the work is an act restricted by the copyright in:

   i) a literary, dramatic, musical or artistic work
   ii) a sound recording or film; or
   iii) a broadcast.

2. References to 'communication to the public' are to communication to the public by electronic transmission, and in relation to a work include:

   i) the broadcasting of the work;
   ii) the making available to the public of the work by electronic transmission in such a way that members of the public may access it from a place and at a time individually chosen by them.

It appears from this section that a communication to the public is restricted whether it be by broadcast, for example, television and radio, or by electronic transmission where the public can access it where and when they like, such as the Internet in general or by the use by the public of virtual world services.

5.7.1.2 The Making Available Right

One significant revision of the 1988 Act is the introduction of the Making Available Right for performers. Section 182CA of the Regulations state that consent is required for making available to the public.

The section states:

> *A performer's rights are infringed by a person who, without his consent, makes available to the public a recording of the whole or any substantial part of a qualifying performance by electronic transmission in such a way that members of the public may access the recording from a place and at a time individually chosen by them.*
>
> *The right of a performer under this section to authorise or prohibit the making available to the public of a recording is referred to … as the 'making available right'.*

Thus, any in-world transmission of media content such as audio or visual works must be undertaken solely with the consent of the media content owner. If a virtual environment featured a movie displayed for example, in an in-world restaurant or bar, the owner of the film rights must have granted express consent for such display.

However, as with all copyright rules that came before the new Regulations, there are certain actions which by their nature do not constitute a significant breach of copyright and are as such permissible under the law.

5.7.1.3 Making Temporary Copies

Section 8 provides that the copyright, in for example a film work, is not infringed by the making of a temporary copy which is transient or incidental, which is an integral and essential part of a technological process and the sole purpose of which is to enable:

a) a transmission of the work in a network between third parties by an intermediary; or
b) a lawful use of the work.

And which has no independent, economic significance. It is not easy to assess whether this exception would include certain in-world activity and thereby exclude a virtual world operator or anyone who makes the content available to others in the environment. It will depend on the facts of the case but one can see that arguments of interpretation of the Regulations will arise in the future as technological developments emerge which render uncertain the status of particular in-world activity.

5.7.1.4 Research and Private Study

The Regulations also alter the definition of so called 'Fair Dealing' in copyright work. The new provision is clear enough. Section 9 now provides that fair dealing with a work for the purpose of research for a non-commercial purpose does not infringe any copyright in the work provided that it is accompanied by a sufficient acknowledgement.

The section goes on to say that no acknowledgment of the kind detailed above is required where this would be impossible for reasons of practicality or otherwise.

Further, fair dealing with a work for the purposes of private study does not infringe any copyright in the work.

A new element to the extent of fair dealing is the clear direction in relation to computer programs. Such programs might, of course, be related to the in-world distribution of media content. The new paragraph says; 'It is not fair dealing to observe, study or test the functioning of a computer program in order to determine the ideas and principles which underlie any element of the program.'

5.7.1.5 Criticism, Review and News Reporting

The Regulations also address the issue of fair dealing in the context of criticism, review and news reporting. Section 10 says that; 'Fair dealing with a performance or recording for the purpose of criticism or review, of that or another performance or recording, or of a work, does not infringe any of the rights ... provided that the performance or recording has been made available to the public.'

Thus, it might be that a social network features user generated content which includes a review of a new film, television series or album release by a band. Such use within the environment would be permitted under this section. The same would apply if that content was featured for similar purpose within a virtual world.

In relation to the exceptions to copyright infringement the Regulations also make clear that certain things can be done with copyright works for the purposes of instruction or examination. The new law says that; 'Copyright in a sound recording, film or broadcast is not infringed by its being copied by making a film or film soundtrack in the course of instruction, or of preparation for instruction, in the making of films or film soundtracks, provided the copying:

a) is done by a person giving or receiving instruction;
b) is accompanied by a sufficient acknowledgement; and
c) provided the instruction is for a non-commercial purpose.

This exception would cover the situation where a virtual environment is used for training purposes. In fact training is one of the areas regarded as most likely to be adopted in virtual spaces.

There are other circumstances where certain copying is permitted. They include provisions relating to the observing, studying and testing of computer programs. This covers the situation where the study or testing of the functionality of the program is done in order to determine the ideas and principles which underlie any element of the program. If this is done while for example, running the program which one is entitled to do then the copying is permitted. This is an interesting issue in the context of virtual worlds and social networks given that they are themselves computer environments and are likely to feature software programs developed by the operator of the environment or other users. It should be appreciated that this exception is very limited and does not mean that one can copy such programs for commercial use.

5.7.1.6 Provisions Relating to Recording for the Purposes of Time Shifting

The Regulations provide for another exception which is useful to examine. They state that where a copy which would otherwise be an infringing copy is made ... but which is subsequently dealt with:

a) it shall be treated as an infringing copy for the purposes of that dealing; and
b) if that dealing infringes copyright, it shall be treated as an infringing copy for all subsequent purposes.

'Dealt with' means sold or let for hire, offered or exposed for sale or hire or communicated to the public.

How might this exception be viewed in the context of virtual worlds and social networks? First it is important to distinguish pure domestic time shifting. The Regulations state:

1. The making in domestic premises for private and domestic use of a recording of a broadcast solely for the purpose of enabling it to be viewed or listened to at a more convenient time does not infringe any right in relation to a performance or recording included in the broadcast.

This is clear enough in its purpose. It does not include therefore an inhabitant of a virtual world or social network uploading media content for use or experience by other users. That situation is prevented by the Regulations which make clear:

1. 'Where a recording which would otherwise be an illicit recording is made in accordance with this paragraph but is subsequently dealt with:

   i) it shall be treated as an illicit recording for the purposes of that dealing; and
   ii) if that dealing infringes any right ... it shall be treated as an illicit recording for all subsequent purposes.'

It is always going to be a question of fact whether certain in-world activity falls within the ambit of this and other provisions of the Regulations. It is likely that whilst the Regulations were drafted for the digital environment, such is the nature of technological advancement, applications may come along which cause uncertainty surrounding the ambit of the Regulations to that new application. Virtual worlds are fertile ground for this kind of ambiguity as they are rich media environments which will undoubtedly develop in sophistication.

5.7.2 CIRCUMVENTING TECHNICAL MEASURES

It is new technologies which have created the problem of Internet piracy. It is new technologies which in many ways are the best form of resistance. The commonly understood form of management is the generic term Digital Rights Management.

It is true that mere imposition of licence terms in virtual worlds and social networks to try to manage the risks presented by digital copying cannot sufficiently prevent consumers from unlawfully dealing with digital content if they are so minded. Given the ease with which unprotected digital content can be copied or distributed, it is argued that Digital Rights Management protection is essential to prevent the collapse of the established sales based revenue model for the exploitation of digital content.

The issue is as relevant to virtual world and social network environments as to any other Internet space. The obvious answer is for in-world companies which offer media or software content to install technology in their files which would monitor when and where they were used.

This would prevent such content being viewed unless the copyright use was identified as legitimate. Huge resources have been put into anti-piracy devices in recent years particularly with the Internet in mind. Techniques include watermarking and other methods to track the copying of content to control it and ensure proper payment.

Other systems seek to create permanent and temporary passwords on computer files which permit only one copy of a file to be made and played on a legitimate player. Making one copy destroys one of the passwords and if an attempt is made to copy once more, the copy will not play because the player can only find one of the required two passwords. Whilst there are many such systems at present they probably only make it more difficult for software pirates rather than solve the problem fully. In many ways, they cause frustration to legitimate users which outweighs the benefits of trying to prevent illegal use.

A useful example is the difficulty presented by installing copyright protection in DVDs. These contain deliberate errors which make it harder to copy the film. However, these errors mean that many legitimate DVDs cannot be used in the DVD drives of some computers.

Digital Rights Management covers a range of issues. The All Party Parliamentary Internet Group[5] defines DRM as 'the generic term for a set of technologies for the identification and protection of intellectual property in digital form.' From a legal perspective DRM has two elements:

- Technological prevention measures which are defined by section 296ZF(1) of the Copyright Design and Patents Act as 'any technology, device or component which is designed, in the normal course of its operation, to protect a copyright work other than a computer program'.
- Rights management information which section 296ZG(7)(b) of that Act defines as 'any information provided by the copyright owner or the holder of any right under copyright which identifies the work, the author, the copyright owner or the holder of any intellectual property rights, or information about the terms and conditions of use of the work, and any numbers or codes that represent such information'.
- It includes encryption of content, licensing, and authentication of identity of users. There are differing forms of Digital Rights Management including the forensic watermarking described above. Geo Filtering is another. This is the technical process which controls where the user is. For example, a credit card merchant can tell where the user is located. Such Geo Filtering makes territorial restrictions on the use of content safe. It is a very important method of ensuring territorial restrictions on legitimate distribution of content are viable even in the Internet environment. Geo filtering is perhaps a more difficult control, however, in the context of virtual world inhabitation. In addition, ISPs can tell where a user is and prevent access as appropriate. This is where operators of virtual worlds and social networks may regain the control they, or inhabitants of their environments who have a legitimate complaint about misuse of their copyright works, need. There are also time limitations. This might apply to how many uses an inhabitant of a virtual world may make of an in-world application before the stated time restriction expires. Copy Protection technology controls how many copies may be made of the content.

Each of these methods of copyright control fall under the generic term Digital Rights Management.

There are some interesting legal issues at play when one considers the use of Digital Rights Management technologies. For example, if you have purchased this book you may read it as many times as you like and wherever you like. However, Digital Rights Management on an Internet download restricts such unfettered use.

---

5 Digital Rights Management – Report of Inquiry by the All-Party Internet Group.

Whilst it may be very difficult to develop technology to prevent infringement, the EU and the UK, by virtue of the Copyright and Related Rights Regulations 2003, insist on strict legal protections for technology driven devices. In essence, the requirement, common throughout the EU, is that member states must provide adequate legal protection against the circumvention of any effective technological measures. This is designed to govern the situation in which the person concerned carries out the circumvention in the knowledge, or with reasonable grounds to know, that he or she is pursuing that objective.

5.7.2.1 The Definition of Technological Measures

Before we consider the point that attempts to get around technical processes which are designed to stop copyright infringement are unlawful, it is worth reviewing how the Regulations define 'technological measures'.

Section 296ZF states that technological measures are any technology, device or component which is designed, in the normal course of its operation, to protect a copyright work other than a computer program. They are 'effective' if the use of the work is controlled by the copyright owner through:

a) an access control or protection process such as encryption, scrambling or other transformation of the work; or
b) a copy control mechanism which achieves the intended protection.

It can be seen that the definition is self-explanatory and certainly would include the various forms of Digital Rights Management outlined above.

For example, when reference is made to protecting media works in virtual worlds this means the prevention or restriction of acts that are not authorised by the copyright owner and which are restricted by copyright; and that use of the media work does not extend to any use that is outside the scope of those acts which are restricted by copyright.

5.7.2.2 Circumvention of Technological Measures which are Applied to in-world Copyright

So, we know that technical developments allow media copyright holders to make use of technological measures which are designed to prevent or restrict actions they have not authorised. The threat, of course, is that illegal activities might be carried out in order to enable or facilitate the circumvention of technical protection provided by these measures.

Section 296ZA of the Regulations applies where:

a) effective technological measures have been applied to a copyright work other than a computer program; and
b) a person (B) does anything which circumvents those measures knowing, or with reasonable grounds to know, that he is pursuing that objective.

In this scenario the following people have legal rights against B:

- a person:

i) issuing to the public copies of; or
ii) communicating to the public.

The work to which effective technological measures have been applied; and:

a) the copyright owner or his exclusive licensee, if he is not the person specified in paragraph (a).

5.7.2.3 Devices and Services which are Designed to Circumvent Technological Measures Applied to in-world Copyright

Under Section 296ZB of the Regulations entitled 'Devices and services designed to circumvent technological measures':

1. A person commits an offence if he:

    a) manufactures for sale or hire; or
    b) imports otherwise than for his private and domestic use; or
    c) in the course of a business:

        i) sells or lets for hire; or
        ii) offers or exposes for sale or hire; or
        iii) advertises for sale or hire; or
        iv) possesses; or
        v) distributes, or distributes otherwise than in the course of a business to such an extent as to affect prejudicially the copyright owner, any device, product or component which is primarily designed, produced, or adapted for the purpose of enabling or facilitating the circumvention of effective technological measures.

This is clear enough in terms of who falls within the ambit of the Regulations. If someone were to so provide a device or product which achieves this circumvention within a virtual world they are acting unlawfully. The definition however goes further:

1. A person commits an offence if he provides, promotes, advertises or markets:

    a) in the course of a business; or
    b) otherwise than in the course of a business to such an extent as to affect prejudicially the copyright owner, a service the purpose of which is to enable or facilitate the circumvention of effective technological measures. So, if someone does not necessarily provide the actual device, but instead provides a service which operates in a virtual environment and has the effect of circumvention then they are also acting unlawfully.

The penalties for such actions are severe as the actions are treated as criminal acts. Under Section (4) a person guilty of an offence under subsections (1) or (2) above is liable:

a) on summary conviction, to imprisonment for a term not exceeding three months, or to a fine not exceeding the statutory minimum, or both;
b) on conviction on indictment to a fine or imprisonment for a term not exceeding two years, or both.

The Regulations do provide for a defence to a charge of circumvention by the above methods. Section (5) states that it is a defence to any prosecution for an offence under this section for the defendant to prove that he did not know, and had no reasonable grounds for believing, that:

a) the device, product or component; or
b) the service, enabled or facilitated the circumvention of effective technological measures.

5.7.2.4 Who can Sue those who use Devices and Services within Virtual Worlds Designed to Circumvent Technological Measures?

The question arises as to who actually has the right to take legal action against someone who attempts to get around the copyright technical safeguards applied to in-world media content? Section 296ZD of the Regulations provides the answer. If effective technological measures have been applied to a media copyright work (for use within a virtual environment) and someone manufactures, imports, distributes, sells or advertises or simply has in his possession a device or provides services which are promoted advertised or marketed for the purpose of the circumvention, then the following people will have legal rights against that person:

- A person issuing to the public copies of or communicating to the public the film work to which effective technological measures have been applied.
- The actual copyright owner or his exclusive licensee.
- The owner or exclusive licensee of any intellectual property right in the effective technological measures applied to the film work.

Each of these people can take legal action against the infringer demanding delivery up, or seizure of, the products in question. Such people may also take legal action against someone who manufactures, imports, distributes, sells or advertises or simply has in his possession a device or provides services which have only a limited commercially significant purpose other than to circumvent, or which are primarily designed to enable circumvention.

5.7.2.5 Electronic Rights Management Information

The Regulations also provide legal protection in the sphere of electronic rights management. Rights Management Information is defined as any information provided by the copyright owner or the holder of any right under copyright, which identifies the work, the author, the copyright owner or the holder of any intellectual property rights, or information about the terms and conditions of use of the work, and any numbers or codes that represent such information.

Section 296ZG says that it is unlawful where a person knowingly and without authority, removes or alters electronic rights management information associated with a copy of a copyright work. It is also unlawful if a person knows he is inducing, enabling, facilitating or concealing an infringement of copyright. So, if someone perpetrates such removal to media work which has copyright protection and which is then distributed within a virtual environment by that person, he or she is acting unlawfully.

In addition, section 296ZG (2) covers someone who knowingly and without authority, distributes, imports for distribution or communicates to the public, copies of a copyright work from which electronic rights management information has been removed or altered, if that person knows or has reason to believe, that by so doing he is inducing, enabling, facilitating or concealing an infringement of copyright. So, again, if that person distributes within a virtual environment such altered media works they are acting unlawfully.

5.7.2.6 Criminal Offences

The Regulations introduce new criminal offences in circumstances where there has been infringement as follows:

A person who infringes copyright in a work by communicating the work to the public:

a) in the course of a business; or
b) otherwise than in the course of a business to such an extent as to affect prejudicially the owner of the copyright, commits an offence if he knows or has reason to believe that, by doing so, he is infringing copyright in that work.

The Regulations state that a person guilty of an offence above is liable:

a) on summary conviction to imprisonment for a term not exceeding three months or a fine not exceeding the statutory maximum, or both;
b) on conviction on indictment to a fine or imprisonment for a term not exceeding two years, or both.

A person who infringes a content owner's making available right:

a) in the course of a business; or
b) otherwise than in the course of a business to such an extent as to affect prejudicially the owner of the making available right, commits an offence if he knows or has reason to believe that, by doing so, he is infringing the making available right in the recording.

A person guilty of an offence above is liable:

a) on summary conviction to imprisonment for a term not exceeding three months or a fine not exceeding the statutory maximum, or both;
b) on conviction on indictment to a fine or imprisonment for a term not exceeding two years, or both.

The Regulations also seek to enforce legal remedies against service providers in the context of copyright infringement.

a) The High Court has power to grant an injunction against a service provider, where the service provider has actual knowledge of another person using their service to infringe copyright. The question arises whether the operator of a virtual world or Internet social network would fall within the meaning of 'service provider'? It is important to note that the definition of service provider in the context of the Copyright and Related Rights Regulations have the same meaning given to it by regulation 2 of the Electronic Commerce (EC Directive) Regulations 2002. In Chapter 4 we consider in detail the legal argument about the liability or otherwise of service providers and indeed whether operators of virtual worlds or Internet social networks might claim immunity from liability. For present purposes we can only consider how the courts in the context of the Copyright and Related Rights Regulations will approach the issue of whether a service provider (it being an open question whether a virtual world or social network provider is such a service provider).

The court clearly will have to determine whether the virtual world service provider has actual knowledge and it will take into account all matters which appear to it in the particular circumstances to be relevant. Amongst other things, the court will have regard to:

a) whether the virtual world service provider has received a notice which includes the full name and address of the sender of the notice and details of the infringement in question.

The High Court also has power to grant an injunction against a virtual world service provider, where that service provider has actual knowledge of another person using their service to infringe a performer's property right. Once again, in determining whether a service provider has actual knowledge the court will apply the same test detailed above.

The Regulations provide certain rights to those who hold merely a non-exclusive license in relation to copyrighted works. A non-exclusive licensee may bring an action for infringement of copyright if:

a) the infringing act was directly connected to a prior licensed act of the licensee, and the licence itself:

   i) is in writing and is signed by or on behalf of the copyright owner; and
   ii) expressly grants the non-exclusive licensee a right of action under the section in the Regulations.

The non-exclusive licensee has the same rights and remedies as the actual copyright owner would have had if it was he who had brought the legal action. The copyright owner still of course has his own rights if he chooses to use them.

5.7.2.7 Duration of Copyright in Sound Recordings

The Regulations amend the Copyright, Designs and Patents Act 1988 on the matter of how long copyright lasts in a work.

Section 29 of the Regulations state that copyright expires:

i) at the end of the period of 50 years from the end of the calendar year in which the recording is made; or
ii) if during that period the recording is published, 50 years from the end of the calendar year in which it is first published; or
iii) if during that period the recording is not published but is made available to the public by being played in public or communicated to the public, 50 years from the end of the calendar year in which it is first so made available.

However, in determining whether a sound recording has been published, played in public or communicated to the public, no account shall be taken of any unauthorised act. So, illegal downloading or use within a virtual world or social network will not extend the period of expiration of copyright.

5.8 Trademark in Internet Social Networks and Virtual Worlds

Trademarks are another form of intellectual property right. However, unlike copyright which arises simply by virtue of a work being original and which need not be registered, trademarks must be registered at the Trademark Registry to be recognised as registered marks having commercial and legal significance. Before considering how trademarks sit within the context of virtual worlds and social networks it is useful to briefly review the attributes of trademarks in general.

There are benefits of seeking registration. Registration of a trademark gives the owner of the mark the right to the exclusive use of that mark and that right is infringed by the unauthorised use of the same or a similar sign for the same or similar services. The right is thus a very valuable, and trademark registration is a far more effective, way of protecting a sign used in trade than company name registration or domain name registration. Trademarks can also be valuable property rights and are often shown as an asset on the balance sheet of a company.

Once a trademark is registered, for example, by a virtual world provider, then in order to maintain that registration, the trademark must be used in the form in which it is registered. If the trademark is used in a form which differs to that registered, it might be cancelled by the Trademark Registry. In addition, if a trademark is not used for a continuous five year period following registration, and there is no genuine reason for the non-use, it might be cancelled until such time as use is resumed.

Following recent expansion of the EU, a European Community Trademark Registration may be obtained which confers upon the proprietor trademark rights in each of the 27 member states being Austria, Belgium, Bulgaria, Luxembourg, Netherlands, Germany, Denmark, Spain, Finland, France, UK, Greece, Ireland, Italy, Portugal, Romania, Sweden, Estonia, Latvia, Lithuania, Poland, Czech Republic, Slovak Republic, Slovenia, Hungary, Malta and Cyprus.

On the basis of a UK registration or Community Trademark Registration, it is possible for example, for the virtual world provider to file an International Trademark application which allows the operator to designate up to 70 countries. The main advantage to this system is that by filing one application in one governing office, the operator obtains one registration, with one registration number but covering a number of different jurisdictions. It is also far more cost effective than filing separate national applications.

The following is a list of all those member states that can be designated.

International Registration of Trademarks Madrid Protocol Member States (as at July 2007)

MEMBER COUNTRIES:

Albania

Antigua and Barbuda

Armenia

Australia

Austria

Azerbaijan

Bahrain

Belarus

Belgium*

Bhutan

Botswana

Bulgaria

China

Croatia

Cuba

Cyprus

Czech Republic

Democratic People's Republic of Korea

Denmark

Estonia

European Union

Finland

France

Georgia

Germany

Greece

Hungary

Iceland

Iran

Ireland

Italy

Japan

Kazakhstan

Kenya

Kenya

Lesotho

Liechtenstein

Lithuania

Luxembourg*

Madagascar

Moldova

Monaco

Mongolia

Montenegro

Morocco

Mozambique

Namibia

Netherlands*

Norway

Poland

Portugal

Republic of Korea

Romania

Russian Federation

San Marino

Serbia

Sierra Leone

Singapore

Slovakia

Slovenia

Spain

Swaziland

Sweden

Switzerland

Syrian Arab Republic

The former Yugoslav Republic of Macedonia

Turkey

Turkmenistan

Ukraine

United Kingdom

United States of America

Uzbekistan

Vietnam

Zambia

* Belgium, Luxembourg and The Netherlands are covered by a single 'Benelux' Trademark Registration.

5.9 Internet Social Network and Virtual World Trademark Use Policies

We examined in Chapter 3 the issues an operator of either a virtual world or social network would want to address in the user terms and conditions. One feature of these networks is the importance of their brand integrity. Whilst the general terms of use will cover intellectual property rights and how they are preserved, some operators go further and adopt a policy outlining the use of its trademarks. These trademarks include more than merely logos, but also the names of various products which might, for example, be certain software applications made available in-world.

In this section we will review the approach taken by operators to such policies. In essence they need to achieve a balance between ensuring that their trademarks remain reliable indicators of quality against the desire to permit inhabitants to discuss the various products and services featured in-world.

We have seen how trademarks may include word marks or brand names often in a distinctive font. If an inhabitant wishes to use a trademark the policy will require them to seek the permission of the operator of the environment. The policy will set out certain guidelines. The guidelines will state how an in-world business, for example, might use certain trademarks to show their association with the virtual world operator. Another expressly permitted use of certain trademarks might be to permit journalists and media organisations use of the same in published articles, blog entries, and news programmes specifically about the virtual world.

The policy may well highlight examples of what would constitute unauthorised use of the operators' trademarks. It may state that the inhabitant cannot use the same in its own branding, in the name of its business, organisation, product, or service. It will make clear that they must not register as a trademark, service mark, or business or organisation name, any trademark owned by the operator or any words or symbols which are near identical or confusingly similar to those trademarks.

The question of Domain name utilisation should also be addressed in the policy. The inhabitant must not use or register any second-level domain name that is identical, near identical, or confusingly similar to a trademark owned by the operator. Second-level domain names are those which identify part of a domain name that commonly refers to the organisation or entity that registered it. For example, 'Lecote.com'.

5.10 Creating in-world Software Platforms for use by other Inhabitants

5.10.1 BACKGROUND

Whatever might be said about the Internet in terms of its being a highly disruptive technology for the media industry, at the same time it is spawning a new era in entrepreneurialism, creativity and innovation. The sheer wealth of content available by the joining of millions of people across the globe and the opportunities that presents is incredible. Not only do social network forums and virtual worlds offer the landscape for developing original works they also form the ready means of distribution to millions of other users or inhabitants of the environment. If one considers for a moment the potential audience reach made possible by these online networks they dwarf the typical consumer or business target customer lists associated with software development. A typical software development company needs to work very hard to identify and then promote its software applications to generate business. Yet virtual worlds and social networks can provide a target base of millions of people.

One of the ways in which social network websites have sought to ensure users stay loyal to their network is to permit the development of software applications in the environment by users themselves. This development uses software tools intrinsic to the network but allows for original thought and intellectual effort on the part of the developer. Thus, new and useful software aids can be made available to other users of the service which have been entirely developed by a user. The interesting thing is many of these home-based software developers are very young, being in their late teens and usually not yet in full-time employment. Much of this content is provided free by those individuals although some of the social network operators provide grants to the best ideas which become applications used by other inhabitants.

There are some immediate questions which arise as a consequence of this phenomenon. It is clear that it has resulted in a huge pool of intellectual property which resides in networks, but how is that intellectual effort to be treated? Who owns the intellectual property rights in the software applications? How is the developer to be rewarded? What happens if the software application then assumes life outside the social network or virtual world?

In this section we will examine how a virtual world operator must address these and other issues in-world if it permits and encourages the development of further software applications using core tools by its inhabitants.

5.10.2 LEGAL TERMS GOVERNING AN INHABITANT'S ORIGINAL DEVELOPMENT WORK

The legal terms and conditions which control this activity in-world will be extensive and this is very important when one considers for a moment the activity they seek to capture. A developer will be allowed to develop and operate a completely new software application and make it available to potentially millions of users, all within an environment operated by a host organisation which will find it difficult to control to a high degree how that independent software works and is utilised by inhabitants. In this book we can only cover some of the issues one needs to address if drafting such terms and conditions and specialist legal advice should be sought.

If the virtual world is designed so as to permit this in-world development the virtual world terms and conditions will extend to govern this aspect of the service. We examined at Chapter 3 the typical provisions covered by the general terms and conditions. Here, we review the matters relating only to in-world software development.

The terms will state that the virtual world possesses a series of tools that provide a way for external applications to access the environment and allow any developer to build an application that integrates with the environment. This, in turn, allows for mass distribution of that software product and even permit the freedom to build a business around the development.

The terms will contain typical provisions such as stating that the virtual world will do its best to keep the environment bug-free but that the developer uses it at their own risk.

The developer will own their application and will be responsible for developing, operating, maintaining and supporting it. They must not infringe anyone else's copyright or intellectual property rights in general. If the application allows for file sharing, the developer must adopt and implement an acceptable copyright use policy. In addition, they must treat other user's privacy with the same degree of security and compliance as the operator of the virtual world. In fact, the developer will be subject to the provisions of the Data Protection Act if their application enables the collection of personally identifiable information.

The operator of the service will need to make available various software and intellectual properties to the developer and these it may term 'Properties'. The developer will be informed that they may use and store any Properties that are expressly identified as storable. However, it may not continue to use the Properties and Properties under its control if the operator gives the developer notice of removal or upon termination of the Agreement to participate in the virtual world development platform.

In connection with termination, generally some Properties will be of an exportable nature. This means that they are items which are capable of being exported to other applications and data repositories. These other applications may be independent of the virtual world operator. Thus, the terms will need to control how these items are surrendered by the developer. They will probably allow for a defined period of continued use following termination.

The developer will be informed that they must not infringe any international laws or use their applications in a manner which is misleading, deceptive or fraudulent, libellous or defamatory. The application must not allow for the personal identification of other virtual inhabitants except with their consent. It must not have as its primary purpose the facility to distribute copyrighted content without the authorisation of the copyright holder.

The application must not interfere with the functionality or proper working of the virtual world environment. The developer must provide the operator of the virtual world with full documentation relating to the functioning of the development if so requested by the operator. The developer must not block access to the work by the operator such as applying technical means to prevent such access. The developer will be asked to provide documentation to assist with access if access is needed on the part of the operator.

The control of the properties provided by the operator will be set out and the developer required not to edit or modify in any way those properties except, for example, in the case of graphics or images, the ability to resize the same to meet the new software product. Similarly the developer will not be able to sell, licence or distribute those properties except within the confines of the virtual world environment to other inhabitants.

Whilst the operator wants its inhabitants to develop their own software products for use by other inhabitant's in-world it will not want the developer to reveal confidential information of the developer to anyone else. Therefore the terms will contain a restriction.

It might be that the in-world developer, in addition to the operator's properties, the developer uses third party software to produce the new product. If so, then that third party product will be licensed. The operator will want the developer to agree to adhere to the copyright of that third party. If there is any claim by a third party that the new product infringes its own work then the developer will be required to suspend its product from use in the environment, typically within 48 hours of such notification. The operator will insist on an indemnity against liability.

The operator may elect to charge a fee to a developer for using its properties and, if so, this must be stated clearly in the terms. Whether or not a fee is charged the developer will be granted a non-exclusive limited and revocable licence to use the properties of the operator to develop the new product. The licence of course, is the proper legal mechanism to control the use of such intellectual works without giving the developer actual ownership of the same. The operator will have the ability to terminate that licence at any time and the developer must surrender up any materials or properties then used in its in-world software application.

The operator will want to reserve the ability to continue to develop its own software applications which may be deployed in-world. These may run alongside the developer products and the terms will make clear that the operator will not be restricted in any way from such activity and owes the developer no obligation.

If the developer does produce new products for use by other inhabitants the operator will need to control and limit its legal exposure for the running of those applications in the virtual environment. The terms will thus specify that the developer is solely responsible for, and that the operator has no liability for, those applications including the technical operation of the same, how they are displayed and the accuracy and appropriateness of the same. In addition, the essential need is for the developer to have a proper privacy policy, stating clearly to inhabitants how the developer collects, uses, and stores personal information about other inhabitants. That privacy policy will also govern the transfer of such in-world collected data to third parties such as advertisers who might then be free to serve advertisements within the virtual world to other inhabitants of the service who have used the developer's software product.

It is true to say at the time of writing that many branded applications have failed to take-off, as members of the social network websites choose not to install them. *Facebook*, for example, in 2008 had around 22,000 applications including branded applications pushing anything from artist album releases to television shows. These can be expensive to develop as pieces of software but in some instances attract only a handful of daily active users. To put the branded applications in context, this year none of them feature in Facebook's 50 most popular on the social network. Quite what this means for brand presence generally within social networks and virtual worlds is unclear. It may be that inhabitants of such environments are not happy to see advertising in this form within the environment. In the alternative, a number of brands are seeking to 'piggyback' on in-world software applications which are already popular though not belonging to major brands.

5.11 Controlling the use of the Virtual World Operators' Branding Material

It is generally understood that the brand style used by a business is very important to the general profile and reputation of the business. One only has to consider for a moment the names of High Street retailers, product manufacturers and service providers to know that huge value is attributed to those names because they become synonymous with quality and reliability. The same is true of leading ISPs, operators of search engine facilities, social networking websites and virtual worlds.

Therefore, the operator of a virtual environment will want to build and retain high levels of goodwill with its inhabitants. It will have adopted a suite of tools to represent that reputation, including its business name and graphical depiction in the form of a logo. These carry enormous weight and form part of the intellectual property assets owned by the virtual world provider. It will want to control their use and the way it can do that is by stating the limitations in the terms and conditions on the website itself. This may be achieved by including appropriate provisions in the body of the terms and conditions generally (see Chapter 3) or by their insertion in related but nonetheless visible sections of the virtual world website.

We will examine here the typical items such provisions will address. This is particularly important since the nature of virtual worlds gives rise to the transfer of, for example, logos to retailers who trade in-world. We have seen elsewhere that virtual retailers may have an in-world shop presence and occupy an island in the environment. However, in order for an inhabitant avatar to complete a purchase of goods the inhabitant must transition by hyperlink to the retailer's e-commerce website outside the environment. It may well be that the retailer wishes to relate the visiting inhabitant to their virtual world source and therefore display the virtual world operators logo on its e-commerce website to reinforce its in-world participation.

The operator will state that the presentation of its logos must be consistent with its own use of its trademarks in comparable media. This means, for example, that if the operator uses certain registered trademark or service mark notices with its logos (for example, ®), the inhabitant of the world will be required to use such notices when it uses the operator's logos. In addition, the inhabitant must include a statement in its material that includes such a logo: for example, ©2007 Company Virtual. All Rights Reserved.

This statement thus makes it clear to third parties that the logo of the operator also has copyright protection as well as its registered trademark status.

The operator will also want to control how its logo should appear within any website or material of an inhabitant. Once again, this is to preserve brand integrity. So, it might state that its logos must appear by themselves, with reasonable spacing and a minimum number of pixels between each of its sides and other graphic or text elements on the inhabitant's e-commerce website or printed material. In addition, the logo must also appear by itself in a manner that does not in any way indicate to viewers of the e-commerce website or printed material that the virtual world operator endorses the products, services, or information provided therein.

There will be activity in relation to the operator's brand which it will wish to expressly forbid. These will include preventing the inhabitant from displaying the operator's logo as the largest logo on the inhabitant's website or printed material, or displaying the operator's logo as the most prominent element on any page of the inhabitant's website or printed material. Displaying that logo in any manner that implies a relationship or affiliation with, or endorsement by the operator will also be prevented. So too will display which might be reasonably interpreted to suggest editorial content has been authored by, or represents the views or opinions of the operator. Clearly, displaying the operator's logo in a manner that is misleading, defamatory, infringing, disparaging, obscene or otherwise objectionable to the operator, will be forbidden. An online technique which will also not be permitted will be to frame or mirror any web page of the operators (including the page that appears in response to a click on the operator's logo). Finally, removal, distortion or alteration of any element of the logo including squeezing, stretching, inverting or discolouring, will be prevented by the operator.

5.12 Licensing Digital Content

Virtual worlds consist of a variety of features, some original to the inhabitant, others owned by commercial entities which choose to have an in-world presence for promotion. The latter group might typically be a well known store which operates an island in-world, or perhaps a media company or artist which wishes to make available musical work or movie images within the environment.

If such content is being made available in the virtual world the question arises on what basis is it to be accessed by inhabitants acting via their avatars?

The proper method of delivery will be by a licence granted by the content owner to consumers of the content. The content owner will want to ensure that it retains all rights of intellectual property ownership in the content and so will simply permit the user to access the content without that inhabitant acquiring any proprietary rights in that content. Licensing is at the core of the marketplace for digital content as it is the legal means by which the content owners can leverage the value of their assets. Likewise the content hungry virtual worlds and networks need to acquire the necessary content to drive traffic and revenues.

Whilst the concept of a licence of rights is commonly understood the precise terms of such a licence are more difficult to craft in the rapidly changing world that is digital media. For example, licensing arrangements relating to media content entered into only a few years ago may not have addressed Internet distribution. Yet, as is now clear, music and film can be distributed with incredible ease across networks and this has revolutionised the music business and film industries respectively. Still less will older licence agreements have broken down the rights granted to various forms of technology such as virtual worlds.

Thus, before drafting a licence of digital content the parties need to examine the underlying rights in the digital content to be licensed and how these will apply to digital content together with the potential ambiguities. The rights to be licensed will not be restricted to copyright but may also include database rights, trademark and image rights.

Linden Lab, the operator of Second Life, decided at the outset to grant users intellectual property rights for their creations which have been made using Second Life's own free software.

The following is a review of the issues which a content owner should consider if it intends to operate in a virtual world and make content available for consumption in that environment.

The use that a bespoke licence is to cover, needs to be clearly understood. For example, it might be that the content features in-world in a particular setting with limited operation. An illustration would be the making available of movie clips on a screen which is featured in the virtual world, perhaps in a virtual store, or in-world cinema. The screen might simply display the movie running on a loop with no ability on the part of the avatar to doing anything other than passively view.

However, the content owner might instead allow for downloading of that movie or perhaps clips from it. Such an ability is of course technically feasible but would fundamentally alter the nature of the digital licence to be granted by the content owner.

Therefore consideration needs to be given to the technical activity in question and provisions limiting the reception of digital content. That reception might also be limited to Internet access rather than mobile phone or portable device access to the virtual world.

The problems virtual worlds introduce on the issue of intellectual property rights, stem not so much from reconciling legally concepts of intellectual property with virtual environments, but in finding the perpetrators of intellectual property infringement.

5.13 The Rise of Social Networking Websites and User Generated Content

Virtual networks it could be argued, for all their risks, have unleashed a storm of creativity, entrepreneurialism, commercial thinking and social thinking. Such activity must surely be of benefit to society at large in the long term. However, those who participate in this manner are often doing so simply to improve both their own and other inhabitants' experience of the virtual environment. They are aloof to the value which might be attributed to their intellectual effort. Many are very young. It is not uncommon for teenagers to write software or other applications for use within their social network. Such applications are persuading inhabitants to devote time to the social networking websites and virtual worlds.

So important are they to *Facebooks's* popularity for example, that it announced grants of up to $250,000 to anyone who wanted to develop a *Facebook* application. In a matter of only months, 14,000 were spawned. The highest ranking application called *'Top Friends'* has almost 3 million users. By opening up the platform to external developers, *Facebook* not only acquired new products online to keep users at their computers for longer, but also fostered a burgeoning new industry. The kind of reach which can be achieved for software applications conceived and developed within virtual worlds and social networks far exceeds the best marketing efforts of most established software development companies. Such software applications may take several weeks to develop. Yet, the majority of this intellectual activity, aside from those who win grants, which is rare, goes unrewarded. Unless the authors regard the mere use of their work as reward itself.

The growth of social networking websites has given rise to another problem – that of copyright infringement in the media content often featured in such networks. In late 2006 Universal Pictures in the US began a legal action against the social networking website *MySpace*. The legal case followed a breakdown in negotiations between the two companies for a content licensing deal. In fact, Universal had similarly threatened legal action against another social networking website *YouTube* because that website specialises in video sharing. However, Universal settled the case against *YouTube f*or an equity share as part of Google's £841m acquisition of the website. All such websites raise questions about the rights of copyright owners in relation to distribution of their content on the websites. In addition, social networking websites attract significant advertising revenue (see Chapter 6) given their huge user base. They have become a major distribution channel for both video and music and hence a target for content owners who are losing revenue as a result.

It is interesting to note an important distinction. Both *YouTube* and *MySpace* began life as user-generated websites rather than peer to peer websites. The same is true of most social networking websites. By contrast, peer to peer websites focus on distributing existing third party material as opposed to new, original material created by network members or virtual world inhabitants.

When Napster collapsed as a free peer to peer network following the successful copyright legal action by A&M Records, the only way for members of the network to obtain free music was to rely on unsigned bands who agreed to make their work available.

User generated websites thus began to develop since their content is created and distributed almost exclusively by their members as non-media professionals. User generated websites also provide a powerful platform for independent content owners to promote their material to other users who can recommend a video to other website users.

However, this distinction between peer to peer websites and user generated websites has more recently become blurred. An increasing amount of content is now uploaded to social networks and virtual worlds which is not user generated. This may take two forms. First, it is often the result of established content owners such as record companies and movie studios, uploading their material in order to gain a greater audience. If one searches websites such as *YouTube* one can find, for example, the entire library of pop music videos belonging to the major record companies. Those companies have authorised this presence as they have recognised that there are indirect benefits to this form of promotion of their artists – perhaps driving or reviving consumer interest in the artist. Those consumers then go on to purchase music tracks of other material featuring that artist. There is therefore a latent commercial market to be won.

The second issue is the problem that a good deal of the content on social network websites consists of copyrighted material being uploaded and circulated without permission of the content owners. Both *MySpace* and *YouTube* show a catalogue of well known adverts, videos and clips from syndicated television programmes.

5.14 Creative Commons

There has been a move of late to design a mechanism for the practical use of copyright material online which recognises the reality of both the risk and opportunities the Internet presents to creative endeavour.

It is known as Creative Commons. Creative Commons began in the US in 2001 with the aim of establishing a fair middle way between the extremes of copyright control, and the unsolicited exploitation of intellectual property. The creator-led scheme encourages writers, musicians and artists to give up some of their rights, for example the right to distribute work or to control derivative works to the 'commons' of the Internet. This is achieved via a system of off the peg licences that are machine readable. Its primary tool is the use of a range of copyright licences which are freely available for public use. The licences allow creators to fine tune control over their work to enable as wide a distribution as possible. In essence, the copyright holder is able to set out terms of use when they create their work. They might for example state that they are content for others to use their work for any reason as long as it is not for commercial purposes. Alternatively they may permit use for commercial purposes. In this way, ideas can be protected, but the author is able to encourage some other uses of their work. It is in effect a label saying 'Some rights reserved' as opposed to the usual copyright protection of 'All rights reserved'. The individual keeps his or her copyright but allows people to copy and distribute their work provided they, as writers, are given credit. The idea is to give the public access to, for example, archive footage from the different archives so they can use it to create new things, for example, make their own video.

Virtual worlds are a sophisticated array of content which spans software development, graphical animation, audiovisual material and text. They comprise both content owned by in-world retailers and the operator of the environment itself, and user generated content. That is, material wholly original to the inhabitants of the environment. This might be in the form of audiovisual content as part of their island presence, or, as we have noted elsewhere in this book, even software products they have developed for use by other inhabitants. In fact, given the ability of inhabitants to manipulate and design virtual assets, those assets may well attract copyright. It may well be that the inhabitant of the environment, having produced a virtual asset which they regard as having some intellectual property worth, decides to allow other inhabitants to interact with the virtual asset but not to replicate it entirely. In such circumstances the creative commons concept may well work. The virtual asset may be 'tagged' with the creative commons licence.

The creative commons concept has just been introduced in the UK following careful work by a legal team at Oxford University's *'Programme in Comparative Media Law and Policy'*. Channel 4 is using the creative commons licences scheme for a music video service which it calls *PixnMix*. The concept behind creative commons is to allow for content to be introduced into the online environment so that it can be shared fully but also protected.

In the UK there are two different licences. One for England and Wales and one for Scotland, to reflect the differing legal jurisdictions. Creative Commons is at an early stage of life but it has already had significant impact on creative industries both in music and film, with some artists being persuaded to release their content under a creative commons licence.

There are some in the entertainment industry who express concern over creative commons fearing that it undermines traditional copyright protection. They believe that content owners may unwittingly give away their rights irrevocably. In addition, it could result in content owners who sign creative commons licences being discounted by a potential acquirer of those rights hostile to the concept. At the time of completion of this book it is not possible to assess the likely impact creative commons will have on Internet content distribution. However, it can be seen that creative commons has clear application to virtual worlds.

The operator of a virtual world may wish to employ the creative commons licence to its management of the environment. More likely still, the inhabitants of the environment may wish to apply such licences to their in-world presence where they provide for example, original music or audiovisual content as part of their virtual existence.

There appears below a typical licence approved by creative commons which might be used perhaps by certain inhabitants to govern in-world copyright use of their content. Clearly, they would need to incorporate the Licence into their virtual presence and provide other users the ability to access the Licence terms. That will be a matter of design of their island presence and will depend on the actual nature of their service in terms of how the Licence might be displayed.

5.14.1 CREATIVE COMMONS SPECIMEN LICENCE

Legal Code

CREATIVE COMMONS CORPORATION IS NOT A LAW FIRM AND DOES NOT PROVIDE LEGAL SERVICES, DISTRIBUTION OF THIS LICENCE DOES NOT CREATE AN ATTORNEY-CLIENT RELATIONSHIP. CREATIVE COMMONS PROVIDES THIS INFORMATION ON AN 'AS-IS' BASIS. CREATIVE COMMONS MAKES NO WARRANTIES REGARDING THE INFORMATION PROVIDED, AND DISCLAIMS LIABILITY FOR DAMAGES RESULTING FROM ITS USE.

Licence

THE WORK (AS DEFINED BELOW) IS PROVIDED UNDER THE TERMS OF THIS CREATIVE COMMONS PUBLIC LICENCE ('CCPL' OR 'LICENCE'). THE WORK IS PROTECTED BY COPYRIGHT AND/OR OTHER APPLICABLE LAW. ANY USE OF THE WORK OTHER THAN AS AUTHORISED UNDER THIS LICENCE OR COPYRIGHT LAW IS PROHIBITED. BY EXERCISING ANY RIGHTS TO THE WORK PROVIDED HERE, YOU ACCEPT AND AGREE TO BE BOUND BY THE TERMS OF THIS LICENCE. THE LICENSOR GRANTS YOU THE RIGHTS CONTAINED HERE IN CONSIDERATION OF YOUR ACCEPTANCE OF SUCH TERMS AND CONDITIONS.

This Creative Commons England and Wales Public Licence enables You (all capitalised terms defined below) to view, edit, modify, translate and distribute Works worldwide, under the terms of this licence, provided that You credit the Original Author.

'The Licensor' (one or more legally recognised persons or entities offering the Work under the terms and conditions of this Licence.)

and

'You'

agree as follows:

1. Definitions

a) *'Attribution'* means acknowledging all the parties who have contributed to and have rights in the Work or Collective Work under this Licence.
b) *'Collective Work'* means the Work in its entirety in unmodified form along with a number of other separate and independent works, assembled into collective whole.
c) *'Derivative Work'* means any work created by the editing, modification, adaptation or translation of the Work in any media (however, a work that constitutes a Collective Work will not be considered a Derivative Work for the purposes of this Licence). For the avoidance of doubt, where the Work is a musical composition or sound recording, the synchronisation of the Work in timed-relation with a moving image ('synching') will be considered a Derivative Work for the purpose of this Licence.
d) *'Licence'* means this Creative Commons England and Wales Public Licence agreement.
e) *'Original Author'* means the individual (or entity) who created the Work.
f) *'Work'* means the work protected by copyright which is offered under the terms of this Licence.
g) For the purpose of this Licence, when not inconsistent with the contracts, words in the singular number include the plural number.

2. Licence Terms

The Licensor hereby grants to You a worldwide, royalty-free, non-exclusive, Licence for use and for the duration of copyright in the Work.

You may:

- copy the Work;
- incorporate the Work into one or more Collective Work; and
- publish, distribute, archive, perform or otherwise disseminate the Work or the Work as incorporated in any Collective Work, to the public in any material form in any media whether now known or hereafter created.

HOWEVER,
You must not:

- impose any terms on the use to be made of the Work or the Work as incorporated in a Collective Work that alter or restrict the terms of this Licence or any rights granted under it or has the effect or intent of restricting the ability to exercise those rights;
- impose any digital rights management technology on the Work or the Work as incorporated in a Collective Work that alters or restricts the terms of this Licence or any rights granted under it or has the effect or intent of restricting the ability to exercise those rights;
- make any Derivative Works;
- sublicence the Work;
- subject the Work to any derogatory treatment as defined in the Copyright, designs and Patents Act 1988.

FINALLY,
You must:

- make reference to this Licence (by Uniform Resource Identifier (URI), spoken word or as appropriate to the media used) on all copies of the Work and Collective Works published, distributed, performed or otherwise disseminated or made available to the public by You;
- recognise the Licensor's/Original Author's rights of attribution in any Work and Collective Work that You publish, distribute, perform or otherwise disseminate to the public and ensure that You credit the Licensor/Original Author as appropriate to the media used; and
- to the extent reasonably practicable, keep intact all notices that refer to this Licence, in particular the URI, if any, that the Licensor specifies to be associated with the Work, unless such URI does not refer to the copyright notice or licensing information for the Work.

Additional Provisions for third parties making use of the Work

Further licence from the Licensor
Each time You publish, distribute, perform or otherwise disseminate

- the Work; or
- the Work as incorporated in a Collective Work.

The Licensor agrees to offer to the relevant third party making use of the Work (in any of the alternatives set out above) a licence to use the Work on the same terms and conditions as granted to You hereunder.
This Licence does not affect any rights that the User may have under any applicable law, including fair use, fair dealing or any other legally recognised limitation or exception to copyright infringement.
All rights not expressly granted by the Licensor are hereby reserved, including but not limited to, the exclusive right to collect, whether individually or via a licensing body, such as a collecting society, royalties for any use of the Work.

3. Warranties and Disclaimer

Except as required by law, the Work is licensed by the Licensor on an 'as is' and 'as available' basis and without any warranty of any kind, either express or implied.

4. Limit of Liability

Subject to any liability which may not be excluded or limited by law the Licensor shall not be liable and hereby expressly excludes all liability for loss or damage howsoever and whenever caused to You.

5. Termination

The rights granted to You under this Licence shall terminate automatically upon any breach by You of the terms of this Licence. Individuals or entities who have received Collective Works from You under this Licence, however will not have their Licences terminated provided such individuals or entities remain in full compliance with those Licences.

6. General

The validity or enforcement of the remaining terms of this agreement is not affected by the holding of any provision of it to be invalid or unenforceable.

This Licence constitutes the entire Licence Agreement between the parties with respect to the Work licensed here. There are no understandings, agreements or representations with respect to the Work not specified here. The Licensor shall not be bound by any additional provisions that may appear in any communication in any form.

A person who is not a party to this Licence shall have no rights under the Contracts (Rights of Third Parties) act 1999 to enforce any of its terms.

This Licence shall be governed by the law of England and Wales and the parties irrevocably submit to the exclusive jurisdiction of the Courts of England and Wales.

7. On the role of Creative Commons

Neither the Licensor nor the User may use the Creative Commons logo except to indicate that the Work is licensed under a Creative Commons Licence. Any permitted use has to be in compliance with the Creative Commons trademark usage guidelines at the time of use of the Creative Commons trademark. These guidelines may be found on the Creative Commons website or be otherwise available upon request from time to time.

Creative Commons Corporation does not profit from its role in providing this Licence and will not investigate the claims of any Licensor or user of the Licence.

One of the conditions that Creative Commons Corporation requires of the Licensor and You is an acknowledgment of its limited roles and agreement by all who use the Licence that the Corporation is not responsible to anyone for the statements and actions of You or the Licensor or anyone else attempting to use this Licence.

Creative Commons Corporation is not a party to this Licence, and makes no warranty whatsoever in connection to the Work or in connection to this Licence, and in all events is not liable for any loss or damage resulting from the Licensor's or Your reliance on this Licence or on its enforceability.

USE OF THIS LICENCE MEANS THAT YOU AND THE LICENSOR EACH ACCEPTS THESE CONDITIONS IN SECTION 7.1, 7.2, 7.3, 7.4 AND EACH ACKNOWLEDGES CREATIVE COMMONS CORPORATION'S VERY LIMITED ROLE AS A FACILITATOR OF THE LICENCE FROM THE LICENSOR TO YOU.

Creative Commons is not a party to this Licence, and makes no warranty whatsoever in connection with the Work. Creative Commons will not be liable to You or any party on any legal theory for any damages whatsoever, including without limitation any general, special, incidental or consequential damages arising in connection to this Licence. Notwithstanding the foregoing two (2) sentences, if Creative Commons has expressly identified itself as the Licensor hereunder, it shall have all rights and obligations of Licensor.

Except for the limited purpose of indicating to the public that the Work is licensed under the CCPL, neither party will use the trademark 'Creative Commons' or any related trademark or logo of Creative Commons without the prior written consent of Creative Commons. Any permitted use will be in compliance with Creative Commons' then current trademark usage guidelines, as may be published on its website or otherwise made available upon request from time to time.

Creative Commons may be contacted at http://creativecommons.org/.

5.15 Image Rights in Virtual Worlds and Social Networks[6]

It is a feature of modern life that celebrity endorsement of products, services and causes has huge impact on the success of each. Whether they be actors, musicians, sports personalities or sports clubs themselves they are all aware of the commercial value their image has. The use of their image has obvious application to visual media such as newspapers and magazines, television and of course the Internet. Given that virtual worlds permit the design of characters in the form of computer generated avatars, it can be seen that the potential for infringement of what we might understand as being image rights, exists.

The question arises therefore is there such a thing as image rights in English law?

In other legal jurisdictions such as the US and Canada the concept of rights in a personality's image is recognised in law. There is a right of publicity which affords the individual the exclusive right to control commercial use and exploitation of their image, likeness and even voice. In France there are robust publicity laws and those laws enabled the footballer Eric Cantona to claim damages for the unauthorised use of his image on the cover of a video.

However, such rights do not exist as such in the UK. Instead, whatever rights may be said to govern an individual's image are a combination of various strands of legal principles none of which are in fact intended to grant image rights. These include copyright infringement, trademark infringement, passing off, libel and malicious falsehood, and the Trade Descriptions Act 1968.

We have noted previously that registration of a trademark gives the owner an exclusive right to use that mark for specified goods and services. Typically, revenue is achieved by the licensing of those marks. The registration also allows the owner to prevent anyone else from using it. However, trademark is a difficult principle to apply in the context of image protection. Typically trademarks are granted not merely in the words but the graphical or stylised depiction of the words. We are all familiar with well known brand logos which are famous not only for the name but the style of logo or even their distinctive colour. If

6 See 'Image Rights – do they exist and who should own them?' By Andrew Braithwaite, *Sports and Technology Monthly*.

one considers the issue it may be seen that applying the principle to a personality's name alone might be difficult.

Another form of intellectual property protection is the offence of Passing Off. This essentially is where someone attempts to pass off their goods or services as someone else's without their consent by taking advantage of that other's brand, goodwill or reputation. It was this law which was used by the Formula One driver Eddie Irvine when a photograph of him holding a mobile telephone was manipulated to replace the phone with a portable radio showing the brand of the radio station 'Talk Radio'.

5.15.1 CASE LAW RELATING TO IMAGE RIGHTS

The first case which, whilst not dealing with virtual world depiction, is nonetheless a useful precedent for review. It is an English law decision of the Court of Appeal.

Irvine and others v TalkSport Ltd[7]

TalkSport operated a commercial news and talk-back radio station. It decided that the station should change its character from news coverage and talk-back to sports coverage. It had acquired the rights to cover a number of prominent sports events, including the 1999 FIA Formula One Grand Prix World Championship. It thus embarked on a promotional campaign to generate interest among advertisers, which included a boxed Formula One pack which contained a leaflet bearing a photographic image of Irvine, a well-known Formula One racing driver, dressed in racing gear and apparently holding up to his ear a small radio on which the radio station's logo clearly appeared. Talksport had, perfectly properly, purchased from an agency a photograph of the claimant listening to a mobile telephone, and had altered that photograph by substituting the radio for the mobile telephone. Irvine knew nothing of the Formula One pack or its contents, and had neither agreed to the use of the image in the leaflet nor to give any kind of endorsement to the radio station.

Irvine sued TalkSport claiming it had passed off its radio station as having been endorsed by him, and that as a result he had suffered loss and damage. TalkSport contended that the image on the leaflet was manifestly intended as a joke, and that its likely effect was not such as to induce its intended recipients to believe that the claimant had endorsed the radio station. It was accepted by the court that celebrities have a property right in their goodwill and that right may be enforced against those who falsely suggest endorsement of their products.

The Court of Appeal held that the image on the front of the leaflet was the clearest representation that Irvine had endorsed Talk Radio. The fact that the whole Formula One pack may have been intended as a joke, and may well have been perceived as such by recipients of it was irrelevant. The court found it difficult to conceive of a clearer way of conveying, by way of a quasi-photographic image, the message that a celebrity had endorsed a particular radio station than by depicting the celebrity listening intently to a radio bearing the station's logo. The court also found on the question of damages due to Irvine that the unchallenged evidence led to the conclusion that TalkSport would in all probability have had to pay at least £25,000 in order to enable it to do lawfully that

7 [2003] EWCA Civ 423; [2003] All ER (D) 05 (April).

which it did unlawfully, that is to say represent by means of the image appearing on the front of the leaflet that Irvine had endorsed Talk Radio. Therefore the court ordered damages of £25,000.

One has to distinguish between this kind of use of an image and the position where a celebrity image is used only to adorn a product and there is no suggestion that the celebrity is associated with it. In that situation no legal remedy exists.

Perhaps the best known footballer of the modern era is David Beckham. Most recently his celebrity has crossed the Atlantic to Los Angeles and he has successfully achieved a following in the US as well as maintaining one in the UK and elsewhere. Whilst at Manchester United, the club agreed to Beckham keeping hold of his image rights and granted him the freedom to choose his own endorsements. The club paid him a significant sum to use his image on club merchandise. He also has many other deals with major retailers and brands to promote products featuring his image. Thus, one can see that the image of a celebrity in certain cases has huge commercial value and, if it is misused, whether in real world advertisement or perhaps virtual world presence, legal action may be possible on the part of the personality.

So, whilst in the UK we lack a direct image right, by a combination of other legal principles the image of a personality can be afforded protection. This means that in the context of a virtual world or social network, any use of such an image must be undertaken with the permission of the personality concerned. The way such use will be permitted will be encapsulated in a legal agreement. The agreement therefore may be between an in-world retailer and the celebrity, or even between the personality and the operator of a virtual world depending entirely on how the image is being utilised within the environment.

There exists case law in the form of a United States Court of Appeal of California decision which serves as a useful guide to how the issue of image rights in the context of computer games has been addressed. Once again, as the case is not an English law decision it does not constitute precedent in the UK but is helpful for the purposes of our review of this subject.

Kierin Kirby v Sega of America, Inc 2006

The case is interesting and it will be seen that when the issue of likeness in the context of image rights is considered it is not merely physical similarities which fail to be considered, but gestures and other mannerisms.

A celebrity sued the distributors of a video game, claiming that the distributors misappropriated her likeness and identity in creating a character for the game, in violation of federal and state law. The celebrity was the lead singer of a retro-funk-dance musical group.

The court concluded that the video game character was more than a mere likeness or literal depiction of the celebrity. The character contained sufficient expressive content to constitute a transformative work and was not a mere imitation of the celebrity. Although the celebrity and the character shared similarities, they also differed in many respects. The character's extremely tall, slender computer-generated physique was dissimilar from the celebrity's. The character's typical hairstyle and primary costume differed from those worn by the celebrity. Moreover, the setting for the game that featured the character as a space-age reporter in the 25th century – was unlike any public depiction of the celebrity. Finally, the dance moves performed by the character were unlike the celebrity's movements in any of her music videos.

To understand the issues considered in the case we need to briefly discuss the American legal principles which formed the subject of the claims made by the plaintiff. The first is the invasion of privacy argument.

In the context of a celebrity, the invasion of privacy tort for appropriation turns on a right of publicity arising from commercially exploitable opportunities embodied in the Plaintiff's likeness. The elements of legal action are founded on two basis. The unauthorised use of a Plaintiff's identity to the defendant's advantage by appropriating the Plaintiff's name, voice and likeness, for commercial gain or otherwise, and which results in injury.

The second limb to the claim is based on legislative prohibition against the unauthorised appropriation of one's likeness. A statutory cause of action for appropriation requires a knowing use of the Plaintiff's name and likeness.

A further basis of claim in the United States exists under The Lanham Act (*15 U.S.C. § 1125(a)*). This is the federal equivalent of a right of publicity claim. It protects against use of a celebrity's image or persona in connection with a product in a manner likely to falsely imply a celebrity product endorsement. It is essential to a claim under the Lanham Act that there be the likelihood reasonable consumers will be confused about the celebrity's endorsement.

There is then another basis for claim in the form of the freedom of expression protected by US Constitution First Amendment. The provision exists to preserve an uninhibited marketplace of ideas and to further individual rights of self-expression. The protections may extend to all forms of expression, including written and spoken words, music, films, and entertainment, whether or not the same are sold for a profit. Importantly, video games are expressive works entitled to the same First Amendment protection as the most profound literature.

There is a defence available to a defendant who may raise the United States Constitution First Amendment as an affirmative defence to an allegation of appropriation of likeness. If the defendant's work adds something new, with a further purpose or different character, or alters the first with new expression, meaning, or message. In essence, the new work must contain significant transformative elements. The transformative test protects the right of publicity. It shields celebrities from literal depictions or imitations for commercial gain by works which do not add significant new expression. A work that has been transformed is less likely to interfere with the economic interests protected by the right of publicity, because a distorted image of a celebrity is a poor substitute for more conventional forms of celebrity depiction. As such, they are less likely to threaten the market for celebrity memorabilia. The real inquiry a court must make is whether the celebrity likeness is one of the raw materials from which an original work is synthesised.

The Plaintiff was Kierin Kirby, professionally known as 'Lady Miss Kier,' Kirby was the lead singer of a retro-funk-dance musical group known as 'Deee-Lite' best known for its song *'Groove is in the Heart'* released in 1990. The song's music video, which received extensive airplay on MTV, features band members clad in 'funky retro outfits, vivid graphics, groovy dance moves, a futuristic setting and an overall party feel'.

In addition to being a musician, Kirby is a dancer, artist, choreographer and fashion designer. Kirby claimed that, as 'Lady Kier,' she had developed a 'specific, distinctive, look,' of a 'fashionable, provocative, and funky diva-like artistic character'. Her 'unique public identity,' which combines retro and futuristic visual and musical styles, results from her signature costumes and lyrical expression. She claimed substantial, commercially valuable, goodwill in her sound, appearance, persona and likeness.

Deee-Lite disbanded by the mid-1990s. Kirby alleged she is regularly approached by advertisers and manufacturers interested in licensing her name and likeness to sell products. She submitted that she declined most offers.

The Defendants were distributors of a video game called *'Space Channel 5'* developed between 1997 and 1999, the main character was originally conceived as a male but was changed to a female in order to develop a video game to appeal to girls. The character was called *Ulala* and had six main dance moves (up, down, right, left, forward and backward). The character's dance moves were created by a Japanese choreographer and dancer who claimed the dance moves were her's alone. Further, at the time she created the moves, the dancer did not know nor had even heard of Kirby.

The game, set in outer space in the 25th century, features the computer-generated image of *Ulala*, a young, fictional, elongated and extremely thin female reporter. *Ulala* wears a few different costumes, but is primarily seen in an almost entirely orange outfit which includes a midriff-exposing top bearing the numeral '5', a miniskirt, elbow-length gloves, and stiletto-heeled, knee-high platform boots. Her hot pink hair is always worn in short pigtails placed high on the back of her head, and she wears a blue headset and jet pack and a blue gun holster strapped to her right thigh. Orange and blue were chosen as the primary colors for Ulala's costume because orange is the official color of Dreamcast, and the corporate color of Sega Japan is blue.

In July 2000, Kirby was contacted by a subsidiary of Sega Japan, in connection with its effort to launch a version of SC5 in England. It was considering using *'Groove is in the Heart'*, to promote the game in England and, possibly, Europe. Kirby was not interested.

Kirby sued Sega in April 2003 and, using US legal principles, alleged; (1) common law infringement of the right of publicity; (2) misappropriation of likeness; (3) violation of the Lanham Act; (4) unfair competition; (5) interference with prospective business advantage; and (6) unjust enrichment. Kirby alleged respondents wrongfully used her name, likeness and identity in developing and marketing the game and, specifically, its *Ulala* character.

The court found that notwithstanding certain similarities, *Ulala* was more than a mere likeness or literal depiction of Kirby. *Ulala* had sufficient expressive content to constitute a 'transformative work'. First, *Ulala* was not a literal depiction of Kirby. *Ulala's* extremely tall, slender computer-generated physique is dissimilar from Kirby's. In addition, the setting for the game that features *Ulala* as a space-age reporter in the 25th century is unlike any public depiction of Kirby. Finally, the dance moves performed by *Ulala* – typically short, quick movements of the arms, legs and head are unlike Kirby's movements in any of her music videos. Taken together, these differences demonstrate *Ulala* is 'transformative,' and the defendants had added creative elements to create a new expression.

5.16 Case Law relating to Virtual World and Social Network Intellectual Property Rights

There are few cases which, at the time of writing, address the treatment of intellectual property rights in virtual worlds. However, it is perhaps unsurprising that one of the most significant cases is first, very recent, and second, was decided in the US. The case is:

MARC BRAGG V LINDEN RESEARCH INC AND PHILIIP ROSEDALE, 2007[8]

A detailed review of the case is instructive because it considered many practical issues relating to how terms and conditions, which seek to govern in-world activity, need to be presented. Whilst the case is a US decision it nonetheless provides a good analysis of the issues which would be a feature of a UK-based virtual world service. It will be seen why certain aspects of such a service must be carefully considered by an operator. The case was about virtual property maintained in a virtual world on the Internet. The Plaintiff, Marc Bragg, claimed an ownership interest in virtual property. Bragg contended that Linden Research Inc. and its Chief Executive Officer as the operators of the virtual world, unlawfully confiscated his virtual property and denied him access to their virtual world. The case thus addressed questions of what rights and obligations grow out of the relationship between the owner and creator of a virtual world and its inhabitant users.

The defendants, as has been noted elsewhere in this book, operate a multiplayer role-playing game set in the virtual world known as Second Life. It is perhaps the best known virtual world at present. Inhabitants of the environment create avatars to represent themselves.

The environment is an interactive computer simulation which lets its participants see, hear, use, and even modify the simulated objects in the computer-generated environment.

In November 2003, Linden announced that it would recognise its inhabitants' full intellectual property protection for the digital content they created or otherwise owned in Second Life. As a result, Second Life avatars may now buy, own, and sell virtual goods and, most significantly, avatars may purchase 'virtual land', make improvements to that land, exclude other avatars from entering onto the land, rent the land, or sell the land to other avatars for a profit.

Although participants purchase virtual property using the virtual currency of 'lindens', lindens themselves are bought and sold for real US dollars. Linden maintains a currency exchange that sets an exchange rate between lindens and US dollars. Third parties, including ebay.com, also provide additional currency exchanges.

Second Life represented a departure from previous virtual environments in that it recognised the inhabitant's right to own intellectual property. Hitherto, any content created by inhabitants essentially became the property of the company developing and hosting the environment. Thus, the move recognised the fact that frequent inhabitants are making significant contributions to building these worlds and should be able to both own the content they create and share in the value that is created.

The Plaintiff claimed that he reviewed and relied on some of these representations about the ability to own in-world property. It was even contended that Mr Rosedale (Second Defendant) created his own avatar and held virtual town hall meetings in Second Life where he made representations about the purchase of virtual land. The Plaintiff attended such meetings and relied on the representations that Rosedale made therein.

In 2005, the Plaintiff signed up and paid Linden to participate in Second Life and began investing in virtual land, also paying real world currency as 'tax' on his land. By April 2006, he had not only purchased numerous parcels of land in his Second Life, he

8 Decided in the United States District Court For the Eastern District Of Pennsylvania.

had also digitally crafted 'fireworks' that he was able to sell to other avatars for a profit. In addition, he_acquired other virtual items from other avatars.

According to the Plaintiff, by June 2004, the Defendant reported that its 'real estate tax revenue on land sold to the participants exceeded the amount the company was generating in subscriptions.'

The dispute ultimately at issue in this case arose on April 30, 2006, when the Plaintiff acquired a parcel of virtual land named 'Taessot' for $300. Linden sent the Plaintiff_an email advising him that Taessot had been improperly purchased through an 'exploit'. Linden took Taesot away. It then froze the Plaintiff's account, effectively confiscating all of the virtual property and currency that he maintained on his account with Second Life.

The Plaintiff sued Linden and Rosedale.

The Plaintiff alleged several breaches on the part of the Defendant's including, under the Pennsylvania Unfair Trade Practices and Consumer Protection Law, the California Unfair and Deceptive Practices Act, California Consumer Legal Remedies Act, fraud, intentional interference with a contractual relations, breach of contract and tortious breach of the covenant of good faith and fair dealing. These are all of course US laws but in the UK similar legislative provisions might form the basis of a claim by a Plaintiff in not dissimilar circumstances.

The Defendants also sought to compel arbitration and compel the Plaintiff to submit his claims to arbitration according to the Rules of the International Chamber of Commerce (ICC) in San Fransisco.

We should at this stage review the sequence of events surrounding the Plaintiff's participation in Second Life. Before a person is permitted to participate in Second Life, he must accept the Terms of Service of Second Life (the 'TOS') by clicking a button indicating acceptance of the TO. (see Chapter 3). The Plaintiff conceded that he clicked the 'accept' button before accessing Second Life. Included in the TOS are a California choice of law provision, an arbitration provision, and forum selection clause. One clause stated '... Notwithstanding the foregoing, either party may apply to any court of competent jurisdiction for injunctive relief or enforcement of this arbitration provision without breach of this arbitration provision'.

The court noted that the TOS are a contract of adhesion. Linden presents the TOS on a take-it-or-leave-it basis. A potential inhabitant can either click 'assent' to the TOS, and then gain entrance to Second Life's virtual world, or refuse assent and be denied access. Linden also clearly has superior bargaining strength over the Plaintiff. Although in this case the Plaintiff was an experienced attorney, who believes he is expert enough to comment on numerous industry standards and the 'rights' of participants in virtual worlds, nonetheless he was never presented with an opportunity to use his experience and legal skills to negotiate terms different from the TOS that Linden offered. This, of course, is a feature of all Internet service legal terms and conditions.

The court noted that although the TOS are ubiquitous throughout Second Life, Linden buried the TOS's arbitration provision in a lengthy paragraph under the benign heading, 'GENERAL PROVISIONS.'

The court then went on to look at the issue of Substantive Unconscionability. Even if an agreement is procedurally unconscionable, 'it may nonetheless be enforceable if the substantive terms are reasonable'. In this case it determined that a number of the TOS's elements lead the Court to conclude that the Plaintiff had demonstrated that the TOS are substantively unconscionable.

The court also considered the mutuality of arbitration clauses. In other words, the fairness or otherwise of a company stating that its customers only remedy is to seek arbitration when the company then states that for its part, it has several options. In this case the court noted that the TOS contained many elements that potentially made the user agreement substantively unconscionable for lack of mutuality. The TOS proclaim that 'Linden has the right at any time for any reason or no reason to suspend or terminate your Account, terminate this Agreement, and/or refuse any and all current or future use of the Service without notice or liability to you'. Whether or not a customer had breached the Agreement was 'determined in Linden's sole discretion'. Linden also reserved the right to return no money at all, based on mere 'suspicions of fraud' or other violations of law. Finally, the TOS stated that 'Linden may amend this Agreement ... at any time in its sole discretion by posting the amended Agreement [on its website]'.

The TOS also provided Linden with a variety of one-sided remedies to resolve disputes, while forcing its customers to arbitrate any disputes with Linden. This is precisely what occurred in the circumstances of this case. When the dispute arose, Linden exercised its option to use self-help by freezing the Plaintiff's account, retaining funds that Linden alone determined were subject to dispute, and then telling the Plaintiff that he could resolve the dispute by initiating a costly arbitration process. The TOS expressly authorised Linden to engage in such unilateral conduct. For all practical purposes, a customer may resolve disputes only after Linden had had control of the disputed funds for an indefinite period of time, and may only resolve those disputes by initiating arbitration.

Also of significance was Linden's right to modify the arbitration clause. The court noted that it was this lack of mutuality which supported a finding of substantive unconscionability.

The Plaintiff also contended that the cost of an individual arbitration under the TOS was likely to exceed $13,540, stating that such arbitration would be cost-prohibitive for him. The Court's own calculations, indicated that the costs of arbitration, excluding arbitration, would total $17,250. These costs might not, on their own, support a finding of substantive unconscionability.

The TOS also require that any arbitration takes place in San Francisco, California. The Court found that a similar forum selection clause supported a finding of substantive unconscionability, because the place in which arbitration was to occur was unreasonable, taking into account 'the respective circumstances of the parties'. The record in this case showed that Linden serves millions of customers across the US and that the average transaction through or with Second Life involves a relatively small amount. In such circumstances, California law dictated that it is not 'reasonable for individual consumers from throughout the country to travel to one locale to arbitrate claims involving such minimal sums'. Indeed, limiting the venue to its own location was yet one more means by which the arbitration clause served to shield Linden from liability instead of providing a neutral forum in which to arbitrate disputes.

A further issue which went to the root of whether the legal terms and conditions used by Linden were reasonable, was the question of arbitration. It was a condition that Arbitration before the ICC, pursuant to the TOS, must be kept confidential pursuant to the ICC rules. The court noted that such confidentiality supported a finding that an arbitration clause was substantively unconscionable. The court reasoned that if the company succeeded in imposing a gag order on arbitration proceedings, it placed itself in a far superior legal position by ensuring that none of its potential opponents had access to precedent. At the same time, the company accumulated a wealth of knowledge on how to negotiate the terms of its own unilaterally crafted contract. Thus, the unavailability of arbitral decisions could also prevent potential plaintiffs from obtaining the information needed to build a case of intentional misconduct against the company.

This does not mean that confidentiality provisions in an arbitration scheme or agreement are, in every instance, per se unconscionable. The court had noted that taken together with other provisions of the TOS, the confidentiality provision gave rise for concern of the conscionability of the arbitration clause. The confidentiality of the arbitration scheme that Linden imposed also therefore supported a finding that the arbitration clause was unconscionable.

The court drew the following conclusions. When a dispute arose in Second Life, Linden was not obligated to initiate arbitration. Rather, the TOS expressly allowed Linden, at its 'sole discretion' and based on mere 'suspicion', to unilaterally freeze an inhabitant's account, refuse access to the virtual and real currency contained within that account, and then confiscate the inhabitant's virtual property and real estate. An inhabitant wishing to resolve any dispute, conversely after having forfeited its interest in Second Life, must then initiate arbitration in Linden's place of business. To initiate arbitration involves advancing fees to pay for no less than three arbitrators at a cost far greater than would be involved in litigating in the state or federal court system. Moreover, under these circumstances, the confidentiality of the proceedings helped ensure that arbitration itself is fought on an uneven field by ensuring that, through the accumulation of experience, Linden became an expert in litigating the terms of the TOS, while plaintiffs remain novices without the benefit of learning from past precedent.

Taken together, the lack of mutuality, the costs of arbitration, the forum selection clause, and the confidentiality provision that Linden unilaterally imposed through the TOS demonstrated that the arbitration clause was not designed to provide Second Life participants an effective means of resolving disputes with Linden. The court found that the arbitration clause was procedurally and substantively unconscionable, and refused to enforce it.

For the reasons set out above, the court denied the Defendant's motion to dismiss for lack of jurisdiction. The court also refused the Defendant's motion to compel arbitration.

The most recent case at the time of writing which deals with the issue of Intellectual Property Rights in the context of computer games is once again a United States decision.

MDY INDUSTRIES, LLC V BLIZZARD ENTERTAINMENT, INC.; AND VIVENDI GAMES, INC.[9]

Blizzard Entertainment, Inc. and Vivendi Games, Inc. (which collectively we will term, 'Blizzard') are the creators and operators of a multiplayer online role-playing game known as *World of Warcraft* (WoW). WoW is the largest and most successful multiplayer online

9 No. CV-06-2555-PHX-DGC, United States District Court For the District of Arizona. This discussion based on Lexis case report 2008 US Dist. LEXIS 53988).

game in the world. WoW currently has some 10,000,000 active players and generates more than $1.5b in revenue annually.

WoW was released in November of 2004. Players control characters within a virtual universe, exploring the landscape, fighting monsters, performing quests, building skills, and interacting with other players and computer-generated characters. Players who succeed acquire in-game assets, experience, and power. They can advance through various levels of skill within the environment.

Blizzard is the owner of the copyright for the WoW software. The software consists of two components: the 'game client' software and the 'game server' software. A user obtains the game client software by purchasing a copy at a retail store or downloading a copy from the WoW website. The user plays WoW by loading the game client software on his personal computer and accessing the game server software through an online account for which he pays a monthly fee.

Use of WoW is governed by an End User License Agreement (EULA) and Terms of Use Agreement (TOU) (see Chapter 3) These agreements are displayed on a player's computer screen when the game client software is loaded and the player seeks online access to the game servers. As we have noted in our review of in-world terms and conditions and contract formation, the players are required to read and accept the terms before proceeding to play the game.

Michael Donnelly was the founder of MDY Industries, LLC ('MDY'). Donnelly created, and MDY owned, a software program known as *WowGlider* (Glider). *Glider* was a computer program known as a 'bot' – a word derived from 'robot.' *Glider* plays WoW for its owner while the owner is away from his or her computer. *Glider* thereby enables the owner to advance more quickly within WoW than would otherwise be possible. MDY began selling *Glider* to WoW users in June 2005.

Blizzard claimed that *Glider* diminished the value of WoW and caused it to lose customers and revenue. It asserted that WoW was a carefully balanced competitive environment where players compete against each other and the game to advance through the game''s various levels and to acquire game assets. Blizzard claimed that *Glider* upset this balance by enabling some payers to advance more quickly and unfairly, diminishing the game experience for other players. Blizzard also claimed that *Glider* enabled its users to acquire an inordinate number of game assets – sometimes referred to as 'mining' or 'farming' the game – with some users even selling those assets for real money in online auction sites, an activity expressly prohibited by its legal terms and conditions.

MDY in reply, claimed that *Glider* actually enhanced the game playing experience of its users and even enabled some disabled users to play WoW. Further, Glider users represented a small fraction of WoW players and that the effect of *Glider* on WoW was thus minimal. MDY claimed that Blizzard sought improperly to use the copyright laws to stifle competition and innovation.

Blizzard claimed contributory and vicarious copyright infringement, violation of the Digital Millennium Copyright Act, and tortious interference with contract.

MDY sought judgment on all claims except trademark infringement.

Blizzard alleged that users of WoW were licensees who were permitted to copy the copyrighted game client software only in conformance with the terms and conditions on the website, and that when users launched WoW using *Glider*, they exceeded the license in the those terms and conditions and thus created infringing copies of the game client software. Blizzard claimed, because it materially contributed to this direct infringement by *Glider* users, MDY was liable for contributory copyright infringement. It claimed that MDY did so by developing and selling *Glider* with the full knowledge that *Glider* users would create infringing copies.

MDY was, according to Blizzard's claim, also liable for vicarious copyright infringement, because it had the ability to stop the *Glider*-caused infringing activity and derived a financial benefit from that activity.

MDY for its part maintained it did not dispute that it promoted the use of *Glider* in connection with WoW, that it controls *Glider*, or that it profited from *Glider*. MDY instead contended that it was not liable for contributory or vicarious copyright infringement because *Glider* users do not infringe Blizzard's copyright. MDY also did not dispute that Blizzard owned a valid copyright in the WoW game client and game server software. Nor that the game client software, which is usually located on the hard drive of a player's personal computer, was copied from the hard drive to the computer's random access memory (RAM) when WoW is played.

The court reached the following conclusions by way of summary judgment. Other of the issues for determination were ordered to be considered at a full trial and at the time of writing that case has not been heard. The court said that Blizzard owned a valid copyright in the game client software, Blizzard had granted a limited license for WoW players to use the software, use of the software with *Glider* fell outside the scope of the license granted in the terms and conditions, use of *Glider* included copying to RAM within the meaning of *section 106* of the US Copyright Act and *Glider* users therefore infringed Blizzard's. The court accordingly granted summary judgment in favour of Blizzard with respect to liability on the contributory and vicarious copyright infringement claims.

The court also granted summary judgment in favour of Blizzard with respect to MDY's liability for tortious interference and held that copyright applied to Blizzard's game client software code. The court however granted summary judgment in favour of MDY on its counter claim for unfair competition.

THE VIACOM CASE[10]

In March 2007 Viacom International Inc. instigated a legal offensive against *YouTube* and its owners Google. The claim sought in excess of $1b in damages for what it argued constituted massive intentional copyright infringement. The case came to epitomise the differing views of how the Internet should be regarded as it continues its unabated evolvement and becomes ever more significant in terms of media distribution. We will only consider the basic principles underlying the case to illustrate how the ever present copyright problems have been argued in the latest manifestation of Internet development.

There are what might be described as two sides to the debate on how the law should treat the use of material which attracts copyright protection within Internet social networks, video sharing websites and virtual worlds.

One side of the argument is represented by those who are most keen to preserve digital rights. These include groups such as broadcasters – like Viacom, and software companies such as Microsoft. Inevitably these organisations see the protection of copyright in the

---

10 Based on e-commerce Law and Policy *'Copyright v Web 2.0: the next digital challenge'* by Richard Graham March 2007 Volume 09 Issue 03.

digital sphere as vital. Elsewhere in this chapter we consider the question of digital rights management and its commercial value in a consumer landscape where users are increasingly reluctant to be restrained by specific media players when accessing music or film content. In 2007 both Apple and EMI began to move away from this restricted approach by allowing Digital Rights Management free music tracks to be distributed via the iTunes platform.

Those on the other side of the digital divide comprise the second generation providers. These are the operators of services such as *YouTube*, *MySpace* and virtual worlds. These groups disrupt the long understood business models for content distribution. They believe revenues come from advertising support. The origins of this argument may be found in the open source software model. Open source software generates revenue from support, maintenance and commercial plug-ins and not software licensing as it is commonly distributed.

Viacom believed that around 160,000 of its programs had been viewed on *YouTube* over 1.5 billion times. It argued that *YouTube* permits its platform to be used to upload infringing content whilst generating revenues for itself from advertising. The complaint against *YouTube* comprised six elements. Direct copyright infringement by public display, direct copyright infringement by public performance, direct copyright infringement by reproduction, inducement of copyright infringement, contributory copyright infringement and vicarious copyright infringement.

The Viacom case was similar in character to the earlier music industry related cases including the Napster case and the later Grokster and Kazaa litigation surrounding MP3 technology. We examine elsewhere the Napster decision and its promotion of peer to peer software with a centralised indexing server allowing users to search and transfer MP3 music files. The success of the litigation led to the further development of peer to peer technology offered by services such as Kazaa and Grokster where the centralised server was removed and the users themselves became responsible for searching and indexing. The ensuing court cases revealed the tendency of the courts to regard peer to peer providers as liable for copyright infringement because of evidence of their knowingly authorising or inducing the infringing acts of the users of their software in sharing MP3s.

In the UK, section 16(2) of the Copyright, Designs and Patents Act 1988 provides that copyright infringement can occur where an individual does or authorises another to do, any of the acts restricted by copyright without the licence of the copyright owner. This would include both the copying and distribution of unlicensed content over the Internet.

One argument which is used by the proponents of free distribution of content via the Internet is analogous to the one used in much earlier cases such as Amstrad. In the context of virtual worlds or video file sharing websites, the argument is as follows. Such websites promote the generation of creative user generated content and that the uploading of infringing programs such as those owned by Viacom, is incidental and peripheral to its aims.

There are other distinguishing elements to distribution of copyright works within social networks or virtual worlds as contrasted with peer to peer networks. These include the following.

Peer to peer distribution platforms carry substantial infringing content. The content of virtual world platforms is generally user generated and that is most likely not to be infringing.

Peer to peer platforms usually allow the user not to purchase the genuine content. However social networks, video sharing and virtual world environments often only permit clips of content. It might therefore be argued (and supported by user evidence) that they thus perform an advertising and revenue generation function for the rights owners. One only has to look at viral campaigns conducted on the Internet to see the strengths of this argument. This though is only a partial argument. Many websites of this kind now make available entire films albeit offered in ten minute segments which can be viewed in succession. Thirdly, peer to peer allows users to share and distribute files, whereas some virtual world and social network content only permits viewing through streaming.

CHAPTER

6 Marketing, Promotion and Advertising of Internet Social Networks and Virtual Worlds

6.1 Background

2008 saw the continued growth of social networks. *Facebook* achieved the most significant growth reaching in excess of 130 million users. Its UK sales operation claims to be running one hundred campaigns a week. These include video and rich media advertisement for O2, Sky and Vodafone.

This adoption of social networks was not restricted to commercial brands. *Facebook* registered 5.4 million US users voting Barack Obama following a push to vote on the website. Indeed the President's use of the community strength the Internet offers and in particular social networks is understood to have fuelled support for his presidential campaign. Younger voters, who are more actively engaged with social media could be reached in ways which not have been possible had such new media techniques not been pursued by the campaign.

In the same year *MySpace* reached 121 million users. Its promotional activity included an online radioshow, gaming channel, third party application platform. The most notable was the launch of *MySpace Music* in the US.

Bebo transitioned into an interactive content portal. It was sold to AOL for £417m. It developed a reputation for branded content. Its interactive web drama *KateModern* achieved 67 million views and was followed by *Sofia's Diary, The Gap Year, The Secret World of Sam King* and *Meet The Freshers*. In addition to running branded campaigns it also drove attention to teenager street violence and drug and alcohol abuse.

Bebo's sale was by no means the only one. Other acquisitions of user generated content forums include New Corporation's acquisitions of *MySpace* in 2005. Viacom/MTV acquired *iFilm*. The following year Viacom/MTV purchased *Atom Films* and, also in 2006, Google acquired *YouTube*.

These enormous transactions were all predicated on a belief that these environments have huge commercial potential. In addition to Internet social networks, Virtual worlds also present opportunities for commercial organisations and brands to promote themselves. Virtual worlds are developing in all directions and not just as commercial environments but there is certainly scope for product placement in-world such as clothing and furniture. However, brands can also create their own spaces and craft their own customised experience.

Advertising potential is not a given at this stage. Disney is implementing a digital strategy with interconnected virtual worlds playing a central role. The company wants to create a connected entertainment experience under the Disney brand. Disney.com is the hub of this and it believes virtual worlds are strategically important in making it immersive. It is launching five virtual worlds globally to complement all its other content formats from theme parks to films, merchandise to video games. To date, *Pirates of the Caribbean, Toon Town* and *Disney Fairies Pixie Hollow* virtual worlds have gone live in the US. Disney's revenue model is primarily free to play for basic content with the option of a subscription for premium content.

Major brands regularly advertise in Habbo and Second Life. L'Oriel Paris offered Second Life residents skins of different make-up looks. The methodology for brand promotion in virtual worlds may be different however. Their adoption by brands is not so much about reaching huge audiences but rather developing interactive relationships with their customers. There are inhibitors to virtual world use on the part of users. For example, it is easier to access a Flash game than to download a virtual world program. Despite this, the dynamic nature of virtual worlds means they must hold appeal for advertisers. The manner of that adoption may take many forms. One example might be advertisers using online three dimensional (3D) posters that, when clicked, will take the user to virtual models of stores, complete with products and services.

6.2 Internet Social Networks and Media Audience Engagement

Before we turn to an examination of the laws surrounding marketing and promotion of Internet social networks and virtual worlds it is useful to briefly consider the impact these forums are already having on mainstream media. This demonstrates that the environments are not simply fringe forums. If they can be interwoven with traditional media, they offer a richer experience for their inhabitants and another outlet for media content owners. The much talked about concept of convergence is, in 2009, becoming reality. The crossover between media platforms is significant. One development is the use by broadcasters and television production companies of Internet social networks to deepen their relationships with audiences. Examples of this include ITV launching its new series of *Primeval* by integrating a live *Twitter* feed into the first episode's online simulcast. ITV also developed for *Primeval* an interactive online experience with additional content and games. It amalgamated *Twitter* feeds about the show and displayed them alongside the simulcast of the show on ITV.com. The television production company Endemol conducted preliminary auditions for Big Brother via *YouTube*. Media companies are using social networks to promote television programmes through character profile pages and clips which can be shared, it worked with *MySpace* on the launch of the E4 series *Skins*. It demonstrated how well social media can build a television brand and assist with audience loyalty. It also worked by, for example, offering *MySpace* members a preview of the first episode. Channel 4 then created associated content for social networkers to consume and share, such as music downloads, character profiles and blogs. The result was said to be an increase in audience levels six times that of the average audience for an E4 show. Broadcasters can use social networks to distribute their content as well as monitor what inhabitants of those networks think about the programmes.

Internet social networks ought to be hugely important to broadcasters simply because of the size of the audiences in *Facebook*, *MySpace*, *Bebo* and other social networks. Indeed, by comparison their own audience reach is small.

One aspect of increased use of Internet social networks is involving audiences in the content creation itself. Collaboration between the audience and producer is known as co-authoring and it is an approach several content makers are exploring. For example, *Routes* is a Channel 4 educational project for Channel 4 Education. It is to educate 14–19 year olds about genetics through a portfolio of elements including an online documentary series, an alternate reality game about the murder of a fictitious genetic scientist, and genetics themed online games. The murder mystery narrative was told through video sequences, and clues spread across 30 specially created websites.

Despite the mixed marketing landscape that is virtual worlds, it can be seen that promotional activity is an ongoing feature of the successful social networks and virtual worlds. The capacity to reach huge audiences is clearly present. However, in common with many other facets of virtual environments, this aspect also carries legal compliance. In this chapter we will consider the law which governs the marketing, promotion and advertising of virtual environments both in-world and real world.

6.3 The Privacy and Electronic Communications (EC Directive) Regulations 2003

6.3.1 INTRODUCTION

There are clear differences in approach between traditional promotion and online marketing. We are entering an era of content abundance which is the Internet. The Internet is the perfect shop window for the promotion of virtual world environments. As the PC leaves the bedroom in most people's homes to join the living room and as those PCs become more media centre than IT device, the Internet thus changes the environment in which we consume information and interact with the world around us.

Although there are opportunities for those wishing to promote virtual world forums to maximise exposure to their target markets using the Internet in many ways, there is no less effort required. The promoter still has to reach out to their email database and find their audience online. There is a huge amount of careful marketing preparation and maintenance associated with direct virtual world promotion.

The increased sophistication of apparatus in the telecommunications sector in recent years is tremendous. In particular, mobile phones have evolved to the extent that they no longer merely serve as voice data instruments permitting telephone conversations from wherever there exists a service. Internet access is possible and with the rapid growth of 3G services, video downloads and broadcast material are accessible directly via the mobile phone. They are also an ideal means through which virtual world experience can be promoted. Factors which make mobile promotion of virtual worlds very significant include, improved handset technology with better screens, memory and battery life, improved data connections with more 3G networks, flat rate data pricing and the fact that it is a widely used technology with three billion phones worldwide and over sixty million in the UK alone

Virtual world development may mirror the evolvement of computer games in general. It was thought that computer games were the preserve of predominantly male users. As a consequence, the characteristics of the game would lend itself to a male audience. However, more recently the style of computer games has altered, not least because of the number of women users. The games industry itself has changed a good deal. There are now more women in senior positions. This is a reflection not merely of the fact that more women are gaming, but also that the workforce is changing. People are growing up with computers now and regard it as an industry that is easier to enter. A leading games developer, GameVision conducted a survey in 2008. It found that in Europe 23 per cent of people aged between six and 55 play computer games. Of those, 41 per cent were female, compared to 37 per cent in 2006. The average male user plays for 8.3 hours per week compared to 6.1 hours for females. 2007 was a record year for video game sales in the UK. 78 million game titles were sold while console unit sales hit 7.4 million, an increase of 45 per cent and equivalent to almost one in three UK households.

Thus, the market for computer games is both well established and growing. The prospect for commercial success of online virtual games is therefore reasonably secure.

As we will see in Chapter 7, the Data Protection Act 1998 is the legislation in the UK which governs the use of personally identifiable information relating to individuals. The principles contained in that Act must still be met by a virtual world operator or social network provider wishing to develop an email marketing campaign targeted at its inhabitant database. However, in addition to the Act such providers must also abide by the provisions of *The Privacy and Electronic Communications (EC Directive) Regulations 2003*.

The introduction of Regulations and the need for them highlight the problem lawmakers face in the world where media technology is developing so quickly. In 1999, for example, hardly an age ago and certainly not ancient by legislative standards, there were Regulations introduced to control the unfettered use of telephone numbers by businesses wishing to sell to consumers. Those Regulations were called Telecommunications (Data Protection and Privacy) Regulations 1999. In the short period following their adoption, email use and mobile phone adoption has been such that it was clearly necessary to revisit the issue of control and come up with a new set of rules more suited to the reality of the marketplace. The result, following a good deal of consultation with industry and consumer groups alike was The Privacy and Electronic Communications (EC Directive) Regulations 2003.

The Regulations came into effect in the UK on 11 December 2003. It is important to emphasise that given their nature as Regulations they are common to the rest of the EU. As such however, their ambit extends only throughout the Member States and they do not and cannot govern activity generated outside the EU.

In our review of the Regulations it is important to make clear that we are referring not only to voice data telephone calls, (telephone conversations) but also SMS text messages and email and other electronic messaging.

Regulation 4 of the new Regulations make clear that they do not relieve a person of any obligations under the Data Protection Act 1998.

6.3.2 TRAFFIC DATA

Regulations 7 and 8 set out certain restrictions on the processing of traffic data relating to a subscriber or user by a telecommunications provider. When one considers the issue it can be appreciated that the study of actual user data can reveal how the subscriber uses their mobile phone. This, of course, is useful to mobile phone service providers so they can market appropriate tariffs to their subscribers. It would also be of interest to those marketing other services, that is, third party companies wishing to sell other goods and services.

'Traffic Data' is defined as 'any data processed for the purpose of the conveyance of a communication or an electronic communications network or for the billing in respect of that communication.' 'Public communications provider' is defined as 'a provider of a public electronic communications network or a public electronic communications service.'

If we consider traffic data from the perspective of a virtual world provider wishing to market and promote its environment via a mobile phone network in order to get to potential consumer purchasers the following explanation is helpful.

Regulation 7 says that Traffic data relating to a subscriber or user may be processed and stored by a provider of a public electronic communications service in certain circumstances. Remember, we are not talking about third party organisations here, only the phone service provider.

They may process and store the data if it is:

a) for the purposes of marketing electronic communications services; or
b) for the provision of value added services to that subscriber; or
c) if the subscriber has given his consent to the processing or storage; and finally
d) if the processing or storage is done only for the duration necessary for the marketing of their services or provision of their value added services.

The phone subscriber must be told by the virtual world provider about the kind of information which the traffic data will consist and the duration of such processing before his consent is given.

The processing considered above can only be done for the following purposes:

a) the management of billing or traffic;
b) customer enquiries;
c) the prevention or detection of fraud;
d) the marketing of electronic communications services; or
e) the provision of value added services.

So, the sophistication which traffic data afford a marketer is restricted only to the phone service provider. It cannot be made available to, for example, a virtual world provider wishing to tailor its marketing message according to how its inhabitants actually use their mobile phone.

Regulation 10 is a provision relevant to virtual world businesses that obtain the mobile number of their target inhabitant by following the appropriate procedure detailed later in this section. It says that the provider of a public electronic communications service shall provide users originating a call with a simple means to prevent presentation of the identity of the calling line on the connected line as respects that call. Thus, the calling virtual world or social network provider could take up this facility so that the consumer would not necessarily know the identity of the company. This service must be provided free by the phone service provider company.

6.3.3 LOCATION DATA

Let us now consider the matter of location data. We stated earlier that the use of location based services by a virtual world provider was possible. Suppose the virtual world or social network provider wishes to provide value added services to the mobile phone consumer via a network and it strikes an agreement with the network provider to offer certain services. Which rules must the virtual world or social network and the phone company provider adhere to when offering such a service?

The Regulations state at 14(2) that location data relating to a user may only be processed where that user cannot be identified from such data or where necessary for the provision of a value added service with the consent of that user or subscriber.

Before obtaining the consent of the subscriber the phone company must provide the following information to the subscriber:

a) the types of location data that will be processed;
b) the purposes and duration of the processing of the data;
c) whether the data will be transmitted to a third party for the purpose of providing the value added service.

The subscriber can withdraw his consent at any time free of charge. The said processing of the location data can only be carried out by:

a) the public communications provider in question;
b) the third party (for example, virtual world or social network provider) providing the value added service in question; or
c) a person acting under the authority of either of the above.

Suppose the virtual world or social network provider wants to set up an automated calling system to contact its target consumer audience. The Regulations also set out how this process must be conducted.

Regulation 19(2) states that the phone subscriber must have previously given his consent to such communications being sent.

6.3.4 UNSOLICITED TEXT MESSAGING FOR DIRECT MARKETING PURPOSES

We now turn to the rules which must be followed strictly if a virtual world or social network provider wishes to contact would-be inhabitants with a view to marketing or promoting its environment. First, let us consider this process assuming the provider wishes to do this on an unsolicited basis using, for example, the mobile phone number of the subscriber.,

The Regulations provide for two mechanisms by which the consumer can ensure no unsolicited phone calls are made to their number. First, the person may have notified the virtual world or social network provider that no such calls should be made to that number. Second, and more likely, the consumer may have registered their phone number with the Telephone Preference Service. This is a register maintained by OFCOM which contains the numbers of individuals who do not wish to receive any unsolicited phone calls.

Provided the consumer has not then either notified the virtual world or social network provider of their objection to marketing calls or has registered with the Telephone Preference Service, it is possible for the company to make unsolicited calls to that individual. Remember, the definition of 'calls' includes both voice data and SMS text messages.

Thus, the rules for making speech calls to a target consumer or indeed sending them a text message are clear. However, with convergence of technology many mobile phones also have the capacity to send and receive email communications. The Regulations also contain rules concerning use of email for marketing purposes.

There was a great deal of consultation by the UK Government before the Regulations were introduced. The concern was to ensure that the proper balance between fair activities of the marketing community were achieved with the legitimate needs of consumers to maintain privacy. It must be understood that the Regulations only apply in the context of business to consumer relationships. That is, they apply solely to situations where a business, such as a virtual world or social network provider, wishes to make unsolicited telephone calls or send unsolicited emails to a target inhabitant. The Regulations do not apply to the situation where that business wishes to market its services to another business – perhaps a would be in-world retailer. This was largely due to the fact that businesses expect to be marketed to and to impose a bar on marketing calls and emails would run counter to the spirit of enterprise. The Government, however, made clear that if the evidence over the next few years pointed to business to business unsolicited communications becoming a significant menace, then further regulation would be considered with a view to combating the problem.

The other point to emphasise is that these laws can only address the problem of unsolicited messages if they originate from within the EU. The rules, of course, do provide a framework for virtual world or social network providers in terms of how they must go about marketing their environment and services using electronic communications. The Regulations have been successful in controlling what was fast becoming a major problem. They cannot however govern virtual worlds and social networks based outside the EU. Therefore such businesses can still send unsolicited communications to consumers and, of course, other businesses without restriction. This is why many readers will doubtless receive several emails a day from businesses based for example in the US.

There are exceptions to the general bar as a virtual world or social network provider on sending unsolicited emails to consumers.

If such a provider can demonstrate that one of the following conditions has been satisfied then it will not be deemed to have infringed the Regulations.

Regulation 22(3) states that:

A person may send or instigate the sending of electronic mail for the purposes of direct marketing where:

(a) that person has obtained the contact details of the recipient of that electronic mail in the course of the sale or negotiations for the sale of a product or service to that recipient;

(b) the direct marketing is in respect of that person's similar products and services only; and

(c) the recipient has been given a simple means of refusing (free of charge except for the costs of the transmission of the refusal) the use of his contact details for the purposes of such direct marketing, at the time that the details were initially collected, and, where he did not initially refuse the use of the details, at the time of each subsequent communication.

These exceptions allow for a degree of flexibility on the part of a virtual world or social network provider which intends to market its titles and merchandise. For example, (a) might be satisfied if the consumer has previously given their contact details to the company as part of a promotional offer or competition. It might be that the provider offered a prize inviting people to enter the competition and asking they complete their address details. Any contact details thus obtained would permit the virtual world or social network provider to commence sending emails to those individuals without infringing the Regulations.

The second exception (b) is also fairly wide. In the case of a supermarket selling a wide range of products it might be difficult for them to start marketing film DVD titles to their consumer database when those consumers have only previously purchased groceries. However, in the case of a virtual world or social network it might be that it has previously marketed its general service to its inhabitants but now wishes to offer a new software application to its inhabitants as part of its service. Such offers would amount to similar goods or services and therefore the virtual world or social network would not infringe the Regulations.

The third exception deals with where a consumer notified his willingness to receive future marketing communications. The individual has to 'opt in' to the receipt of such messages. In the past, a marketing department could regard an individual's silence as acceptance. Thus, the virtual world or social network could draft a response form for the inhabitant to complete which required the inhabitant to tick a box to indicate their objection to receiving material in the future (Opt out). If the inhabitant did not tick that box, the company was entitled to assume that consent had been granted and they could continue to send material. Now, the Regulations require the inhabitant to tick expressly that they have no objection to receiving marketing communications.

If a virtual world or social network wishes to instigate a publicity and marketing campaign using electronic communications it must follow the above procedures. It should also state clearly the precise means by which it may market its merchandise or services to the target consumer in the future. Thus, if it intends to send SMS text messages to the individual's phone, this must be made clear. If, in addition or in the alternative, it wants to send emails, this must be clarified.

One interesting point of note is that the Regulations, as we have said, only apply to individuals. However, the definition of individuals also includes 'an unincorporated body of such individuals' which could include a legal partnership.

Another important restriction on a tactic which might be thought useful is contained in Regulation 23. This prohibits the sending of communications by means of email for the purposes of direct marketing where the identity of the person on whose behalf the communication is made has been disguised or concealed or an address to which requests for such communications to cease may be sent has not been provided.

The important thing to note is that a virtual world or social network provider cannot seek to exclude a consumer's rights under the Regulations by contractual term. So, for example, in the website terms and conditions (Chapter 3) the provider could not include a clause which informed their inhabitant that they could expect to receive future marketing communications without offering that person the ability to register their express consent.

There are penalties which will be imposed on a virtual world or social network provider which infringes the Regulations. Regulation 30 allows a claim for damages to be brought by the person receiving the messages. The provider can mount a defence if it can prove it took such care as in all the circumstances was reasonably required to comply with the relevant requirement.

The Regulations also add an obligation on those providers who wish to use cookies or other similar software tracking devices to notify their use to their inhabitants. A cookie is an electronic tag which permits website operators to identify the buying habits of their online consumers. They allow for very sophisticated marketing. They are widely deployed on commercial retail websites. Internet users will be familiar with such technology if for example they use Amazon to purchase film DVDs. The Regulations do not forbid the use of such technology in a website but the virtual world or social network provider must include a clause in its website terms and conditions notifying the visitor to the website that the website uses cookies for these purposes.

For a virtual world or social network, mobile marketing has the appeal of the precision of direct marketing, the tracking potential of the Internet with massive publicity and advertising cost savings. Some in the new media sphere believe that the mobile phone could become one of the most important media for advertisers and marketers. The mobile phone industry actually has a huge market advantage in the new media world in that they already have a ready made single billing system for their subscribers. Those subscribers expect to pay for content such as music ringtones. Therefore, for the virtual world or social network wishing to access new markets using new media the approach to mobile phone service providers is perhaps a route to consider.

The potential for virtual worlds and social networks to be marketed via mobile phones has been ushered in by two principal factors. First, fast networks and high functionality phones. Second, the sheer ubiquity and importance of the mobile phone among consumers. Indeed, some research suggests that people were more willing to do without television than their mobile phones. The evidence also suggests that children and young people upon returning from school or college do not switch on the television, but rather log on to the Internet. The world which the media industry understands is rapidly changing. Audiences are becoming fragmented.

It is thus useful to consider how a virtual world or social network provider might go about marketing its environment by the use of mobile phones. As we have seen, the telephone service provider can use the traffic and billing data it holds about its subscribers for the purpose of marketing further services to them. It cannot, however, release that data to a third party company. It can, though, release the mobile phone number of a subscriber to a third party company such as a virtual world provider where the telephone service company has included a clause in its network access contract with the subscriber.

That clause might state that the phone company is entitled to release numbers to third party companies with a view to those companies sending marketing messages.

If the mobile phone service provider has included this notification, then the virtual world provider might acquire (for a fee) that database of mobile phone numbers. However, the provider would then have to send an initial message to the subscriber stating that they intend to send marketing messages in the future and the means by which those messages will be sent. This is known as a Data Protection Notice. The subscriber must then expressly signify their agreement to receiving those messages. This acceptance might be given by visiting the virtual world or social network provider's website to register consent. Provided the subscriber does give consent in this way the provider can commence marketing its environment to the mobile phone subscriber. The subscriber can refuse their consent at any time and, if so notified, the virtual world provider must cease transmission of material or face legal penalties.

6.4 In-world Advertising and Marketing

6.4.1 WHY IS IN-WORLD ADVERTISING SO IMPORTANT?

The staggering sums of money paid by News Corporation and Google for user generated websites is made more remarkable by the fact that only five years ago social networking websites did not exist.

Online advertising, or digital signage, is growing in sophistication and significance. In Chapter 7 we examine the concerns which in-world behavioural targeting raises in the context of privacy laws. However, the capacity to deliver highly targeted advertisements is likely to become more commonplace in virtual worlds and Internet social networks. To place the online advertising industry in today's context it can be seen there is a plethora of tools available to Internet users and those companies who want to advertise online. Most of the Internet industry leaders offer advertising platforms. AOL has Adtech, and Advertising.com which is a display advertising network. AOl's Buy.at is an affiliate marketing tool, Lightingfast is its video advertising platform, Quigo is its contextual advertising tools and Third Screen Media its mobile marketing platform.

Microsoft operates AdECN as its advertising exchange, Atlas for its advertising serving, Microsoft Live is paid search and Screen Tonic is for mobile marketing which enables advertisements to be placed across MSN portals and services such as Hotmail.

Google has AdSense for its contextual advertising network, AdWods as its paid search platform, DoubleClick for advertisement serving and exchange and Google Andriod as its mobile operating system.

Yahoo has Yahoo Advertising as its display, rich media, mobile and behavioural targeting platform. Yahoo Search Marketing for paid search and Yahoo Go3.0 for mobile services.

The question arises how can social network websites command such values? The answer is that they offer a previously impossible proposition for advertising inventory. They transform the online experience for advertisers, media companies and consumers. *Bebo*, for example, claims at the time of writing to have more than 40 million worldwide users making it one of the top social network sites in English speaking nations. The website is one of the leading networks in the UK, and top ranked in Ireland and New

Zealand. It is suggested that the average *Bebo* user spends 40 minutes a day on the site and it is this that makes it and other social network websites highly attractive to media companies. They represent a tremendous opportunity to bring advertisers solutions that fit their marketing.

At the same time some social network websites also offer media companies the opportunity to put their content on the pages of the network in whatever form they want and keep the advertising revenue. CBS, MTV Networks, the BBC, Turner Broadcasting Systems and Yahoo were among the first companies to adopt this facility when *Bebo* made it available via its new open platform.

A company's digital presence goes beyond digital signage to include everything an organisation does digitally to promote itself or its products. It is fast becoming as significant to advertisers and broadcasters as commercial broadcast television. Social networking websites, and virtual worlds are attractive to advertisers because many such environments are an educated, affluent demographic. Further, they are very compelling because they are a part of people's day. These online environments are capturing millions of users worldwide who each spend a portion of their day interacting with others in-world. To reach people in such numbers by, for example, television advertising would be hugely expensive. However, there might be a careful balance to be achieved. If an online network becomes too large it risks losing its attraction. For many users, the bigger their network gets, the less relevant and meaningful it becomes. Niche networks are thus finding new users. Virtual worlds are the definition of niche in the online environment.

In this chapter we will consider the controls which exist in the UK on the use of advertising in virtual worlds.

The point to appreciate about social networks is that they allow more targeted advertising for brands than banner advertisements placed on Yahoo or Google for example. Traditional online advertising is inefficient, with only around one in every two hundred people bothering to click on the advertisements and a fraction of those actually going on to buy.

The first thing to note, which is central to understanding how virtual environments operate and hence how best to approach them, is their particular characteristic. Virtual worlds are an extension of the world we live in. However, they are also very different. Every participant in a virtual world can construct his or her own custom lifestyle and select their ideology from a large number of choices. Thus, rather than pushing the same objects to a mass audience, marketing now has to target each individual separately. Virtual worlds shift the model of mass communication and radically shape the way participants interact and communicate with each other. In-world avatars establish relationships and experience a sense of belonging despite temporal and special boundaries.

Once it became clear that the Internet was a natural medium for the conduct of business, then it was inevitable that advertising would find a home online. The advertising industry has capitalised on the proliferation of new media with large agencies running multi-million pound interactive advertising subsidiaries. However, the early attempts at Internet advertising were unsophisticated and unsuccessful. It was the widespread adoption of broadband technology in the home which catapulted Internet use into the mainstream and in turn made the attraction of online advertising inescapable. What has been added to this is the huge increase in advertising spend on the Internet. In the past year, major advertisers are setting aside much more of their budget for digital advertising. Television advertising is suffering not least because of this trend. It is a development which is unlikely to diminish in the years ahead. Advertisement funded content is the becoming the mainstay of online media distribution.

Given the impact advertising now has in the online environment it is likely that it will come to encroach on virtual worlds as well. Second Life, for example, has its own currency, the Linden dollar. Whilst one does not have to earn money within the Second Life platform in order to exist therein, it appears that most participants desire the same things in the virtual world as they do in the real world. They may not actually need anything but this does not prevent them from wanting it and they will spend their earned dollars purchasing drinks, furniture and clothing, for example. The attraction of Second Life to advertisers is its sheer scale of users and they are highly engaged. Some users spend as much time in Second Life as the average American spends watching television. The number of Second Life participants is also growing hugely. There are agencies now established to assist major corporate brands gain entry into virtual worlds. Brands and marketing companies are eager to exploit this new phenomenon. The question remains just how?

The obvious form would be in-world billboard-style advertising. Such an approach has been adopted by Coca-Cola and IBM who maintain pitches in Second Life. However, it is important for advertisers to recognise the differing characteristic of virtual world participation contrasted even with typical Internet browsing. Some feel that blatant advertising will not work. Whilst one may have come to acknowledge the presence of advertising on a website the entry into a virtual world is often based on a more focused interest in knowledge share and business inspiration. Users may thus object to elements of marketing infiltrating their world. Advertisers may have to be far more subtle if they are gain benefit from in-world presence.

There is clear evidence of the increasing use of Virtual worlds by major brands. For example, in 2009, 20th Century Fox launched a digital version of the Smithsonian Museum in the virtual world *Habbo* to promote the cinema release of *Night at the Museum 2*. The film company partnered with *Habbo* to create a branded room along with an avatar of actor Ben Stiller's character to attempt to engage with the website's teenage audience.

In the same year Sony Computer Entertainment Europe extended its PlayStation campaign onto the virtual world *Home*. Sony intends to create a virtual community on *Home* where gamers can discuss and share official and user generated content around the campaign. *Home* is a virtual world which allows PlayStation Network users around the world to interact with each other, download and play external games and access external partner content.

It is possible that avatars, as virtual animated representatives of individuals, could start wearing branded clothing, visiting branded clubs and restaurants and drinking branded drinks. Covert sales representative avatars could enter into online communities and subtly drop brand names into conversations.

Whether such an approach would be effective is questionable.

One potential attraction to advertisers is the possibility that avatars will roam between virtual worlds carrying their personal data and branded guide with them thus offering further visibility for the brand across platforms. Indeed, many software applications developed by users of virtual worlds themselves easily allow advertisers to sift through the personal data on social network websites and virtual worlds to identify and market to potential customers. There is a generation of young people who appear not care about personal privacy despite the existence of laws designed to protect the same (see Chapter 7).

Without straying into the realms of how law reflects the society it seeks to protect, there is an interesting argument that in the years ahead the very laws which are designed to provide so much privacy protection will not be regarded as essential by a generation of adults who have disclosed personal information in social networks for years without much thought.

The trend for online advertising to become highly targeted is increasing and virtual worlds will be no exception. Online advertising campaigns may be based around time, location and weather. Companies such as Renault, Wagamana and Lastminute.com launched online advertising campaigns using live data such as the weather, where the person viewing the advertisement is, or the time of day, in an effort to make them more relevant to the customers' needs.

Wagamama is the Japanese style noodle bar chain. It launched a location-based campaign using online map site Multimap. When a user searches an area that is near a Wagamama restaurant, a message pops up saying 'Click for Noodles in this area'. Wagamama logos linking to its website then appear at restaurant locations on the map.

It is clear, that in this pioneering era with respect to virtual worlds, brands need to carefully assess how best to gain presence. If a major company were considering entry in Chinese markets, for example, in the real world, it would research the Chinese people and their culture. The same vigorous study applies to virtual worlds.

Virtual worlds offer a company a much more personalised way of marketing to people, enabling more accurate delivery of messages to the target consumer.

The Internet has radically changed the nature of marketing and advertising, just as it has changed the media industry in general. There are opportunities for promotion using viral marketing techniques which no one could have foreseen even two or three years ago. The use of social networking websites such as *YouTube* has created vast markets for film content and in the main user generated content. These websites have proved remarkably effective in spreading a message simply by their users posting and transmitting messages about films, or sending the film content itself. In effect, the audience does the marketing for you. The implications in terms of reduced costs are easy to grasp.

Virtual worlds however offer the more imaginative advertisers the opportunity to explore new techniques. When Diageo, the drinks business, entered virtual worlds they decided to recreate the feeling that consumers got from the company's brands, rather than concentrate on the act of drinking itself, which is meaningless in a virtual world. The result was a virtual bar kit that owners could buy. It enabled avatars to share a drink, propose toasts and engage in social networking or dialogue with other drinkers.

There are a host of virtual worlds, each targeting a different user audience. *Habbo Hotel* is aimed at teenagers. *Club Penguin* has around eight million 10–13 year old users. There.com claims an average user age of 22 equally split between male and female. It has run pioneering virtual brand experiments with companies such as Levi's and Nike. Nike introduced a range of shoes which enabled users to run faster, while Levi's created a limited edition denim jacket. These items could be purchased by members through There.com's web catalogue or from in-world kiosks. Levi had product pages in-world which asked 'Want the real thing? Only at Levis.com'. This linked to the Levi's e-commerce website.

Entertainment brands have been among the first to harness the alternative worlds, particularly since social networking websites such as *MySpace* and *YouTube* have diverted the attention of their audience. MTV has experimented in virtual domains.

As an aside, there are a number of digital agencies which, in addition to offering website development and related Internet services such as viral marketing campaigns, search engine optimisation, and pay per click advertising services also offer advice on virtual world presence. Legal advice should be taken on the effect of the Service Level Agreements which such agencies seek to impose.

A company's advertising in-world will be interactive and based on a model in which the consumer's avatar comes to it. Until the advent of the Internet, interactive advertising or marketing activity has been conducted face-to-face. The worldwide web enables companies to engage their consumers in the advertising itself. Virtual worlds once more allow face-to-face dialogue, albeit avatar to avatar.

Before considering in-world advertising, it is as well to briefly set out the legal background to advertising production in the UK, where advertising is regulated by voluntary codes. There are also many statutes which affect advertising. There should be no reason why any company wishing to promote itself in virtual worlds should not be subject to these rules and so it is important to review the real world legal landscape.

6.4.2 THE BRITISH CODE OF ADVERTISING, SALES PROMOTION AND DIRECT MARKETING

The British Code of Advertising, Sales Promotion and Direct Marketing is now in its eleventh edition and came into force on 4 March 2003. It replaces all previous editions. This is the principal voluntary code in the UK. It is drawn-up by the Committee of Advertising Practice.

The Advertising Standard Authority (ASA) is charged with the duty of monitoring compliance with the Code. The ASA is independent of the advertising industry.

The Code applies to traditional media such as advertisements in newspapers, magazines and mailings, but it also covers emails, text transmissions and other electronic material. In addition the Code governs advertisements in non-broadcast electronic media including online advertisements in paid for space, for example, banner and pop-up advertisements.

Therefore, a company wishing to embark on an in-world advertising campaign should abide by the provisions of the Code.

We will now examine the principal terms of the Code as they apply to an in-world company. It is important to appreciate that the ambit of the Code is wide and it does not simply apply to advertisements in the traditional sense. The Code contains various definitions. For example products which fall within its domain encompass goods, services, ideas, opportunities, prizes or gifts. Promotions are also covered. Thus, an in-world company wishing to offer a prize to win merchandise, or run an opportunity to claim a gift, perhaps via its e-commerce website as in the Levis example above, must comply.

There are some general rules which will apply to a promotion or advertisement for goods or services conducted in a virtual world. These include:

- All marketing communications should be legal, decent, honest and truthful.

- All marketing communications should be prepared with a sense of responsibility to consumers and to society.
- All marketing communications should respect the principles of fair competition generally accepted in business.

6.4.3 TESTIMONIALS

There are many other requirements. For example, on the matter of testimonials and endorsements. An in-world company should hold real world signed and dated proof, including a contact address for any testimonial it uses. Unless they are genuine opinions taken from a published source, in-world testimonials should be used only with the written permission of those giving them.

The testimonial must relate to the product being advertised.

Testimonials alone do not constitute substantiation and the opinions expressed in them must be supported, where necessary, with independent evidence of their accuracy. Fictitious testimonials should not be presented as though they are genuine.

There are clear guidelines on the protection of privacy of people the in-world company might wish to associate with the virtual advertisement. If referring to people with a public profile, for example a well known actor, references that accurately reflect the contents of books, articles or films may be acceptable without permission.

Prior permission may not be needed when the in-world marketing communication contains nothing that is inconsistent with the position or views of the person featured.

However, an in-world company which implies any personal approval of the advertised product should recognise that those who do not wish to be associated with the product may have a legal claim. In addition, how the in-world company depicts the celebrity by avatar needs very careful consideration.

6.4.4 PRICING OF PRODUCTS BOTH REAL AND VIRTUAL

On the matter of pricing, any virtual world advertising must ensure that stated prices should be clear and should relate to the product advertised. The in-world company must ensure that prices match the products illustrated in, for example, the virtual graphical representation in the advert. It is important to state here that we are referring to price information for items one can purchase by, perhaps, a link to an e-commerce website from the virtual world environment. For these purposes we are not speaking of virtual currencies such as Linden dollars or Therebucks. However, it is an interesting concept to consider. If those currencies can be redeemed against the purchase of actual goods or the balance which a virtual world user has on their currency account is reduced by the misinformation on pricing then the controls over pricing information would apply to these virtual currencies.

All real world prices quoted in marketing communications addressed to the public should include VAT and other non-optional taxes and duties imposed on all buyers.

A recommended retail price (RRP) or similar, used as a basis of comparison should be genuine, it should not differ significantly from the price at which the product is generally sold. DVDs, for example offered via the virtual island of a well known retailer at a discount from the RRP in their real world shops must be a genuine reduction.

6.4.5 AVAILABILITY OF REAL WORLD PRODUCTS OR SERVICES PROMOTED IN-WORLD

The in-world company must make it clear if stocks are limited. Products must not be advertised in-world unless it can be demonstrated that the company has reasonable grounds for believing that it can satisfy demand outside of the virtual environment and in real time. If the merchandise becomes unavailable, the in-world company will be required to show evidence of stock monitoring, communications with outlets and swift withdrawal of marketing communications from the virtual world, whenever possible.

Real world goods which cannot be supplied should not be advertised in a virtual world as a way of assessing potential demand by avatars unless it is made clear that this is the purpose of the in-world marketing communication.

The virtual world company must not use the technique of switch selling. For example where its avatar sales staff criticise the advertised product or suggest that it is not available and recommend the purchase of a more expensive alternative. They should not place obstacles in the way of purchasing the product or delivering it promptly in the physical world.

6.4.6 PRODUCT GUARANTEES IN VIRTUAL WORLDS

If a virtual environment company is offering a Guarantee to avatars it will still be legally binding. The word 'Guarantee' should not be used in a way that could cause confusion about a virtual world user's rights as a consumer. Any substantial limitations on the guarantee should be spelled out in the marketing communication. Before commitment, the consumer avatar should be able to obtain the full terms of the guarantee from the in-world company. This, of course, brings into question the use of placing advertisements in-world where there may be limitations on screen size or graphical depiction of content within the virtual environment. In such cases, clear reference to the in-world company website and the legal terms and conditions which appear on the website must be made. It can be seen, however, that such a seamless transition from virtual world to e-commerce website ought to be entirely possible thus still using the virtual environment to capture customers.

If it is a money back guarantee, the virtual world operator must provide a cash refund or cheque promptly to those claiming redress under the offer.

Remember it is necessary for the virtual world operator to ensure its target users recognise it is a marketing communication. The email message or mobile broadcast should be designed and presented in such a way that it is clear they are marketing communications. Unsolicited email marketing communications should be clearly identifiable as marketing communications without the need to open them.

6.4.7 IN-WORLD SALES PROMOTIONS

As stated above, the Code also applies to sales promotions and regulates the nature and administration of promotional marketing techniques. Those techniques usually involve providing a range of direct or indirect additional benefits, usually on a temporary basis, designed to make products or services more attractive to purchasers.

The in-world company must conduct any virtual world promotion equitably, promptly and efficiently and should be seen to deal fairly and honourably with consumers acting through their respective avatars. The company should avoid causing unnecessary disappointment.

The company wishing to promote products or services should be able to demonstrate that it has made a reasonable estimate of likely response and that it was capable of meeting that response. This, of course, is a difficult issue in the context of virtual worlds because wholly different criteria apply. For example, there are inevitable attitude shifts required of an in-world company when working in the virtual world. Primarily the small number of consumers involved and the open-ended nature of a virtual campaign which may not have a clearly defined start and end points. However, whilst the actual user numbers in virtual worlds may be less, the average user spends much longer in-world. These users may send blogs to other users or within their broader social networking sphere. Thus, the volumes can grow dramatically from the in-world environment. Therefore, the company needs to consider such issues.

Using phrases such as 'subject to availability' would not relieve in-world promoters of their obligation to take all reasonable steps to avoid disappointing virtual world participants.

The in-world company should not encourage consumers acting through their avatars to make a purchase or series of purchases as a precondition to applying for promotional items if the number of those items is limited. Once again, this concept can apply to the virtual environment if by the transaction the same misrepresentation takes form.

If the company promoting its products in-world is unable to satisfy demand for a promotional offer because of an unexpectedly high response or some other anticipated factor outside its control, it should offer refunds or substitute products. How this message to avatars is conveyed in-world needs to be considered by the company.

The virtual promotion should be conducted under proper supervision and adequate resources should be made available to administer it. The company should allow adequate time for each phase of the in-world promotion, distributing the goods in physical form, collating email or blog messages from avatars and announcing results in-world.

The appeal of virtual world promotions to both consumers acting through their avatars and to in-world companies is that they are capable of immediate response by avatars. However, that means the company must be able to fulfil with similar speed.

A free offer may be conditional on the purchase of other items. An avatar's liability for costs should be made clear on the in-world material featuring the offer. These costs which will apply to the real world satisfaction of the promotion. An offer should be described as free only if avatar consumers pay no more than:

a) the minimum, unavoidable cost of responding to the promotion, for example, the current public rates of postage, the cost of telephoning up to and including the national rate or the minimum, unavoidable cost of sending an email or SMS text message.
b) the true cost of delivery.

The in-world company should not charge for packing, handling or administration.

6.4.7.1 Essential Conditions for a Virtual World Promotion

A virtual world promotion should specify clearly before any purchase (or before or at the time of entry or application), the following detail if no purchase is required:

- How to participate, including significant conditions and costs either to the virtual currency or real world funds, and any other major factors reasonably likely to influence the avatar consumers' decisions or understanding about the promotion.
- The start date and the closing date, if applicable, for purchases and submissions of in-world entries or claims. Prize promotions and promotions addressed to or targeted at children in virtual worlds always need a closing date.

All other restrictions must be stated. For example, if there are any geographical restrictions which apply and personal restrictions, such as age. Technological limitations must be made clear, suppose the in-world company made it a condition that the promotion is only available to an avatar visiting a specified island within the virtual world. Other technical restrictions such as email only response and not text message must be made clear. The in-world company should state any need to obtain permission to enter from an adult or employer.

6.4.8 FURTHER REGULATORY DEMANDS FOR IN-WORLD ADVERTISING

Computer games and advertising are linked very closely. In part this is because of a desire on, the part of the games developer to create a realistic environment featuring well known brands on, for example, billboard advertisements on the track siding of a road race game. Integrating commercial messages into games is well understood. There has been a change in the relationship, however, between software developers and advertisers. Hitherto advertisers had to be approached by the developers for permission to use a particular brand in the game. The developer would have to pay money for such use. Today it is the other way round. Advertisers are very keen to secure a place in a computer game.

There are different forms of advertising within computer games. The first is a static feature which is incorporated into the game's source code and cannot be altered. The billboard adverts described above are an example of this kind of advert. It is common for advertisers to actually commission certain computer games which will then feature the brand in some form. Then there are banner advertisements. These are of course common on many websites. Dynamic virtual world advertising has the advantage that the advertisements can be switched in the course of the environment experience. This is achieved by incorporating into the environment of a program, surfaces that are either empty or designed to be switched and that can later be covered dynamically with advertising.

Another form of advertising is in the nature of product placement. This is also used in virtual worlds and takes the form of objects which replicate the appearance of real life products. For example, a Coca-Cola drink can or even a motor car.

There are, however, other regulatory requirements which impact on advertising in virtual worlds to those considered above.

6.4.8.1 The Protection of Young People

Virtual worlds may well fall within the perview of the Audiovisual Media Services Directive. If this is the case, then, in relation to the inclusion of advertising, attention must be paid to Article 3e (1) (a) and to Article 3(g) in the case of product placement. This means that in-world advertising must be recognisable as such. In addition, surreptitious advertising is not permitted in virtual worlds.

The question of what might amount to product placement is interesting in the context of virtual worlds as they relate to children. First, if we take the Directive as applying to such environments then the next issue to determine is what constitutes a children's programme. Is it is only programmes made for children only. If so, then some virtual worlds which the whole family may inhabit, will not be covered. Therefore product placement would be permissible in such worlds.

The issue of whether a world is or is not a children's environment in some cases will be obvious. For example, there are a number of virtual worlds which are clearly only made available for participation by children. These environments will not be able to practice product placement. In other, perhaps more ambiguous environments, the issue might be determined thus. It is the point at which children become capable of understanding the distinction between advertisements and programmes, and of recognising the intentions behind commercial communications. So, virtual worlds with an age rating of 12 years or above ought, under this criterion, to lie outside the definition of environments for children only which would mean that product placement could occur. It is of note that today, young people are far more exposed to commercial messaging than ever before. It is probably not possible for a child to experience one day without encountering advertisements of some description, whether on children's commercial television channels, on the back of cereal packaging, and of course via mobile phones or the Internet.

This means that many, as they become teenagers, are more tolerant of advertisements than adults of today. They will accept the intrusive nature of certain forms of advertisements, such as those delivered via mobile phones. It is likely that this acceptance will simply mean that over time a change in culture will evolve so that commercial messages are just regarded as routine experience but it plays a more prominent place in daily life. This increased use of media means that children and young people ought, by the age of 12, be capable of distinguishing between programmes and advertising.

There is further regulation of advertisements aimed at children. This time it is not the Audiovisual Media Services Directive, but the provisions of Directive 2005/29/EC on unfair commercial practices. Articles 5(1), 5(4)(a) and 5(5) of that Directive create a prohibition on misleading advertisements. This may extend to virtual worlds where the Audiovisual Directive may not. So, editorial content which is intended to promote a product where a trader has paid for the promotion without making that fact clear in the content, or by images or sound clearly identifiable, is classed as a misleading commercial practice. In-world product placement is likely to be treated as advertising in the guise of information.

For the most part, however, virtual worlds tend to feature content which is not disguised as information. Rather it serves to 'decorate' a form of visual depiction and it would not therefore fall within the unfair commercial practices Directive's scope. It is worth bearing in mind though as one can see that, even in scenarios which are unclear as to whether in-world content constitutes product placement, there is likely to be some legal governance tending to suggest it is. Therefore, any virtual world operator or retailer in the children's virtual world setting, should assume legal controls exist and then take specialist legal advice before proceeding with planned activity.

6.4.8.2 The Protection of Human Dignity[1]

If the Audiovisual Media Services Directive does apply to virtual worlds then there is another issue which will impact on the content of such environments. The provisions of Articles 3(a) to 3(g) of the Directive must be adhered to.

Article 3(b) states that audio visual media services must not incite hatred on grounds of race, sex, religion or nationality. The Directive also states that audiovisual communications must not prejudice respect for human dignity and must not include or promote any discrimination based on sex, racial or ethnic origin, religion, nationality or belief, disability, age or sexual orientation.

There has been much media commentary on computer games which feature extreme violence. Some games involve the killing of human characters. One particularly high profile example was a game called *Counterstrike*. This involved the user engaging in systematic killing of human characters from the perspective of a marksman, with the weapon and the target always in view. The game featured sounds including gun fire and the impact on the human character. In Germany this game was cited as fuelling a murderous rampage by a former grammar school student in Erfurt in 2001 although never demonstrated to have been in any way causal. It is possible that virtual worlds could replicate this kind of depiction.

There exists a self regulatory system of age rating for computer games in operation since 2003. A new system for online and mobile games is being introduced.

Clearly, virtual worlds have the potential as works of software animation to feature violent content and in some ways would represent a more disturbing manifestation of gaming. This is because computer games are probably experienced by users individually or perhaps playing with one other individual using the games console. However, virtual worlds, of course, involve the participation of several inhabitants of the environment acting through avatars contemporaneously. Each manouvering the action in-world. Thus, if such environments featured extreme violence they would be a form of movement and that might be of more concern. There would be methods for law enforcement agencies to identify such participants if the activity constituted unlawful actions and the operator of the virtual world could be ordered to take down the website. The legal mechanisms used in such action by law enforcement agencies include a variety of legislative tools but would be assisted if the virtual world environment could be shown to fall within the ambit of audiovisual media services regulations as well.

1 See article by Paul Gottlich, *'Online Games from the Standpoint of Media and Copyright Law'*, IRIS Plus, Issue 2007–10).

6.4.9 SENDING ELECTRONIC MARKETING MESSAGES TO PROMOTE A VIRTUAL WORLD TO UNDER 16S

It is perhaps easy to understand why a young technology should appeal to young minds. Virtual worlds are certainly used by those with a lower age profile and indeed many such worlds are specifically designed to be populated by children. If the virtual environment is to be actively promoted to a young audience, special care needs to be taken when addressed to children (people under 16). It is particularly important that those promoting such virtual worlds understand their legal obligations when sending electronic promotional messages.

The way in which children perceive and react to marketing communications is influenced by their age, experience and the context in which the message is delivered. So, marketing communications which are acceptable for young teenagers will not necessarily be acceptable for young children. This needs to be taken into account.

Marketing communications addressed to, targeted at or featuring children should not exploit their credulity, loyalty, vulnerability or lack of experience. They should not be made to feel unpopular or inferior for not inhabiting the advertised virtual world. They should not be made to feel that they are lacking in loyalty if they do not buy or do not encourage others to buy a particular product which is offered in the environment.

The advertisement should be made easy for them to judge the size, characteristics and performance of any product advertised and to distinguish between real-life situations and fantasy. This requirement is probably harder to fulfil in the context of a virtual world since the whole experience is based on a fantasy realm. The in-world marketing of products therefore can easily slip into the borders of what is unacceptable under law when promoting to children.

The permission of an adult should be obtained before the child is committed to purchasing complex and costly products.

Promotions, either of virtual worlds or products offered therein addressed to or targeted at children, should not encourage excessive purchases in order to participate and among other things should contain a prominent closing date.

6.4.10 PENALTIES FOR BREACHING THE CODE

There is a much stricter regime relative to advertising regulations in contrast to the general law. Advertisements of a virtual world or products offered through it require a level of justification in excess of that necessary for general editorial content.

If an online advertisement breaches the Code, the ASA will ask a virtual world operator or in-world advertiser to withdraw or amend its advertisement. Other sanctions include adverse publicity, the refusal of further space, removal of trade incentives and finally legal proceedings.

These sanctions are by referrals from the ASA to the Office of Fair Trading (OFT) under the Control of Misleading Advertisements Regulations 1988 (CMAR). The OFT can obtain an injunction against a virtual world operator or in-world advertiser to prevent it from repeating the same or similar claims in future advertisements.

The first problem which in-world advertising highlights is the proper application of Advertising Standards in the right circumstances. The distinction between advertising material and editorial in a virtual world can become blurred. Such environments may well feature text which forms part of the user experience and which offers guidance about aspects of the service or particular islands owned by virtual inhabitants. This text may not constitute advertisements as we commonly understand them but it may not be easy to make the distinction. In addition, because the very nature of virtual worlds inspire advertisers and marketers to develop sophisticated techniques to reach inhabitants, one can see how problems in interpretation can arise.

This is exacerbated by the seamless linking of pages from virtual world environments to perhaps e-commerce websites of in-world retailers which might render it difficult to separate the two. This difficulty may lead to the inadvertent extension of advertising content restrictions to editorial content.

At the time of writing, there is no reported case concerning how an English court would approach the question in the context of a virtual world. However, the issue was considered in the Irish case of *Dunnes Stores Limited v Mandate*:

> *The case was founded on the Irish equivalent to the UK Control of Misleading Advertising Regulations 1988. A trade union representing a claimant's work force placed an advertisement in the National Press seeking to justify strike action by the Union's members over Christmas pay. The Irish Supreme Court held that the trade union's advertisement had nothing to do with the promotion of the supply of goods or services and so was not advertising.*

When considering advertising and virtual worlds one of the most vexing issues is jurisdiction. The difficulty in properly regulating in-world advertising is trying to apply national frameworks of laws and regulations to adverts disseminated to the world at large.

A virtual world advertisement is, in theory, subject to the laws of every country in which it is accessed by an inhabitant. Thus far, the ASA have focused on websites which originate in the UK and the same approach is likely to be taken to virtual worlds in the UK. However, if it is faced with a foreign virtual world, it may be able to refer the complaint to an equivalent regulatory body in the foreign jurisdiction.

The breach of non-domestic regulations as a result of the global 'reach' of the Internet was illustrated in *US v Thoms*, a US court case.

In that case, the operators of a pornographic electronic bulletin board in California were convicted of criminal obscenity laws by a federal court in Tennessee. The conviction was founded on Tennessee standards of decency.

At present there is no international unanimity on the issue of which countries' law applies to virtual world advertising. The approach which seems to be adopted is that the laws of the country of 'publication' will apply. That is, the country in which there is evidence of 'directed' activity. This is illustrated by an incident involving the English registered Virgin Atlantic Airways:

In 1996 Virgin was fined by the United States Department of Transportation for a misleading advertisement on its UK server. The inaccuracy related to the quoting of erroneous fares and listing a fare that was no longer available on flights from the US.

The simple inclusion of information on the virtual world operator's website, or that of an in-world advertiser will not, of itself, be conclusive evidence of directed activity if there is something about the information making it clear it is targeted at customers in a particular country.

The language of an in-world advertisement may be relevant to an extent. A disclaimer contained on the website may help to clarify who is included in the target audience. An example might be 'this offer is only available to in-world inhabitants in France'. Such a disclaimer will however be construed narrowly and have no legal effect in some countries.

Whilst it will be impractical to obtain legal clearance in every jurisdiction throughout the world, there are some general principles a virtual world advertiser may adopt.

One is to obtain legal and trademark clearance in each target country and in countries in which the in-world advertiser has a presence or assets.

On a purely practical level, the in-world advertiser might consider how costly it might be to change its virtual world advertisement if it were challenged.

Would a competitor in fact be able to prove actual damage?

Finally, it may well be the authorities in a given country will take a 'laissez-faire' approach to a virtual world advertisement.

If the in-world advertiser engages the services of an advertising agency, the issue of the company's virtual world advertising strategy must be discussed fully with the agency.

The risks that a company could incur liability for breach of foreign advertising regulation makes it essential for the contract with the agency to lay down clear lines of responsibility for ensuring legal compliance of advertising materials in the context of virtual worlds.

6.4.11 THE VIRTUAL WORLD ADVERTISING AGREEMENT

The business world is now recognising that Internet advertising in general is no longer a fantasy but an integral part of advertising strategy. A significant development of the commercialisation of the Internet has been the commercial sponsorship of websites.

Some website advertising activity is successful because it is integrated with a broader media promotion campaign. One only has to reflect on the plethora of television advertisements which promote corporate and retail websites.

We have seen how retailers are already using virtual worlds to promote their brand. This may be use of island occupation in-world where the retailer builds a virtual store in the environment. How that depiction is governed may fall outside the scope of the standard user terms and conditions (see Chapter 3) and require legal control in the form of a specific agreement between the in-world retailer and virtual world operator. The same will be true if the advertiser is not featured at all in the environment as occupying virtual real estate, but simply wishes to advertise on the website. This might be by simple banner advertisement, hyperlinks and browser windows which start automatically, or other more sophisticated representation.

The operator may wish to distinguish between a 'sponsor', who is entitled to a more prominent place on the website, and other advertisers who will receive lesser billing.

From the point of view of the advertiser, it will want to be clear not only about the rights it receives in isolation but also its position within the hierarchy of rights.

If an operator is entering into an arrangement with another company to enable that other company to advertise on its website, the Internet Advertising Agreement should cover the following:

The rights being granted in respect of the virtual world website should be determined. Is the advertiser to have exclusive rights? Are there categories of advertising within which the advertiser will have exclusivity, for example, that it will be the only video games developer on the site. It may well be necessary to consider whether an exclusive deal with an advertiser on the website will be affected by the virtual store presence of another competitor advertiser.

The payment structure and triggers should be considered. Whether payment will be calculated on a base fee, or per display, click through or upon ultimate sale. The Agreement should set forth how this is to be achieved.

We noted earlier that online advertisements are subject to very clear advertising code compliance requirements. Therefore, the responsibilities of the advertiser in relation to appropriateness of adverts should be clearly understood.

The advertiser will need to permit the use of graphics or trademarks in the production of the advertisement. It would be prudent to enter into a limited licence for the use of graphics and/or text and trademark used in the advertisements.

The presence of advertisements on a virtual world website still brings possible exposure to legal liability on the part of both the operator and advertiser. Inclusion of indemnities in the Agreement to limit liability should be considered.

How the Agreement may be terminated must be clear. In addition, the Agreement should set out what will happen upon termination. Usually, materials should be destroyed and web pages changed. If the Agreement is terminated at short notice, all payments due under the same should become immediately due and payable.

The precise nature of the relationship between the Advertiser and the Virtual World Operator must be made clear. The Agreement will only be for advertising co-operation. It should state clearly that it does not create an agency or joint venture between the parties.

The positioning and size of the advertisement on the virtual world website must be understood at the outset. An advertiser will wish to specify where on the website its advertisement will appear. It may be that the advertiser wants the advertisement to appear in certain sections of the virtual world which feature virtual landscape associated with the advertiser's business. For example, a rural setting in the environment depicting open landscape, hills and trees may be suitable for the retailer of agricultural products.

The form and size of the advert relative to other text and graphics should be clear. Internet advertising involves the consideration of the working of hypertext mark-up language and the operating web browsers which will be used to access the sites. An advertiser may wish to set up the technical details of how, in particular, its logo is created so as to ensure that it both downloads at an acceptable speed and is attractive.

Updating of the virtual world website should be addressed. Some advertisers may want some contractual assurance that the web page itself will be changed over time to keep up with new versions or releases of relevant browsers. Conversely, that the webpage will remain useable with older versions.

Hypertext links. Both the virtual world operator and the advertiser will have concerns relating to the hypertext links from the advertisement to the advertiser's own web page. Advertisers will want to make sure that the link is correctly created and the virtual world operator is obliged to update it correctly if there is a change in the URL of the advertiser's website. The advertiser may also wish to ensure that the link can be triggered either from the text message or a graphic. The virtual world operator should ensure that the link to the advertiser's website will not give rise to any liability to third parties for defamation.

Intellectual property. Advertisers will wish to specify the extent of the right of the virtual world operator to use any trade or service marks on the website and to ensure that it applies the marks consistently with any standard guidelines. The form of the advertising in general may concern the advertiser and they will wish to have prior approval of relevant copy. The virtual world operator should seek an indemnity in respect of third party claims arising from use of the advertisers marks on the Internet.

Information about visitors to the virtual world. It will be of interest both to the advertiser and the operator of the virtual world to know who visits the website. This is because the operator will need to justify its advertising rate card. The advertiser will need to judge whether the virtual world webpages are an appropriate place to advertise.

6.4.12 GUIDANCE FOR SOCIAL-NETWORKING SERVICE PROVIDERS ON ENHANCING CHILD SAFETY

In 2008, the UK government published *Good practice guidance for providers of social-networking and other interactive services*. The guidance sets out various good practice recommendations on how providers of social-networking and other user-interactive services can enhance the safety of children and young people using their services. It also includes safety tips regarding the use of such services for children, young people and their parents. At the same time as publishing the guidance, the government also launched a new *Kitemark* certification mark to set a standard for filtering software for home computers, and announced plans to introduce secondary legislation to require child-sex offenders to notify police of their email addresses, so that they can be passed on to social-networking sites to enable them to stop offenders from using their sites.

6.4.13 THE BUSINESS PROTECTION FROM MISLEADING MARKETING REGULATIONS 2008

These Regulations came into force on 26 May 2008 and once again, given they are Regulations, they originate from Europe and broadly will exist in the same form throughout the European Union and are not therefore simply English law.

They are designed to provide consumers in the EU protection from misleading advertisements and they will apply to in-world advertising or that represented within Internet social networks. However, only those advertisers based in the EU and consumers in that territory are subject to them. That, of course, presents some legal jurisdiction challenges in the context of a virtual world which typically is accessible throughout the world. We therefore consider in this review of the Regulations the position which will apply in the scenario where the operator of and advertisers within the virtual world or social network are based in the EU. Given the increased number of such environments and their gathering focus on niche offerings it will be appreciated that many such environments will fall into the category.

Advertising for the purpose of the Regulations means any form of representation which is made in connection with a trade, business, craft or profession in order to promote the supply or transfer of a product and 'advertiser' is construed accordingly. The Regulations also cover comparative advertising meaning advertising which, in any way, either explicitly or by implication, identifies a competitor or a product offered by a competitor.

It is interesting to note how this new law is framed by its Definitions of what falls within its ambit.

'Premises' includes any place and any stall. It can be seen for example that in an in-world retail island whilst only a virtual representation of a stall it is in fact a point of advertising and could therefore be regarded as a stall within the Regulations.

'Product' means any goods or services and includes rights and obligations.

'Trader' means any person who is acting for purposes relating to his trade, craft, business or profession and anyone acting in the name of or on behalf of a trader. Once again, it may be seen that there is no reason why a virtual retailer operating from an island within the environment should not be included within this definition.

The Regulations create a prohibition of advertising which misleads traders. Advertising is misleading which:

a) in any way, including its presentation, deceives or is likely to deceive the traders to whom it is addressed or whom it reaches; and by reason of its deceptive nature, is likely to affect their economic behaviour; or
b) for those reasons, injures or is likely to injure a competitor.

In determining whether advertising is misleading, account is taken of all its features, and in particular of any information it contains concerning the characteristics of the product, the price or manner in which the price is calculated, the conditions on which the product is supplied or provided; and the nature, attributes and rights of the advertiser.

The 'characteristics of the product' include availability of the product, nature of the product, method and date of manufacture of the product, fitness for purpose of the product, uses, specification and quantity of the product. In addition the geographical or commercial origin of the product is included in its characteristics as defined in the Regulations. That in itself may present interesting issues given that virtual worlds transcend geographical borders. There may be differing treatment of the characteristics in different countries – even within the European member states which are governed by the Regulations. Other things which impact on its characteristics include the results to be expected from use of the product or results and material features of tests or checks carried out on the product.

The nature, attributes and rights of the advertiser as defined in the Regulations include the advertiser's identity, assets, qualifications, ownership of industrial, commercial or intellectual property rights; or awards and distinctions. For example, if the product offered in-world itself a software application or download, the issue of who owns the intellectual property rights will be important.

The other principal element of the new Regulations is the issue of comparative advertising. Comparative advertising shall, as far as the comparison is concerned, be permitted only when conditions are met which include the following:

a) it is not misleading;
b) it compares products meeting the same needs or intended for the same purpose;
c) it objectively compares one or more material, relevant, verifiable and representative features of those products, which may include price;

d) it does not create confusion among traders:

   i) between the advertiser and a competitor; or
   ii) between the trademarks, trade names, other distinguishing marks or products of the advertiser and those of a competitor.

e) it does not discredit or denigrate the trademarks, trade names, other distinguishing marks, products, activities, or circumstances of a competitor;
f) for products with designation of origin, it relates in each case to products with the same designation;
g) it does not take unfair advantage of the reputation of a trademark, trade name or other distinguishing marks of a competitor or of the designation of origin of competing products:

   i) it does not present products as imitations or replicas of products bearing a protected trademark or trade name. This for example is particularly pertinent in the context of virtual worlds where it is possible to model products to replicate well known brands such as cars, sports shoes and other consumer items. Care must be taken therefore by a virtual retailer in how they depict their goods in-world and of course on this issue they must be mindful of the intellectual property rights of the owner which relate to those items.

A virtual retailer is guilty of an offence if he engages in advertising which is misleading under Regulations.

There are Penalties for the offence and a person shall be liable to a fine or on conviction, to a fine or imprisonment for a term not exceeding two years or both.

Where this offence is committed by a body corporate and it is proved:

a) to have been committed with the consent or connivance of an officer of the company; or
b) to be attributable to any neglect on his part;
c) the officer as well as the company is guilty of the offence and liable to be proceeded against and suffer the same penalty accordingly.

An officer of a company includes a director, manager, secretary or other similar officer; and a person purporting to act as a director, manager, secretary or other similar officer. This again is significant for in-world retailing as an inhabitant of the environment engaged in retailing may not be a director but might, acting via their avatar (where they are content to be depicted so, but also open about their true identity) still be responsible under the Regulations.

There are time limits for prosecution. No proceedings for an offence can be commenced after:

a) the end of the period of three years beginning with the date of the commission of the offence; or
b) the end of the period of one year beginning with the date of discovery of the offence by the prosecutor, whichever is earlier.

The Regulations do contain defences for a retailer in the physical world and indeed an in-world retailer. In any proceedings against a person for an offence under Regulation 6 it is a defence for that person to prove:

a) that the commission of the offence was due to:

   i) a mistake;
   ii) reliance on information supplied to him by another person;
   iii) the act or default of another person;
   iv) an accident; or
   v) another cause beyond his control.

   and:

a) that he took all reasonable precautions and exercised all due diligence to avoid the commission of such an offence by himself or any person under his control.

   However, a person shall not be entitled to rely on this defence unless:

a) he has served on the prosecutor a notice in writing giving such information identifying or assisting in the identification of that other person as was in his possession; and
b) the notice is served on the prosecutor at least seven clear days before the date of the hearing.

Another defence is called the Innocent publication defence. In any proceedings against a person for an offence committed by the publication of advertising which will include an in-world advertisement, it is a defence for that person to prove that:

a) he is a person whose business it is to publish or to arrange for the publication of advertising;
b) he received the advertising for publication in the ordinary course of business; and
c) he did not know and had no reason to suspect that its publication would amount to an offence under the Regulations.

The Office of Fair Trading in the UK may authorise, if it thinks it appropriate to do so, proceedings for an injunction (in which proceedings it may also apply for an interim injunction) against any person appearing to it to be concerned or likely to be concerned with the breach. However, where an enforcement authority considers that there has been or is likely to be a breach of the Regulation, it may accept from the person concerned or likely to be concerned with the breach an undertaking that he will comply with the Regulations.

The court on an application by an enforcement authority may grant an injunction on such terms as it may think fit but, before granting an injunction, the court will take into account the interests of all involved and in particular the public interest. An injunction may relate not only to particular advertising but to any advertising in similar terms or likely to convey a similar impression.

The court may also require any person against whom an injunction is granted to publish for the purpose of eliminating any continuing effects of the advertising:

a) the injunction; and
b) a corrective statement.

In considering an application for an injunction the court may require the person who it is claimed has produced the advertisement to confirm the accuracy of any factual claim made as part of the advertising of that person if, taking into account the legitimate interests of that person and any other party to the proceedings, it appears appropriate in the circumstances.

If, that person:

a) fails to provide such evidence; or
b) provides evidence as to the accuracy of the factual claim that the court considers inadequate, the court may consider that the factual claim is inaccurate.

The court may grant an injunction even where there is no evidence of proof of actual loss or damage or of intention or negligence on the part of the in-world advertiser.

CHAPTER 7 Protecting Personal Privacy in Virtual Worlds and Social Networks

7.1 Background

The principal attraction of the Internet is that it is an open environment. It is the superdistribution channel of the modern age. In its more recent history and with the development of so called Web 2.0 it is becoming clear that audiences are becoming forms of community and people are consuming goods and services in more and more contexts.

Internet audiences are more fragmented but, equally, online visitors leave a more visible footprint about their interests, dreams and desires. Virtual world visitors are in a sense a more captive group, bounded as they are by the dimensions of their virtual environment. Whether you are a business or an individual player, participating in a virtual world requires the surrender of a certain amount of personal data. The key for a business wishing to promote its brand is identifying that in-world audience so that content can be targeted precisely.

Virtual worlds offer opportunities for a company to deploy ever more sophisticated means by which personal information about a consumer audience can be obtained. The richness of the content of this data and how it may be measured is simply incredible and was not possible only a few years ago.

The pace of change is staggering. The success of social networking websites such as *MySpace*, *Facebook* and *Bebo* depend on users posting online a whole range of information about themselves. Their personal interests, their occupations, their personal status.

It is a fascinating phenomenum and one which is changing the way younger people relate, particularly to their peers, and generally interact with the world around them.

We have not yet grasped the true significance of what is happening but it cannot be easily dismissed as simply a short term novelty or passing fad. The technology is too significant an enabler. The Internet is about communication and that is what people do to experience life. In these networks, individuals generate vast networks of friends and they transcend geographical boundaries, ethnicity and cultural differences. In a few clicks, dialogue can take place within the networks regardless of the time of day and there is an expectation of an almost immediate response from within the group.

The ability to use this information and share it with others is a significant attraction of the site. However, such websites bring with them issues of data protection, data security and data sharing. Social networking websites however are just one aspect of the issue of data collection online.

Companies which wish to offer goods and services over the Internet, need to be able to target users properly.

Virtual worlds are the next stage of development of social networks. The virtual world could become the first point of contact between companies and customers and could transform the whole experience. However, they do not exist in a legal vacuum. In the EU, at least, they reside in a heavily regulated data protection regime.

In this chapter we will examine why privacy laws have huge significance in relation to the virtual world experience.

There are legitimate concerns by consumers over marketers buying and selling their personal information generally. The rise of e-commerce has sparked increasing fears, due to the ease with which all types of sensitive data may be gathered, copied, shared and misused via the Internet.

In the context of virtual worlds sometimes valuable data is obtained through covert surveillance by other in-world participants or the operators of the virtual environment. Questions inevitably arise as to whether this constitutes personal data and whether in any event personal data can be protected in virtual worlds. How can users be protected from exploitation?

It is important that a company understands how it may operate within a virtual world and adhere to the legal protection afforded to individuals in the EU. Moreover, given the pan national nature of the Internet, and the fact that information gleaned in-world can then be exploited using the Internet more generally, the company needs to know how it can process personal information in a way which does not fall foul of the data protection regime of other countries.

These problems are particularly acute for a company with an international reach. In addition to possible fines there is a risk of negative publicity for breaching data protection laws. No company can afford to ignore the issues.

It is necessary to examine the basis of data protection principles as they apply within the EU and to consider how they relate to virtual worlds. In addition, the rules for transfer of data from the UK (and indeed from any country in the EU) to a country outside the EU will be explained.

It is fair to say that the EU has one of the most stringent data protection regimes in the world. Some feel that there is an absence of connection between this restricted approach and the realities of the global nature of the Internet.

The information gathering ability of companies has caused concerns over invasion of citizen's rights for many years. In most countries, the unlawful processing of personal data represents a violation of fundamental human rights.

In the UK, company directors are personally liable for the accuracy of their organisation's databases. Individuals can sue, not merely for financial loss directly resulting from inaccurate or wrongly disclosed data, but for any breach of data law and resultant distress.

The Internet permits companies to monitor profiles and information provided directly by its online audience. The process of tracking every click the consumer makes on the Internet and leaving behind 'cookies' on their computers to help the system remember each consumer is hugely valuable. Companies can gather a startling amount of personal information with which to sell consumers film merchandise and services. The vast majority of commercial websites are dependent on cookies to customise the site to users preferences, without them, sites become almost unusable.

Illustration of the technology, for example, lies in a purchase of a DVD on Amazon.com. In time, the site will begin to suggest new purchases each time the consumer visits based on the buying pattern that individual has established.

The argument in favour of online marketing is that it helps consumers find the right products efficiently and with convenience. There are controls on the use of cookies which we have seen elsewhere in this book. In addition, many browsers allow users to block cookies and to delete them from their PCs.

Virtual worlds can provide their operators with an ability to monitor to an even greater extent and degree of accuracy participant behaviour in-world. Legal landscape which governs the issue of data protection. That landscape inevitably shapes how virtual worlds and social networks must operate. However, because these mediums are new and it is therefore very likely their innovative functionality will bring into review existing legal principles and raise questions how those principles can be applied to the technology. For example, Second Life was compelled to adapt its user interface so that its inhabitants could optionally confirm aspects of each other's identity including age and jurisdiction. This move was prompted by fears that it was being used for illegal activities (in the US) such as Internet gambling. The change allowed Internet casinos and other Second Life businesses to restrict access to avatars that are under age, or are from real world US states which prohibit certain activities. It also ceased accepting classified advertisements, place listings or event listings that appear to relate to simulated casino activity.

Many people who venture into virtual environments probably do not even consider how their digital footprint is visible to any operator who cares to investigate.

7.2 The Data Protection Act 1998

In the UK the law which governs the processing of personal data is embodied in the Data Protection Act 1998 (the Act). This Act came into force on 1 March 2000. It replaced the Data Protection Act 1984 and it implements the principles of EU Directive 95/46/EC.

In 1995 the European Parliament and Council issued the EU Directive on Data Protection (95/46/EC). The Directive sought to protect individuals with regard to the processing of personal data and free movement of such data. The Directive led to the introduction of the 1998 Act which is more extensive than the 1984 legislation. Whilst the Act sets forth the overall legal framework, much of the detail is contained in secondary legislation.

The most significant difference to previous legislation is the new definition of 'processing'. This is defined as 'obtaining, recording or holding the information or data or carrying out any operation or set of operations on the information or data'.

Thus, for the operator of a virtual world or social network, the Act imposes a significant compliance program.

The Act applies in the following circumstances:

a) If the virtual world or social network is 'established' in the UK, that is, it is ordinarily resident, a UK Limited company, partnership or unincorporated business. In addition, the Act applies if that business has an office, branch or agency which carries on any activity in the UK.

b) If the virtual world or social network is not established in the UK but uses equipment in the UK for processing data.
c) If data is exported to the virtual world or social network from the UK.

As is the case with much of the law relating to online film strategies featured in this book, there is corresponding legislation in place throughout the EU subject only to minor variation.

The information covered by the legislation is 'Personal data'. That is data relating to a living individual who can be identified directly or indirectly. Employees, suppliers, customers and business contacts all fall within the definition.

7.2.1 THE EIGHT DATA PROTECTION PRINCIPLES AND HOW THEY APPLY TO VIRTUAL WORLD AND SOCIAL NETWORK ACTIVITY

The 1998 Act and related EU regulation set out eight principles. Operators of virtual worlds and Internet Social networks who are based in the UK must follow these.

The first principle states that all personal data which is held must be processed fairly and lawfully. It must not be processed unless one of the conditions at schedule (2) is met. Typically, operators of virtual worlds and social networks will wish to gather a certain degree of information about their users at the point at which those users first register with the service. Such data will be fairly basic. However, more stringent conditions apply to the processing of sensitive personal data. These are set out in Schedule 3 to the 1998 Act. The Act defines 'sensitive personal data' as 'personal data consisting of information as to a data subject's racial or ethnic origin, political opinions, religious beliefs, or other beliefs of a similar nature. In addition, membership of a trade union, physical or mental health or condition, sexual life are examples of sensitive personal data. It can be seen that the operator of a virtual world should not usually have need of such information in order to provide an effective service to its users or inhabitants. It is important to remember though we are not just considering the operators of such environments as we examine the data protection laws. Those laws will apply with equal force to in-world retailers and other inhabitants of the environment who seek to gather personal information about other users for any purpose.

Processing sensitive data will only be legitimate if the data subject has given his 'explicit consent'. If sensitive personal data is used, at least one condition at schedule (3) must also be met. It is clear that personal data will not be considered to be processed 'fairly' unless certain information is provided, or made readily available to the individual concerned.

The information to be given to data subjects must include the identity of the data controller, the purposes for which the data is intended to be processed and any further information which is necessary having regard to the specific circumstances in which the data is to be processed, to enable processing in respect of the data subject to be fair. Where data is obtained directly from the data subject, the requisite information should normally be provided at, or be made available from, the time of data collection.

The Principles include the following:

1. Personal Data shall only be obtained for one or more specified and lawful purpose. It should not be further processed in a manner incompatible with that purpose.

2. Personal data must be adequate, relevant and not excessive in relation to the purpose for which it is processed. Whilst an online enquirer may be willing, in the course of a transaction, to give a film company a great deal of personal information, that business has a duty to protect enquirers from themselves and their generosity. Clearly this has implications for data collection by a virtual world or social network via the Internet. Many websites require regular visitors to register before gaining access. It is very important that the virtual world or social network make clear precisely why non-essential questions are being asked and whether a response is optional. For example, capturing an email address may be necessary for the provision of a particular service, whereas collecting information about gender, marital status, income and age may be irrelevant or excessive.
3. Personal data must be accurate and kept up to date where necessary.
4. Personal data processed for any purpose shall not be kept for longer than is necessary for that purpose.
5. Personal data must be processed in accordance with the rights of data subjects under the Act.
6. Appropriate technological and organisational measures will be taken against unauthorised or unlawful processing of personal data. Such action will also be taken in the case of accidental loss, destruction or damage to personal data.

This principle needs to be considered carefully by the virtual world or social network. If the virtual world or social network uses a data processor such as an Internet Service Provider (ISP) or other third party which processes data on its behalf – for example by hosting the website – it will be in breach of the principle requiring that appropriate technological measures be implemented against unauthorised or unlawful processing of personal data, unless both of the following criteria are satisfied:

i) The processor provides sufficient guarantees in respect of the technical and organisational security measures governing the processing to be carried out, and the virtual world or social network takes reasonable steps to ensure compliance with those measures.
ii) The processing is governed by a written contract requiring the processor to act only as instructed by the controller and to comply with security obligations equivalent to those imposed on the controller. In the context of the Internet, the virtual world or social network will therefore need to ensure it has appropriate and properly documented contractual arrangements in place with, amongst others, its ISP and website hosters.

7.3 Data Processing Principles

1. Purpose limitation: Personal data may be processed and subsequently used or further communicated only for purposes described in Annex B or subsequently authorised by the data subject.
2. Data quality and proportionality: Personal data must be accurate and, where necessary, kept up to date. The personal data must be adequate, relevant and not excessive in relation to the purposes for which they are transferred and further processed.

3. Transparency: Data subjects must be provided with information necessary to ensure fair processing (such as information about the purposes of processing and about the transfer), unless such information has already been given by the data exporter.
4. Security and confidentiality: Technical and organisational security measures must be taken by the data controller that are appropriate to the risks, such as against accidental or unlawful destruction or accidental loss, alteration, unauthorised disclosure or access, presented by the processing. Any person acting under the authority of the data controller, including a processor, must not process the data except on instructions from the data controller.
5. Rights of access, rectification, deletion and objection: As provided in Article 12 of Directive 95/46/EC, data subjects must, whether directly or via a third party, be provided with the personal information about them that an organisation holds, except for requests which are manifestly abusive, based on unreasonable intervals or their number or repetitive or systematic nature, or for which access need not be granted under the law of the country of the data exporter. Provided that the authority has given its prior approval, access need also not be granted when doing so would be likely to seriously harm the interests of the data importer or other organisations dealing with the data importer and such interests are not overridden by the interests for fundamental rights and freedoms of the data subject. The sources of the personal data need not be identified when this is not possible by reasonable efforts, or where the rights of persons other than the individual would be violated. Data subjects must be able to have the personal information about them rectified, amended, or deleted where it is inaccurate or processed against these principles. If there are compelling grounds to doubt the legitimacy of the request, the organisation may require further justifications before proceeding to rectification, amendment or deletion. Notification of any rectification, amendment or deletion to third parties to whom the data have been disclosed need not be made when this involves a disproportionate effort. A data subject must also be able to object to the processing of the personal data relating to him if there are compelling legitimate grounds relating to his particular situation. The burden of proof for any refusal rests on the data importer and the data subject may always challenge a refusal before the authority.
6. Sensitive data: The data importer shall take such additional measures (for example, relating to security) as are necessary to protect such sensitive data in accordance with its obligations under clause II.
7. Data used for marketing purposes: Where data are processed for the purposes of direct marketing, effective procedures should exist allowing the data subject at any time to 'opt out' from having his data used for such purposes.
8. Automated decisions: For purposes hereof 'automated decision' shall mean a decision by the data exporter or the data importer which produces legal effects concerning a data subject or significantly affects a data subject and which is based solely on automated processing of personal data intended to evaluate certain personal aspects relating to him, such as his performance at work, creditworthiness, reliability, conduct, and so on. The data importer shall not make any automated decisions concerning data subjects except when:

   i) such decisions are made by the data importer in entering into or performing a contract with the data subject; and

ii) the data subject is given an opportunity to discuss the results of a relevant automated decision with a representative of the parties making such decision or otherwise to make representations to that parties; or

iii) where otherwise provided by the law of the data exporter.

7.3.1 EXPORTING DATA FROM THE UK TO A COUNTRY OUTSIDE THE EU

The Eighth Data Protection Principle and Transborder Data Flows

There is one facet of privacy legislation which causes some confusion and can easily be overlooked by a virtual world or social network. In particular, virtual worlds or social networks with an international dimension to their operation. The problem is particularly manifest in the context of electronic communications. The ease with which information can be passed around the globe at the press of a button is contributing to the widespread oversight of the laws which control export of personal data. In many ways the enabling technology which permits the easy transfer of information is to blame in that the effortless process does not prompt an investigation of the law which controls the action.

The Act introduces a new principle. It prohibits the transfer of personal data outside the EU unless there is an adequate level of protection in the receiving country, or the individual concerned has consented to the transfer.

There are a number of factors which determine the adequacy of legislation in other legal jurisdictions. These include the purpose for which data will be used and the risk involved. There is a problem. Few countries outside the EU in fact operate adequate data protection provisions. Since the Internet permits the global transfer of data, monitoring of data flow is difficult, thereby exacerbating the problem. First it is necessary to consider the broad ambit of the Act.

A virtual world or social network might infringe the law relating to the export of personal information in ways quite common to everyday business operation.

The legal basis of control lies within the Act.

Section 4 (4) of the Act provides that '...it shall be the duty of a data controller to comply with the data protection principles in relation to all personal data with respect to which he is the data controller.'

It is the Eighth Principle which governs transborder data flows, which is relevant here.

The Eighth Principle states; 'Personal data shall not be transferred to a country or territory outside the European Economic Area unless that country or territory ensures an adequate level of protection for the rights and freedoms of data subjects in relation to the processing of personal data.'

The European Economic Area consists of the 27 EU Member States together with Iceland, Liechtenstein and Norway. The Eighth Principle prohibits the transfer of personal data to any country or territory outside the EEA, a so called 'third country' unless the third country in question ensures this 'adequate level of protection for the rights and freedoms of data subjects' for transfers of their personal data to such countries. The Act does not define 'transfer' but the ordinary meaning of the word is transmission from one place or person, to another. It is important to appreciate that transfer does not mean the same as mere transit. Thus, the fact the electronic transfer of, for example, a virtual world inhabitant database may be routed through a third country on its way from the

UK to another EEA country does not bring such transfer within the ambit of the Eighth Principle, unless some substantive processing operation was being conducted upon the personal data in the third country in question.

A virtual world or social network can fall within the ambit of the restriction very easily without realising it. If information is provided by, for example, the marketing manager in a virtual world or social network in the UK over the telephone to his counterpart in a third country who then enters the information on a computer, the legislation will be breached. Another problem area would be mass data transfers from computer to computer using telecommunications systems.

'Processing' is widely defined by the Act and includes the obtaining, using, recording or holding of information, as well as adaptation or retrieval and disclosure of data. In effect, the obligations and principles apply to almost any use or collection of data regarding an individual.

Certain information is classified as 'sensitive', and there are additional obligations in relation to sensitive personal data. If the virtual world or social network wished to include data regarding its inhabitant's racial or ethnic origin, political beliefs, religious beliefs or sex life these are regarded as sensitive. A UK virtual world or social network intending to transfer data to a third country must assess the question of adequacy. To most companies, this will appear convoluted. In assessing adequacy the data controller in the virtual world or social network is required to make a judgment as to whether the level of protection afforded by all the circumstances of the case is commensurate with the potential of personal risks to the rights and freedoms of its consumer database (the data subjects) in relation to the processing of personal data. There are detailed guidelines which assist all companies in making the assessment and in adhering to good practice. These are too numerous to detail for the purposes of this book, but can be found at the website of the UK Information Commissioner at www.ico.gov.uk. There are however several forms of international transfer which have been identified by the Confederation of British Industry (CBI) where it may be possible for exporting controllers to approach the Adequacy Test with a strong presumption in favour of adequacy in terms of assessing the risk involved in the transfer. In the context of a virtual world or social network these might include:

- Transfers to a third party processor who remains under the control of the exporting data controller in the virtual world or social network.
- Transfers within an international or multi national virtual world or social network where an internal agreement, policy or code is more appropriate than a potentially large number of contracts.
- Transfers between the providers of professional services such as lawyers or accountants, whose clients' affairs are international in scope.
- Transfers which amount to a licence for use and probably a rental payment in respect of personal data used, for instance, in direct marketing, and
- Transfers which constitute a sale of data to a third party where there is no continuing relationship either with the data subject or the purchaser.

All Member states in the EU must take the measures necessary to prevent any transfer of data of the same type to the country in question where the European Commission finds no adequate level of data protection exists. Of particular relevance to a virtual world or social network is the market in the US for artists. However, the US is deemed to be a country where no adequate level of protection exists. So, if the virtual world or social network wishes to transfer data from the UK to the US, two methods of data transfer have been developed. The so called, safe harbor and the EU model clauses. There are a number of alternative options.

First, signing up to the US Privacy safe harbor will legitimise transfers to the US.

A second route to compliance is by putting in place contracts between the virtual world or social network and the importing business. This is a common route to compliance within a corporate group. However the standard terms which must be included may not prove palatable to many virtual world operators, given how weighted they are in favour of the individual consumer.

A third option to addressing transfer may be developing as a variant to a contract on the European Commission's approved terms. In the UK at least, it is open to a virtual world or social network to adopt a policy on privacy compliance which is applicable throughout the company. This policy may be sufficient to address transfer issues provided the policy is binding. This means some form of external dispute resolution mechanism. However this can drafted more favourably to the virtual world or social network than the equivalent provisions in the European Commissions approved terms.

7.3.2 THE UNITED STATES SAFE HARBOR PROCEDURE

US Safe Harbor was the result of five years of negotiation between the US Department of Commerce and the European Commission adopting a decision regarding safe harbor principles. The principles came into effect on 1 November 2000. It is intended to ensure the adequate level of privacy necessary to allow transfers of data from the EU to the US. Essentially Safe Harbor provides a set of privacy principles which replicate, the data protection principles enshrined by the EU data protection regime. These include:

- Notice (of intended use and intended recipients, and of how to limit use and make enquiries and complaints).
- Choice (both opting out and opting in).
- Security.
- Data integrity.
- Data subject access rights.
- Enforcement mechanisms (including effective follow-up procedures).

It is important to emphasise that Safe Harbor only applies between the EU and the US. It is fair to say that the reaction of most businesses in the US to the Safe Harbor principles has been unenthusiastic. Comparatively few US corporations have notified the Department of Commerce that they adhere to them. Notable corporations that have registered include Microsoft and Hewlett Packard.

7.3.3 THE EU MODEL CLAUSES

As we have seen, the Safe Harbor principles only extend to transfers of data between the EU and the US. The European Commission also released a separate scheme for any transfer out of the EU. A set of what are called 'Model Clauses' enable parties to transfer data outside the EU to other parties located in countries falling short of the adequate level of protection by means of a private contractual arrangement.

Both parties must execute a fixed, prescribed agreement distinct from any other commercial agreement that they may be entering into. Thus, whatever the nature of the commercial deal being struck between a virtual world or social network in say the UK, and the US, the parties must enter into a separate legal agreement which incorporates the prescribed Model Clauses. A good deal of experience has been gained since the Model Clauses were first introduced. For example, a number of business groups such as The International Chambers of Commerce (ICC) and Confederation of British Industry (CBI) wanted to adapt the clauses to make them more commercially relevant. As a result, in December 2004 the EU issued new Model Clauses to facilitate data flows from the EU. The Model Clauses ensure that data controllers are able to perform data transfers globally under a single set of data protection rules. The new Model Clauses are set out below for reference but specific legal advice must be taken to establish whether in fact the Clauses apply to the circumstances under which the virtual world or social network may operate. In the specimen Clauses set out, we have assumed a transfer of data between a UK virtual world or social network perhaps of its inhabitant database, to a US-based company.

It will be appreciated that the issue of transferring data from the UK to any country outside the EU is complex and it is sufficient for the purposes of this book to highlight that a virtual world or social network wishing to export data must be mindful of the law and take specific legal advice on how to proceed.

Specimen Clauses to include in commercial transactions involving virtual worlds.

Definitions

For the purposes of the clauses:

a) 'Personal data', 'Special categories of data/sensitive data', 'process/processing', 'controller', 'processor', 'data subject' and 'supervisory authority/authority' shall have the same meaning as in Directive 95/46/EC of 24 October 1995 (whereby 'the authority' shall mean the competent data protection authority in the territory in which the data exporter is established);
b) the 'data exporter' shall mean the controller who transfers the personal data;
c) 'the data importer' shall mean the controller who agrees to receive from the data exporter personal data for further processing in accordance with the terms of these clauses and who is not subject to a third country's system ensuring adequate protection;
d) 'clauses' shall mean these contractual clauses, which are a free-standing document that does not incorporate commercial business terms established by the parties under separate commercial arrangements.

The details of the transfer (as well as the personal data covered) are specified in Appendix B, which forms an integral part of the clauses.

I. Obligations of the Data Exporter

The data exporter warrants and undertakes that:

a) The personal data have been collected, processed and transferred in accordance with the laws applicable to the data exporter.
b) It has used reasonable efforts to determine that the data importer is able to satisfy its legal obligations under these clauses.
c) It will provide the importer, when so requested, with copies of relevant data protection laws or references to them (where relevant, and not including legal advice) of the country in which the data exporter is established.
d) It will respond to enquiries from data subjects and the authority concerning processing of the personal data by the data importer, unless the parties have agreed that the data importer will so respond, in which case the data exporter will still respond to the extent reasonably possible and with the information reasonably available to it of the data importer is unwilling or unable to respond. Responses will be made within a reasonable time.
e) It will make available, upon request, a copy of the clauses to data subjects who are third party beneficiaries under clause III, unless the clauses contain confidential information, in which case it may remove such information. Where information is removed, the data exporter shall inform data subjects in writing of the reason for removal and of their right to draw the removal to the attention of the authority. However, the data exporter shall abide by a decision of the authority regarding access to the full text of the clauses by data subjects, as long as data subjects have agreed to respect the confidentiality of the confidential information removed. The data exporter shall also provide a copy of the clauses to the authority where required.

II. Obligations of the Data Importer

The data importer warrants and undertakes that:

a) It will have in place appropriate technical and organisational measures to protect the personal data against accidental or unlawful destruction or accidental loss, alteration, unauthorised disclosure or access, and which provide a level of security appropriate to the risk represented by the processing and the nature of the data to be protected.
b) It will have in place procedures so that any third party it authorises to have access to the personal data, including processors, will respect and maintain the confidentiality and security of the personal data. Any person acting under the authority of the data importer, including a data processor, shall be obligated to process the personal data only on instructions from the data importer. This provision does not apply to persons authorised or required by law or regulation to have access to the personal data.
c) It has no reason to believe, at the time of entering into these clauses, in the existence of any local laws that would have a substantial adverse effect on the guarantees provided for under these clauses, and it will inform the data exporter (which will pass such notification on to the authority where required) if it becomes aware of any such laws.
d) It will process the personal data for purposes described in Annex B, and has the legal authority to give the warranties and fulfil the undertakings set out in these clauses.
e) It will identify to the data exporter a contact point within its organisation authorised to respond to enquiries concerning processing of the personal data, and it will cooperate in good faith with the data exporter, the data subject and the authority

concerning all such enquiries within a reasonable time. In case of legal dissolution of the data exporter, or if the parties have so agreed, the data importer will assume responsibility for compliance with the provisions of clause I(e).

f) At the request of the data exporter, it will provide the data exporter with evidence of financial resources sufficient to fulfil its responsibilities under the clause III (which may include insurance coverage).
g) Upon reasonable request of the data exporter, it will submit its data processing facilities, data files and documentation needed for processing to reviewing, auditing and/or certifying by the data exporter (or any independent or impartial inspection agents or auditors, selected by the data exporter and not reasonably objected to by the data importer) to ascertain compliance with the warranties and undertakings in these clauses, with reasonable notice and during regular business hours. The requests will be subject to any necessary consent or approval from a regulatory or supervisory authority within the country of the data importer, which consent or approval the data importer will attempt to obtain in a timely fashion.
h) It will process the personal data, at its option, in accordance with:

    i) the data protection laws of the country in which the data exporter is established; or
    ii) the relevant provisions of any Commission decision pursuant to Article 25(6) of Directive 95/46/EC, where the data importer complies with the relevant provisions of such an authorisation or decision and is based in a country to which such an authorisation or decision pertains, but is not covered by such authorisation or decision for the purposes of the transfer(s) of the personal data; or
    iii) the data processing principles set forth in Annex A.

i) Data importer to indicate which option it selects:_______________
j) Initials of data importer:_______________
k) (i) It will not disclose or transfer the personal data to a third data controller located outside the European Economic Area (EEA) unless it notifies the data exporter about the transfer and:

    i) the third party data controller processes the personal data in accordance with a Commission decision finding that a third country provides adequate protection; or
    ii) the third party data controller becomes a signatory to these clauses or another data transfer agreement approved by a competent authority in the EU; or
    iii) data subjects have been given the opportunity to object, after having been informed of the purposes of the transfer, the categories of recipients and the fact that the countries to which data is exported may have different data protection standards; or
    iv) with regard to onward transfers of sensitive data, data subjects have given their unambiguous consent to the onward transfer.

III. Liability and Third Party Rights

a) Each party shall be liable to the other parties for damages it causes by any breach of these clauses. Liability as between the parties is limited to actual damage suffered. Punitive damages (that is, damages intended to punish a party for its outrageous conduct) are specifically excluded. Each party shall be liable to data subjects for damages it causes by any breach of third party rights under these clauses. This does not affect the liability of the data exporter under its data protection law.

b) The parties agree that a data subject shall have the right to enforce as a third party beneficiary this clause and clauses I(b), I(d), I(e), II(a), II(c), II(d), II(e), II(h), II(i), III(a), V, VI(d) and VII against the data importer or the data exporter, for their respective breach of their contractual obligations, with regard to his personal data, and accept jurisdiction for this purpose in the data exporter's country of establishment. In cases involving allegations of breach by the data importer, the data subject must first request the data exporter to take appropriate action to enforce his rights against the data importer; if the data exporter does not take such action within a reasonable period (which under normal circumstances would be one month), the data subject may then enforce his rights against the data importer directly. A data subject is entitled to proceed against a data exporter that has failed to use reasonable efforts to determine that the data importer is able to satisfy its legal obligations under these clauses (the data exporter shall have the burden to prove that it took reasonable efforts).

IV. Law Applicable to the Clauses

These clauses shall be governed by the law of the country in which the data exporter is established, with the exception of the laws and regulations relating to processing of the personal data by the data importer under clause II(h), which shall apply only if so selected by the data importer under that clause.

V. Resolution of Disputes with Data Subjects or the Authority

a) In the event of a dispute or claim brought by a data subject or the authority concerning the processing of the personal data against either or both of the parties, the parties will inform each other about any such disputes or claims, and will cooperate with a view to settling them amicably in a timely fashion.

b) The parties agree to respond to any generally available non-binding mediation procedure initiated by a data subject or by the authority. If they do participate in the proceedings, the parties may elect to do so remotely (such as by telephone or other electronic means). The parties also agree to consider participating in any other arbitration, mediation or other dispute resolution proceedings developed for data protection disputes.

c) Each party shall abide by a decision of a competent court of the data exporter's country of establishment or of the authority which is final and against which no further appeal is possible.

VI. Termination

a) In the event that the data importer is in breach of its obligations under these clauses, then the data exporter may temporarily suspend the transfer of personal data to the data importer until the breach or the contract is terminated.

b) In the event that:

   i) the transfer of personal data to the data importer has been temporarily suspended by the data exporter for longer than one month pursuant to paragraph (a);
   ii) compliance by the data importer with these clauses would put it in breach of its legal or regulatory obligations in the country of import;
   iii) the data importer is in substantial or persistent breach of any warranties or undertakings given by it under these clauses;
   iv) a final decision against which no further appeal is possible of a competent court of the data exporter's country of establishment or of the authority rules that there has been a breach of the clauses by the data importer or the data exporter; or
   v) a petition is presented for the administration or winding up of the data importer, whether in its personal or business capacity, which petition is not dismissed within the applicable period for such dismissal under applicable law; a winding up order is made; a receiver is appointed over any of its assets; a trustee in bankruptcy is appointed, if the data importer is an individual; a company voluntary arrangement is commenced by it; or any equivalent event in any jurisdiction occurs then the data exporter, without prejudice to any other rights it may have against the data importer, shall be entitled to terminate these clauses, in which case the authority shall be informed where required. In cases covered by (i), (ii), or (iv) above the data importer may also terminate these clauses.

c) Either party may terminate these clauses if (i) any Commission positive adequacy decision under Article 25(6) of Directive 95/46/EC (or any superceding text) is issued in relation to the country (or a sector thereof) to which the data is transferred and processed by the data importer, or (II) Directive 95/46/EC (or any superceding text) becomes directly applicable in such country.

d) The parties agree that the termination of these clauses at any time, in any circumstances and for whatever reason (except for termination under clause VI(c) does not exempt them from the obligations and/or conditions under the clauses as regards the processing of the personal data transferred.

VII. Variation of these Clauses

The parties may not modify these clauses except to update any information in Annex B, in which case they will inform the authority where required. This does not preclude the parties from adding additional commercial clauses where required.

VIII. Description of the Transfer

The details of the transfer and of the personal data are specified in Annex B. The parties agree that Annex B may contain confidential business information which they will

not disclose to third parties, except as required by law or in response to a competent regulatory or governmental agency, or as required under clause I(e). The parties may execute additional annexes to cover additional transfers, which will be submitted to the authority where required. Annex B may, in the alternative, be drafted to cover multiple transfers.
Dated:__________

7.3.4 THE RIGHTS OF INDIVIDUALS AGAINST A VIRTUAL WORLD OR SOCIAL NETWORK

Individuals (or Data Subjects) have extensive rights under the Act and a virtual world or social network must comply. The consumer may write to the virtual world or social network and ask to be supplied with a description, purposes and any disclosures made of or a copy of any personal data being held. The virtual world or social network must respond to that request within 40 days on receipt of a single fee (the fee levels are set by regulations and may alter). The consumer also has the right to prevent processing likely to cause damage. In addition, the consumer has the right to claim compensation from the virtual world or social network if it contravenes certain requirements of the Act. In the case of inaccurate data, the consumer can apply to the court for correction, blocking, erasure or destruction. Consumers must also be notified when data is being collected and be told how it may be used and who is collecting it.

7.3.5 PENALTIES FOR A VIRTUAL WORLD OR SOCIAL NETWORK FOR BREACHING THE DATA PROTECTION ACT

It is a criminal offence not to register where a film company holds appropriate data. A larger threat is that of having to pay compensation where damage has been caused by the loss, unauthorised destruction or disclosure of personal data. There is of course also the potential for damaging adverse publicity resulting from such action.

7.4 Database Right and the Virtual World or Social Network

We have seen how the rights of individuals are protected by the data protection regime in the EU and what a virtual world or social network must do to abide by the Data Protection Act.

We will now examine what protection the virtual world or social network has in the database it has sought to compile and concerning which it has gone to great lengths to meet the requirements of the Data Protection Act. Clearly, the database which the virtual world or social network compiles could have enormous commercial value and will likely be the result of considerable effort over a long period of time on the part of that business. We will review the law which governs databases as works which attract financial value.

On 1 January 1998 the *Copyright and Rights in Databases Regulations 1997* ('the Regulations') came into force in the UK. The aim was to improve the protection given to databases and harmonise such protection throughout the EU.

A database is defined by Regulation 6 as: 'a collection of independent works, data or other materials which (a) are arranged in a systematic or methodical way, and (b) are individually accessible by electronic or other means.'

The definition captures hard copy databases but it also applies to online collections.

A database right arises automatically, in common with copyright. However, there are two prerequisites to be met before the right can exist;

In the first place, Regulation 13(1) states that there must have been 'a substantial investment in obtaining, verifying or presenting the contents of the database' Next, the 'maker' or if it was complied jointly, one of its makers, must be a national or if a company, incorporated in the European Economic Area. The 'maker' is defined by Regulation 14(1) as: 'the person who takes the initiative in obtaining, verifying or presenting the contents of a database and assumes the risk of investing in that obtaining, verification or presentation.'

It is the maker who will usually be the first owner of the database right. It is important to point out that if the maker is an employee, then it is the employer who will be the first owner.

Database right lasts for 15 years from the end of the calendar year in which it was either completed or first made available to the public. It is also possible that a substantial change to the contents of a database will result in this 15 years period commencing once again from that time as being considered substantially a new investment. In effect therefore it is entirely possible that databases will enjoy a rolling period of protection which could extend for many years beyond first compilation.

Regulation 16 grants the owner the right to prevent the extraction and/or re-utilisation of the whole or a substantial part of the contents of the database. 'Extraction' is defined as the permanent or temporary transfer of any contents of a database to another medium by any means or in any form. 'Re-utilisation' means making those contents available to the public by any means.

As with copyright law there are a number of defences available to the person or company who is alleged to have infringed the database of an owner. These include 'insubstantiality'. This is defined as meaning 'substantial in terms of quantity or quality or a combination of both'. However, it is possible to infringe an owner's database right by a series of what might be insubstantial copying acts. Another defence is that of 'lawful user' in relation to the database. This would include an express licence granted by the owner or possibly an implied licence. This might be where the owner has not actually given consent for the use of its database but its conduct might lead a court to conclude that the right can be deemed to have granted.

The virtual world or social network should ensure that the arrangement of its data is systematic or methodical and that the data is individually accessible. In addition, it should maintain a record of the investment it has made in obtaining, verifying or presenting its database. This record must be kept safely. This will be necessary if the virtual world or social network is ever called upon to prove its investment was 'substantial' and thus attract the protection of the Regulations. As noted the continued additions to a database could mean that its period of protection runs well beyond the 15 year right.

7.5 Virtual World and Social Network Privacy Policies

It is important that a company which receives personally identifiable information about its online customers include a Privacy Policy in its website terms and conditions. This is to comply with the Data Protection Act 1998. We examined at Chapter 3 the typical provisions one would find in such terms and conditions. The development of virtual worlds presents some interesting questions in the context of data protection and they are more difficult to conceptualise. This is because with more traditional e-commerce websites a company is dealing with online consumers who are individuals who by the information they disclose when purchasing goods or services can be readily identifiable.

With virtual world environments one of the principal attractions to the participants is the degree of anonymity which they can adopt in-world. It is this form of disguise, if you will, which allows users to enter into the world to a degree of their choosing before they might reveal their identity.

Do virtual worlds enable sufficient biographical information about a person acting through their avatar to be constructed which in effect breaches that person's privacy?

In this section the broad ambit of the Privacy Policy the virtual world company would use is examined.

The in-world company will confirm it is committed to protecting and respecting the privacy of its website visitors and will set out the basis on which any personal data it collects or that is provided to it, will be processed.

For the purpose of the Data Protection Act 1998, the data controller will be the in-world company. It will state that it may collect and process the following data about its visitors.

Information that they provide by filling in forms in-world. This includes information provided at the time of registering to participate in the virtual world where is necessary, subscribing to the service, posting material or requesting further services. It will also ask participants for information when they report a problem with the virtual world experience.

In the Second Life, virtual world Linden Lab (which operates the virtual world) specifies the information it collects from its users, which includes:

- IP address and cookie data from visitors.
- Email address from mailing list members.
- Personal data and usage information about registered members.
- Non personally identifiable information about users.

> *We track usage of customer service resources in order to ensure high quality interactions.*
>
> *This is in addition to the personal data and billing information collected during the registration process.*

The in-world company will confirm it may keep a record of that correspondence

It may also ask users to complete surveys that it uses for research purposes, although they will be informed they do not have to respond to them.

As has just been seen by the Second Life example, details of visits to the Virtual world including, but not limited to, traffic data, location data, weblogs and other communication data, whether required for the company's own billing purposes or otherwise, and the resources that its visitors access will be retained by the company and this explained to the user.

Similarly, as has been noted in the Second Life extract the in-world company may collect information about the visitor's computer including, where available their IP address, operating system and browser type, for system administration and perhaps to report aggregate information to the company's advertisers. (see Chapter 6 on advertising). This is statistical data about the users' browsing actions and patterns, and does not identify any individual.

For the same reason, the company may obtain information about its visitor's general Internet usage by using a cookie file which is stored on the hard drive of the user's computer. The company will explain that cookies enable it:

- To estimate its audience size and usage pattern.
- To store information about visitor's preferences, and so allow it to customise its website according to visitors' individual interests.
- To speed up visitors searches.
- To recognise visitors when they return to the website.

The visitor will be invited to refuse to accept cookies by activating the setting on their browser which allows them to refuse the setting of cookies.

The company will explain that unless the visitor has adjusted their browser setting so that it will refuse cookies, the system will issue cookies when the visitor logs on to the website.

The in-world company will state that the data it collects from visitors may be transferred to, and stored at, a destination outside the European Economic Area ('EEA') (see Section 7.2). The data may also be processed by staff operating outside the EEA who work for the company or one of its suppliers. Such staff may be engaged in, among other things, the fulfillment of the virtual world visitor's order made when that visitor transitions from the virtual world to the company's e-commerce website. Or, those staff might be involved with the processing of the virtual world participant's payment details and the provision of support services. By supplying their personal data, the in-world visitor will be asked to agree to this transfer, storing or processing. The company will confirm it will take all steps reasonably necessary to ensure that this data is treated securely and in confidence with the privacy policy.

The company should confirm that all information provided to the company by its virtual world visitors is stored on its secure servers, and that although it does its best to protect personal data, it cannot guarantee the security of such data transmitted to its virtual world environment.

The way the company uses the in-world data should be made clear in the privacy policy. For example:

- To ensure that content in its virtual environment is presented in the most effective manner for participants and for their computer.
- To provide in-world participants with information, products or services that they request from the company or which it feels may interest them, where the visitor has consented to be contacted for such purposes.

- To carry out obligations arising from any contracts entered into between the company and its in-world visitors. These may arise again at the point at which the participant moves from the virtual world to the company's e-commerce website.
- To allow visitors to participate in interactive features of the company's service, when visitors choose to do so.
- To notify visitors about changes to the virtual world service.

The film company will state that it may also use data, or permit selected third parties to use data, to provide visitors with information about content, goods and services which may be of interest to the visitor and that the company or the third parties may contact the visitor about these by email, post or telephone.

The policy should explain that if visitors do not want the virtual world or social network to use their data in this way, or to pass details on to third parties for marketing purposes, the visitor must tick the relevant box situated on the online form on which the company collects the data.

Linden Labs for example uses the following text in its user terms:

You acknowledge and agree that Linden Labs, in its sole discretion, may track, record, observe or follow any and all of your interactions within the Service.

Linden Labs may share general, demographic, or aggregated information with third parties about user base and service usage.

But that information will not include or be linked to any personal information without your consent.

The virtual world or social network will explain that it does not disclose information about identifiable individuals to its advertisers, but it may provide them with aggregate information about users. For example, it may inform them that 200 women aged under 30 have clicked on their advertisement on any given day. The virtual world or social network may also use such aggregate information to help advertisers reach the kind of audience they want to target, for example, men in certain post codes. The virtual world or social network may make use of the personal data it has collected from inhabitants to enable it to comply with its advertisers wishes by displaying their advertisement to that target audience.

The virtual world or social network will explain that it may disclose the personal information of its online visitors to any member of its group, which means its subsidiaries, its ultimate holding company and its subsidiaries, as defined in section 736 of the UK Companies Act 1985.

Further, it may disclose that personal information to third parties:

- In the event that it sells or buys any business or assets, in which case the virtual world or social network may disclose the personal data to the prospective seller or buyer of such business or assets.
- If the virtual world or social network or substantially all of its assets are acquired by a third party, in which case personal data held by it about its inhabitants will be one of the transferred assets.

- If the virtual world or social network is under a duty to disclose or share the inhabitants personal data in order to comply with any legal obligation, or to protect the rights, property, or safety of the company, its customers, or others. This may include exchanging information with other companies and organisations for the purposes of fraud protection and credit risk reduction.

The rights of the virtual world or social network's inhabitants will be set out in the privacy policy. For example, they will have the right to ask the company not to process personal data for marketing purposes. The company will say that it usually informs visitors (before collecting their data) if it intends to use their data for such purposes or if it intends to disclose that information to any third party for such purposes. The inhabitant will be told they can exercise their right to prevent such processing by checking certain boxes on the forms the virtual world or social network uses to collect such data.

The virtual world or social network will state that its website may, from time to time, contain links to and from the websites of its partner networks, advertisers and affiliates. If the inhabitant follows a link to any of those websites, it will be made clear that those websites have their own privacy policies and that the virtual world or social network does not accept any responsibility or liability for those policies. The inhabitant will be advised to check these policies before they submit any personal data to such websites.

The Data Protection Act 1998 gives individuals the right to access information held about them. Thus, the virtual world or social network will confirm the inhabitant's right of access can be exercised in accordance with the Act. Any access request may be subject to a fee, not excessive, for example £10, to meet the costs in providing inhabitants with details of the information held about them.

7.6 The Vulnerability of Social Networks and Virtual Worlds to Computer Hacking

In 2009 *Facebook* was targeted by malicious hackers seeking to steal valuable data from members of the Internet social network. The attacks were perpetrated by the creation of fake messages, augmented with details of *Facebook* members. Whilst malicious computer hacking is hardly new, what makes the attacks on social networks more striking is the fact that such environments thrive on the trust and social links that drive the networks. The very popularity of social networking sites makes them a tempting target.

Essentially the rogue applications directed at social networks all try to steal saleable information from the profiles of those members who open up the messages. Once installed the malicious program hunts for cookies on a victim's computer and uses the details it finds in the small text files to log into other social sites that person may be a member of.

The development highlights the importance for operators of social networks and virtual worlds to review their policy of approving applications. We consider elsewhere in this book that many social networks allow users to write a software application. The problem arises that most of these third party applications are not verified before they are released to other users. They are only vetted after they are offered to members and have been reported as causing problems. The reasoning behind this approach is that offering an open system in which anyone can participate is one of the attractions of the environments.

The risk of malicious attacks of this kind might be curtailed by members and inhabitants of the networks and virtual worlds being vigilant in not revealing their password.

7.7 The Data Retention (EC Directive) Regulations 2009

7.7.1 SOCIAL NETWORK DATA MONITORING PLANS

Example of how dynamic an area of law of virtual worlds and Internet social networks represents in the UK, The Home Office in 2009 announced proposals to require Internet social networking sites such as *Facebook* and *MySpace* to retain details of their users' movements on the Internet.

The plans are contained in a set of draft Regulations called The Data Retention (EC Directive) Regulations 2009.

Under the proposals, operators of such websites could be required to hold data about every person whom users correspond with via the websites, This latest move by the Government follows plans to store information about every telephone call, email and Internet visit made by anyone in the UK on a central database.

The Government is considering acting on social networking sites by modernising the intercept programme because they were not covered by new proposals featured in a draft EU Directive. The plans have, however, raised fresh concerns about the right to privacy. The interface between retaining data, private security and issues of privacy is important and the government is seeking to balance this with maintaining a capability and a capacity to deal with crime and issues of national security. The government state that there are no plans for a database containing the content of emails, texts, conversations or social networking websites.

7.7.2 WHAT THE DATA RETENTION REGULATIONS INTRODUCE

The draft Regulations have been issued pursuant to and implement what is known as the Data Retention Directive (Directive 2006/24/EC of the European Parliament and of the Council of 15 March 2006). This is an EU-wide Directive designed to harmonise Member States' laws relating to the retention of data generated or processed in connection with the provision of publicly available electronic communications services or networks.

The Regulations apply to communications data if the data is generated or processed in the UK by public communications providers in the process of supplying the communications services concerned.

There is an obligation to retain data communications. This obligation extends to communications data for:

1. Fixed network telephony.
2. Mobile telephony.
3. Internet access, Internet email or Internet telephony. It is this element which thus impacts Internet Social Networks or virtual worlds.

This data must be retained by the public communications provider for twelve months from the date of the communication in question.

The public communications providers must observe the following principles with respect to data retained in accordance with the Regulations. The retained data must be of the same quality and subject to the same security and protection as those data on the public electronic communications network. Next, the data must be subject to appropriate technical and organisational measures to protect the data against accidental or unlawful destruction, accidental loss or alteration, or unauthorised or unlawful storage, processing, access or disclosure. Third, the data must be subject to appropriate technical and organisational measures to ensure that they can be accessed by specially authorised personnel only. Finally, except in the case of data lawfully accessed and preserved, the data retained solely in accordance with the Regulations must be destroyed at the end of the retention period.

It is the Information Commissioner in the UK who is charged with monitoring the application of the provisions of the Regulations with respect to the security of stored data.

In terms of the destruction of data at the end of the retention period the duty of the public communications provider is to delete the data in such a way as to make access to the data impossible. It is sufficient for a public communications provider to make arrangements for the operation of so deleting data to take place at such monthly or shorter intervals as appear to the provider to be convenient.

Access to the retained data may only be obtained in specific cases and in circumstances in which disclosure of the data is permitted or required by law. The data retained must be retained in such a way that it can be transmitted without undue delay in response to requests.

A public communications provider must provide the Secretary of State as soon as practical after 31 March in any year, with the following information in respect of the period of twelve months ending with that date:

1. The number of occasions when data retained in accordance with the Regulations has been disclosed in response to a request;
2. The time elapsed between the date on which the data were retained and the date on which transmission of the data was requested;
3. The number of occasions when a request for lawfully disclosable data retained in accordance with the Regulations could not be met.

The expenses incurred by the public communications provider in complying with the Regulations may be reimbursed by the Secretary of State but this may be conditional upon the expenses having been notified to the Secretary of State and agreed in advance. The provider may be required to comply with any audit that may be reasonably required to monitor a claim for reimbursement.

It is Part 3 of the Schedule to the Regulations which deals with data which is obtained from Internet access, Internet email or Internet Telephony and this is the area of direct relevance for our purposes. The requirements are broken down into categories as follows.

First, Data necessary to trace and indentify the source of a communication.

This means the user ID allocated. The user ID is the unique identifier allocated to people when they subscribe to or register with an Internet access service or Internet communications service. The user ID and telephone number allocated to the communication entering the public telephone network. The name and address of the subscriber or registered user to whom an Internet Protocol (IP) address, user ID or telephone number was allocated at the time of the communication.

Second, Data necessary to identify the destination of a communication.

This means in the case of Internet telephony, the user ID or telephone number of the intended recipient of the call. In the case of Internet email or Internet telephony, the name and address of the subscriber or registered user and the user ID of the intended recipient of the communication.

Third, Data necessary to identify the date, time and duration of a communication.

This means in the case of Internet access:

a) the date and time of the log in and log off from the Internet access service, based on a specified time zone;
b) the IP address, whether dynamic or static, allocated by the Internet access service provider to the communication; and
c) the user ID of the subscriber or registered user of the Internet access service.

Also, in the case of Internet email or Internet telephony, the date and time of the log in to and log off from the Internet email or Internet telephony service, based on a specified time zone.

Fourth, Data necessary to identify the type of communication. In the case of Internet, email or Internet telephony, the Internet service used.

Finally, Data necessary to identify users' communications equipment. In the case of dial-up access, the calling telephone number and in any other case, the digital subscriber line (DSL) or other end point of the originator of the communication.

7.8 Privacy and In-World Behavioural Targeting

We saw in Chapter 6, the legal landscape within which online advertising and in-world advertising in particular must sit. Recently, there has been a new development which sees advertisers serve highly targeted advertisements to Internet users. There is an old adage which says that fifty per cent of all advertising works – the trick is knowing which fifty per cent will work. The Internet makes possible the identification of users to a degree previously not possible. The technology thus answers one of the advertising industries longest desires which is the ability to make advertisements relevant not only to a group profile of consumers, but to the individual. The problem is, however, that in common with so many other facets of Internet delivery, this ability brings into play important legal issues. In the case of targeted in-world advertising, the issue is privacy.

In this chapter we have examined the broad data protection regime as it applies in the UK to online collection of personal data. We now need to examine how the data protection law impacts on behavioural targeting.

It is an interesting issue. If your local supermarket offers you products they know you enjoy that is called good service. If, however, even better targeting of your needs is undertaken online it makes consumers wary. The difference, of course, lies in the degree to which your personal information is utilised in the online sphere.

The issue is complex because the concept of behavioural targeting is not restricted to an Internet user's visit to one website. The consumer's pattern of transition between different websites falls within the ability of the technology to map patterns of behaviour. So, for example the user of a social network website or virtual world may be also be a member or inhabitant of other such forums. That user may also transition between the in-world environment and the e-commerce websites of the in-world advertisers who maintain an island presence in the virtual world.

To an extent the unease about behavioural targeting rests on the degree of knowledge online advertisers are equipped with and the nature of that knowledge. Again, if one visits the high street supermarket and is offered your favourite apples or magazine, it improves the shopping experience. If, though, one visits the Pharmacy in that same supermarket to be met with an enquiry from a stranger behind the counter of how a physical rash is behaving, it is quite another thing.

The capacity for websites to deliver targeted products to entice users is not new and is achieved not least by the use of cookies which permit the suggestion of related products to those previously ordered by the user via the particular website. We examine elsewhere in this book how the use of cookies must be explained to inhabitants.

The technology that permits behavioural targeting in the manner we are considering here is very clever. It is being adopted by many ISPs and other online commercial organisations. The question whether the technology gathers personally identifiable information is what concerns regulators and consumers alike.

The proponents of the technology argue that it functions by allocating a number to customers who opt in to its free anti-phishing service and then stores the categories of content visited by each of those numbers. Thus, for example the in-world users browsing history is not retained by the operator of the technology, nor are the website URLs which the user has visited. The technology itself does not take any data from the ISPs which deploy it.

The argument in defence of behavioural targeting is that the in-world inhabitant who moves about the environment and between e-commerce websites is not revealing personally identifiable information. The inhabitant is simply a cookie number to an advertising network.

Despite the above explanation of how the technology operates there remains unease not only from consumers but certain advertisers and website operators. Such operators contend that they have devoted great attention to creating trust and confidence on the part of their users to visit their website and that confidence is risked if inhabitants believe they are being spied upon.

It is clear that inhabitants of virtual worlds and Internet social networks and the commercial Internet in general do not object to advertising being highly targeted to their needs and relevant to them. However, they profoundly object to being tracked online if they believe they will be identified personally. In many ways there should be a demand for in-world behavioural targeting. This is because, whilst inhabitants and members of social networks recognise that a good deal of in-world content, particularly media related, is advertising funded, only a very few regard that advertising as relevant. In addition, most Internet users recognise that tracking is technically possible and might be deployed to a degree in general use. However, when the issue is openly raised it still causes reluctance.

This distrust is fuelled not so much by unease about what the virtual world or social network operator may do with the data the inhabitant reveals to permit better targeted advertising. It is based more on their fear that their IPS may not adequately distinguish between what is personally identifiable information – and thus protected under the Data Protection Act 1998 – and anonymous data, which is not.

At the time of writing the issue is not yet settled either in terms of the precise legal position on how behavioural targeting is to be treated, or indeed on the evidence revealed by user attitudes toward the tracking technology. If, however, the history of the Internet – which shows its capacity to disrupt and then prevail over established principles of law or conduct, is followed by this latest development, behavioural targeting will become a feature of in-world activity in time.

CHAPTER 8 The Distance Selling Regulations and Sales Through Virtual Worlds

8.1 Background

The sale of products over the Internet is now commonplace. Consumers have gained confidence in ordering goods and services online and for many the Internet is as significant as the High Street in terms of meeting their retail requirements.

These products can be distributed to a worldwide audience if desired and with modern logistics most can be dispatched and delivered to the consumer within a matter of days anywhere across the globe.

Many items so ordered are low risk in the eyes of the purchaser in that they are probably already aware of the product and its content and the modest value of the unit means they are more willing to consider an online purchase. The same risk assessment to a large extent pertains to inhabitants of virtual worlds who are presented with in-world retail opportunities to buy products. Or does it?

Virtual worlds depict products often by means of computer graphics which is in many instances represents an approximation of what the physical merchandise looks like. Thus, the decision on the part of the inhabitant of the environment to buy particular goods may be shaped by the portrayal of those goods. There is perhaps more scope on the part of the in-world vendor for misleading descriptions, albeit unintended.

In this chapter we will consider the protection afforded by the law to consumer inhabitants of virtual worlds where those avatars are based in the EU and buy goods within or through the environment.

It is important to clarify what form of sale we refer to here. Virtual worlds, as we have seen elsewhere, allow for the trading of items within the environment such as property and virtual assets which only exist and have consequence in-world. That is one of the major attractions of the forums because they permit a form of inventive exchange simply not possible in any other setting.

This kind of sale is not what fails to be considered here. We will examine the consumer law which does impact on virtual world sales but those laws only relate to sales of physical products which may be made either directly from in-world retailers or indirectly by such retailers by a hyperlink from the virtual world to their principal e-commerce website.

There are important legal considerations which an in-world retailer must be aware of before offering merchandise for sale to avatars via the forum. The laws we are about to consider do not apply where merchandise is sold through virtual worlds to other businesses.

The background to the consumer protection legislation forming the subject of this chapter lies in the EU's desire to protect consumers who enter into contracts for the purchase of goods or services away from business premises. It was considered that people should have the opportunity to examine the goods or services being offered, as they would have done if buying in a shop. Thus, a cooling off period was considered desirable.

The legislative tool by which contracts concluded at a distance are governed is *The Consumer Protection (Contracts Concluded by Means of Distance Selling) Regulations 2000.* Given the date these Regulations were introduced one might be forgiven for thinking that they were written with sales over the Internet in mind because by definition an Internet sale is a distance contract. However, they were not, and certainly the concept of virtual worlds could never have been within the contemplation of legislators. The regulations apply to online sales of goods and services by businesses based in the EU to consumers similarly based anywhere in the EU. The Regulations are commonly referred to as the 'Distance Selling Regulations'.

8.2 The Consumer Protection (Contracts Concluded by Means of Distance Communication) Regulations 2000 and How They Relate to Virtual Worlds

The Distance Selling Directive was adopted by the European Parliament and Council in May 1997 and has been implemented by the UK by The Consumer Protection (Contracts Concluded by Means of Distance Communication) Regulation 2000 (SI 2000 No. 2334) (the 'Regulations').

The Regulations came into force in the UK on 31 October 2000. However, on 6 April 2005, The Consumer Protection (Distance Selling) (Amendments) Regulations 2005 also came into force. These change the original Regulations in relation to certain issues.

8.2.1 THE AIM OF THE REGULATIONS IN THE CONTEXT OF THE IN-WORLD RETAIL EXPERIENCE

The Distance Selling regulations give avatars certain rights and protection when they shop for goods or services in-world. The purpose of the legislation is to:

- give avatars confidence in purchasing goods and/or services where there is no face-to-face contact with the seller;
- ensure that all in-world traders meet certain basic requirements.

In brief, the Distance Selling Regulations say that the in-world retailer must always give its avatar customers certain clear information. This is so they have the information they need to decide whether to buy from that retailer. In most cases the retailer must also give avatar customers the right to a cancellation period.

The information the virtual retailer must give includes details about:

- its business;
- its goods or services;

- its payment arrangements;
- its delivery arrangements;
- its avatar customers' right to cancel their orders.

8.2.2 THE DEFINITION OF A 'DISTANCE CONTRACT'

Distance Contracts are defined broadly as:

> *Any contract concerning goods or services concluded between a supplier and consumer under an organised distance sales or service provision scheme run by the supplier, who, for the purpose of the contract, makes exclusive use of one or means of distance communication up to and including the moment at which the contract is concluded.*

The key to the applicability of the Regulations is a contract where the supplier and the consumer do not come face to face prior to the conclusion of the contract. They provide protection for consumers in the UK shopping for goods and services by telephone, mail order, fax, interactive TV, the Internet and virtual worlds.

The Regulations harmonise laws in all member states so that all European consumers have equality of access to goods and services in other member states.

8.2.3 INFORMATION TO BE PROVIDED BY AN IN-WORLD RETAILER TO INHABITANTS OF VIRTUAL WORLDS UNDER THE REGULATIONS

The Regulations in effect specify that prior to the conclusion of any distance contract entered into in-world a consumer avatar must be provided with the following information. The virtual retailer is required to provide certain clear and comprehensible information in good time before the virtual world sale is made.

This detail should be included on the virtual retailer's e-commerce website. Once again, it is important to make clear that, in our analysis of the Distance Selling Regulations in the context of virtual worlds, we are assuming the sale of real world goods or services in circumstances where the avatar is directed by hyperlink from the virtual world to the e-commerce website of an in-world retailer. The information which must be displayed on that website includes the following:

1. The in-world retailer's identity must be supplied. If the contract requires payment in advance, the company's address should be displayed on its e-commerce website. We have seen at Chapter 4 that in any event under The Electronic Commerce (EC Directive) Regulations 2002 a virtual world retailer which sells merchandise or services via its website must provide this detail.
2. The principal characteristics of the in-world retailer's goods or services should be specified.
3. All prices including taxes should be specified.
4. Details of how payment can be made must be made clear.
5. For how long the price or any special offers, perhaps those offers only available to inhabitants of the virtual world, remain valid.
6. The minimum duration of the contract in the case of contracts for the supply of goods or services to be provided either permanently or recurrently.

7. Delivery costs must be clear, as should all payment arrangements.
8. If it proposed to supply substitute merchandise or services of equivalent quality and price in the event of merchandise or services ordered by the consumer avatar being unavailable.
9. The right of the consumer avatar to cancel must be specified.
10. If the avatar is to use a premium rate telephone number the cost of the call must be specified before charges are incurred for the telephone call.
11. Any costs of using the Internet or the virtual world as a means of distance communication must be highlighted.

All the above information can be supplied by the in-world retailer to the consumer avatar by email. However, in theory, there would be nothing to prevent the in-world retailer from communicating this information to its customer directly to that customer's avatar within the virtual world environment. Whether this method was used would depend on the degree to which the retailer wishes to truly integrate its virtual world presence with its e-commerce website. Some retailers may simply choose to communicate necessary information to the email address furnished by its customer just as it would if that customer had come to the e-commerce website by web search rather than via a virtual world environment.

8.2.4 CARRYING OUT THE VIRTUAL WORLD CONTRACT

Any in-world contract for the delivery of merchandise to the consumer must be carried out within the time limits agreed with the customer as stated in the e-commerce website terms and conditions. If no period has been agreed, the statutory time limit is within a maximum of 30 days from the day after the day the customer sends the order to the in-world retailer.

If the retailer is unable to meet the deadline, it must inform the customer before the expiry of the deadline and refund any money paid in relation to the contract. The refund should be made as quickly as possible and certainly within 30 days, including weekends and public holidays. It is open to the in-world retailer and the customer to agree a revised date for delivery of the goods. The customer however is not under an obligation to agree a revised date. If the customer does not agree to a revised date the contract must be treated as if it had not been made. Any money paid in relation to the contract must be returned to the customer as quickly as possible and certainly within 30 days from the date of cancellation.

8.2.5 CANCELLING ORDERS WITH THE IN-WORLD RETAILER

Provided the in-world retailer gives its customer the required written information latest at the time the goods are delivered, cancellation rights end seven working days after the day on which the goods have been received.

If the virtual retailer does not give its customer the required information latest at the time the goods are delivered, but does so within three months from the day after the day the customer receives the goods, then the customer's cancellation rights will end after the day on which the customer received the required written information.

Where the in-world retailer has not provided the required written information, the customer's cancellation rights will end after the three months and seven working days counting the day after the customer received the goods.

8.2.6 VIRTUAL WORD CONTRACTS WHICH FALL OUTSIDE THE CONSUMER PROTECTION (CONTRACTS CONCLUDED BY MEANS OF DISTANCE COMMUNICATION) REGULATIONS 2000

It is important to note that certain contracts are excluded from the Regulations. Their exclusion is founded on common sense. They include contracts for the supply of foodstuffs, beverages or other goods intended for everyday consumption, supplied to the real world home of the consumer, to his residence, or to his workplace.

Thus, sales through virtual worlds of perhaps branded foodstuffs such as sweets will not be subject to the Regulations because of the perishable nature of the goods concerned.

Audio or video recordings or computer software which the virtual world consumer has 'unsealed' are also excluded.

Another type of contract excluded are contracts for the provision of accommodation, transport, catering or leisure services, where the in-world supplier undertakes, when the contract is concluded, to provide these services on a specific date or within a specific period. For example, hotel and travel bookings are not caught by the Regulations. So, if the in-world retailer makes available via its website a facility for audiences to make bookings for music concert tickets combined with travel and overnight hotel stay, such an offer will not fall under the Regulations.

Other exceptions to the general right to withdraw from contracts concluded in-world include those:

a) for the provision of services if performance has begun, with the consumer's agreement, before the end of seven working days;
b) for the supply of goods or services, the price of which is dependent on fluctuations in financial markets that cannot be controlled by the virtual world retailer;
c) for the supply of goods made to the in-world consumer's specifications or clearly personalised or which, by reason of their nature, cannot be returned or are liable to deteriorate or expire rapidly. For example, an in-world retailer might, via its e-commerce website, make an exclusive offer to the first thousand visitors to its website who transit from the virtual world environment for a personalised item of merchandise. Such merchandise falls outside the scope of the Regulations;
d) for the supply of newspapers, periodicals and magazines;
e) for gaming and lottery services.

The question arises does the provision of a link in a virtual world website operated by an in-world retailer from where users, on payment, can download a film or music, or arrangements for virtual world users to buy ring tones and screen savers for mobile phones, for example by texting or telephoning a particular number, fall within the cancellation exemptions referred to above?

In such cases the inhabitant of the virtual world is not receiving physical goods as such. If the supply is therefore not of an actual goods but rather of a service, the exception to the right to cancel would only apply if the in-world retailer has the user's agreement to start the service before the end of the cancellation period. The retailer must have provided the user with the required written information before it starts the service, including information that virtual world user's cancellation rights will end as soon as the service begins.

Another issue to understand when interpreting the Regulations is whether the above exceptions apply to products which may be the subject of copyright, for example, music CDs. The answer appears to be no. Copyright considerations may underlie the partial exceptions provided in the Regulations for the supply of audio, video/DVD recordings or computer software that the in-world consumer has unsealed. However, there is no general exception for copyright products and the exception probably would not extend to other products that may lend themselves to copying, such as books

This does not, however, stop the in-world retailer from specifying in its website, terms and conditions (see Chapter 3 on retailer terms and conditions) what it considers to be reasonable care, in virtual world customers examining such goods. However, if the customer has done no more than examine the goods as they would have in a shop and, if that requires opening the packaging and trying out the goods, then they would not have breached their duty to take reasonable care of the goods. In a real world shop, for example, books are usually displayed unsealed.

A review of the exceptions listed above should enable a virtual world retailer to establish whether their services offered within the environment, fall outside the Regulations and thus do not allow their avatar customers to withdraw from the contract. It is important to note that full treatment must be given on the matter of cancellation rights in the virtual world retailer's website terms and conditions and legal advice should be taken as to the contents of those terms and conditions as they will cover items not capable of comprehensive review in this book.

8.3 The Consumer Protection (Distance Selling) (Amendments) Regulations 2005

The principal aim of the changes to the Distance Selling Regulations is to make the right of cancellation clearer in the context of the provision of services. Prior to the amendments there was a requirement on a virtual world retailer to inform the in-world consumer in writing or by other durable medium, before the contract is made, that the user will not be able to cancel the contract once performance of the services has begun with his agreement. This created problems for some in-world businesses who receive orders from inhabitants of virtual worlds over the phone for services which those users want straight away or within a couple of days. In such cases compliance with the Regulations was impracticable or unduly costly if necessary information needed to be faxed or sent by post or even couriered urgently. It also meant that performance of the services could well be delayed. The whole point of a virtual world retailer having such a presence is to permit instantaneous, easy conduct of business from a unique platform. Delays to that objective would render the attractions of the retail experience redundant.

The overcome these problems the right to cancel has been amended. For an in-world retailer the new provisions could be important to understand if the business is offering some form of service and this service is available to avatar consumers not only via the virtual world but perhaps by telephone request. This is most likely to arise by the use of mobile phones where the user is required to call whilst operating within the environment, to take advantage of an offer of services and the contract is effectively concluded via that phone call. We will therefore now examine the effect of the changes in that context.

The in-world retailer is no longer required to inform the consumer, prior to the conclusion of a contract for services, that the user will not be able to cancel once performance has begun with his agreement. Under the revised provision, the in-world retailer must, in such cases, provide the user with information as to how the right to cancel may be affected if the user agrees to performance beginning less than seven working days after the contract was concluded. This information must be provided prior to or in good time during the performance of the contract. The question arises, of course, how can the in-world retailer make this known within the confines of a virtual world? The best method, if such notification proves impractical to impart in-world, would be to direct the user by hyperlink to the e-commerce website of the retailer where the information could be made clear.

The next model to consider is where the virtual world retailer providing services gives information as to how the right to cancel may be affected, as set out above, before performance of those services begins and the user agrees to such performance beginning before the end of the cooling off period. In this scenario there is no right to cancel on the part of the in-world consumer user.

Where the in-world retailer which provides services gives information as to how the right to cancel may be affected as set out above, in good time during the performance of the services, there is a right to cancel even if the consumer user agrees to performance beginning within the seven working days of the contract being concluded, but the cooling off period begins when the user receives the information, and ends seven working days later or when performance is completed, whichever is sooner.

The virtual world retailer can still exclude the right to cancel by including terms in their contracts with avatar consumers to the effect that the consumer agrees that the services will begin before the end of the cooling off period. In order to do this, the retailer will need to inform consumers about the loss of the right to cancel prior to the contract being concluded unless agreement is sought from the avatar consumer otherwise than as part of the contract.

Where however the in-world retailer is happy not to exclude the right to cancel, information concerning the right to cancel can be provided in good time during the performance of the services rather than prior to the conclusion of the contract.

The avatar consumer's right to cancel is lost when the performance of the services is completed. This may prove difficult though where there is not 'good time' to provide information about the cancellation right before the services are completed. Where the information is not provided in good time but the services have been substantially performed or are completed, the right of cancellation is preserved.

8.4 Guidance For The Distance Selling Regulations

The Office of Fair Trading (OFT) and the Department for Business, Enterprise & Regulatory Reform (BERR) have issued joint guidance that will update and inform those selling online of their duties under the Distance Selling Regulations. The guidance seeks to clarify some ambiguities after the Regulations came into force. It is felt there are still some areas of confusion.

It is clear what the virtual world or social network must do on the matter of refunds for the supply of, for example, DVDs or other merchandise. If an inhabitant cancels an order for merchandise by email but fails to return the item, the virtual world or social network cannot delay making the refund. The refund must be made as soon as possible after the inhabitant cancels and within 30 days at the latest. Interestingly, even if the inhabitant returns merchandise which is damaged they still do not lose their right to cancel under the Regulations. Clearly, the virtual world or social network or its in-world retailer still has a right of action against its inhabitant for failing to take reasonable care of the merchandise but this could prove difficult and on occasion hardly worth the time and money involved in the effort.

There is also the question of how much the refund should be to the inhabitant. If an in-world retailer supplies merchandise the full price paid for the items including the cost of delivery must be refunded. However, what if the in-world retailer also offers other services. It is recommended that the in-world retailers service should be structured so that there is one contract for the supply of goods where a refund is available and another for a supply of services that is non-refundable.

CHAPTER 9 Agreements between Virtual Worlds or Social Networks and Infrastructure Providers

9.1 Background

For any virtual world to operate properly, a high level of software functionality and complex programming is required. From the inhabitant's perspective this will script language which will be an intrinsic element of the environment that provides an internal, event-driven, computer language which allows the user to control object and avatar behaviour. Typically, the virtual world operator will also provide an in-world live tutorial on a daily basis.

At the same time, broadband's ability to handle vast quantities of data enables virtual world providers the ability to offer new content and services and to create additional markets.

However, in addition to the enrichment of the in-world user experience, the operator will need to consider external links with other service providers in order to capture further revenue and offer a more accessible environment. It is important for the virtual world operator to understand how it can engage with the new breed of telecommunication companies, Internet Service Providers (ISPs), mobile platforms and content aggregators to open up new channels for the virtual world. These gatekeepers to the market are themselves looking for new ways to retain and increase market share. Virtual world environments may be one such route. In essence, the mobile phone operators need content they can package in different forms. There is a consumer demand for more made-for-mobile content. That might include mobile versions of the environment. The mobile operators for their part can concentrate on delivering the best possible experience of that environment to their customers. They can tailor the content for different formats using their knowledge of the customer. At this stage of the development of new media content developers and content aggregators are engaged in a period of experimentation since there is not yet a perfect model. The content developer such as operators of virtual worlds need to ensure that they do not jeopardise their existing relationships with established platforms but, at the same time, yield financial reward in other new media properties. They must strike this balance in the absence of hard data about the actual Whatever commercial model the virtual world operator seeks to implement with the content aggregator, there will be several issues to understand.

These matters require careful consideration and, once strategic partners have been identified by the virtual world or social network, properly drafted legal agreements need to be implemented. We will now consider some of those agreements.

9.2 The In-world Avatar Design and Development Agreement

As has been noted there are an increasing array of established virtual worlds wherein one can participate and interact with fellow users. However, for many businesses a more strategic option might be to create their own virtual environment to achieve its particular objectives. This might be to offer a forum for staff to collaborate on commercial projects or explore new and innovative initiatives.

If a company wishes to produce a virtual world then it will need to employ the technical expertise to build the environment according to its requirements. Thus, the relationship which is vital to the online activity of a film company is that with its virtual world designer and developer. These are companies which have the necessary competence to create electronic spheres and which can advise upon the features which will make the world function. They are not necessarily the same companies which can advise upon how a business can make best use of the marketing potential of a virtual world presence. The latter are typically digital agencies which usually have their roots in website development and online promotion and, prior to that, often in mainstream marketing and advertising. The companies which build virtual worlds may belong to that category but more likely will be purely technically focused.

Just as in the early years of e-commerce, few businesses which elected to operate online gave much thought to the key terms they should have with their website designers, the same applies to the early phase of virtual world creation. However, perhaps what distinguishes the first stirrings of e-commerce from the development of virtual worlds is that in the former case the industry was new and many website development firms had not grown from other businesses. Thus, on both sides of the arrangement, potential problems could not be appreciated. There is now the benefit of over a decade of experience gained from pure website development which will undoubtedly have educated the minds of corporates in how they relate to external online agencies.

A common issue tended to be around what happened when the website designer's services were to be dispensed with. There were disputes over ownership of intellectual property rights in the website, domain name transfer and hosting of the website. The same considerations must be addressed when designing and developing a virtual world.

Most website developers work to standard contracts with their clients and the majority of clients now expect to sign such an agreement and are clearer as to what they wish to see in the contractual relationship. Similarly the company engaged to build the virtual world will more than likely have such terms and conditions.

However, the mainstream business world and the software development world are very different environments and each consist of professionals who may not be hugely experienced with the other. The potential for misunderstanding in the relationship is thus significant. In addition, whilst many virtual world designers will present their standard terms to their client company, it is important to state that these should always be capable of being amended to reflect the commercial imperatives of the your business.

Careful legal advice needs to be obtained on the negotiation of this relationship and the Agreement which records its terms.

In the context of virtual worlds, the company which engages a developer needs to understand the options with regard to land types in-world, location restrictions for such virtual property. There are covenants for such use just as there are covenants which govern the use of land in the real world. Therefore, the virtual world developer needs to understand land and prime usage rights, as well as design, transactional capabilities, security, testing and acceptance, Intellectual Property ownership, ongoing training, development and maintenance and liability considerations.

So, there are some key issues to consider in the contract to be entered into with its virtual world design and development company. In this section we will examine those matters from the perspective of the business seeking to enter the virtual environment as opposed to the design company which it will need to engage. It is important to emphasise this as there are a number of issues where the designer and a business will have different commercial expectations. It will often be a question of negotiation as to what forms the final contract. We will review those matters which a business would find desirable.

The designer will be appointed on the basis of the terms and conditions in the Virtual World Design and Development Agreement. ('the Agreement'). The designer will be required to design the world in accordance with an agreed specification and an agreed time period. This question of the specification is of course very important and has the potential as a source of dispute. This is particularly so because a company will, of necessity, rely heavily on the advice, guidance and experience of the designer. Whilst the business may have a broad objective for its virtual world presence or even some very clear features, it will still be entering into uncharted waters and, therefore, the process of deciding upon just what its virtual world will comprise and how it will function must be given very significant time and attention. This effort needs to be undertaken pre-contract so that at the stage the Agreement is to be prepared there is a well defined specification with development phases fully understood on both sides. On occasion, a business may require certain functionality of the virtual world but may not communicate its aims sufficiently to the designer. The full functionality of the environment must be set clearly and the place to do this is in the technical specification. The specification usually forms a schedule to the Agreement as this is the part which will change for each virtual world produced by the designer whereas the contractual terms may well remain substantially the same from deal to deal.

Agreements of this kind will be technically complex both from a legal and IT perspective. The business must approach the relationship with very clear business and technological objectives. Both issues will determine the content of the Agreement. Sometimes the lawyers engaged by the business to help with the negotiation of the Agreement will not be able to comment to any significant degree upon the technical specification for the virtual world and may assume that its business client can do so. Thus, the business must spend time with the developer in understanding what is meant by certain technical terms.

The Agreement will cover the fees which are to be paid by the business for its virtual world. It is not uncommon for those fees, once agreed to, be met over various intervals of the design process. For example, a certain percentage will be paid upon signing the Agreement, further payments to be made upon presentation of the look and feel stage of the design of the world, or at other testing phases, and the remaining sum within 30 days after live operation of the virtual world.

The business will want to retain as much control over the content of its world as possible and this impacts on the question of intellectual property rights. To enable the development of the environment the business will provide the designer with a good deal of material including text, photographs, video images, logos, and trade names. In addition, it may present photographs of its various personnel so as to enable the designer to create virtual character depictions of those personnel to feature in the world. In themselves, such representations are of great significance and the approval of the individual concerned should be sought by the business before the virtual character can be introduced into the world. People are understandably sensitive about their image in real life and will be similarly concerned in virtual environments.

The intellectual property rights in that content will reside with the business or be otherwise licensed to it by a third party. It will not belong to the virtual designer. The form of that intellectual property may be copyright in the corporate information, such as company documents, text or photos and perhaps trademarks in the name of the business, or services it provides.

Conversely, the virtual world designer is being asked to design an environment and the functionality of the website and the underlying software code may well be the result of original work by the designer which in itself attracts copyright. Virtual world designers will usually only grant a licence to their clients of these rights but retain ownership themselves. This is because those rights represent the value to the designer in its enterprise. There are circumstances where the business will want to expressly acquire the intellectual property rights in its entire virtual world. If the contract between the two were silent on the point the designer would be deemed to own the rights in the software as original author. Therefore, if the business does wish to hold the rights this must be made clear in the Agreement. It should be stated that, typically, the designer would charge a premium for the release of the rights to the business.

The business and, almost certainly its personnel who are be featured in virtual guise, will wish to approve all content in its world before it goes live and this right should be stated in the Agreement. One issue which is not uncommon between the parties is the constant shifting of requirements usually on the part of the virtual world designer's client. This can lead to at the very least, problems in the smooth progress of the design process, and at worst, insurmountable issues which can be costly. It is not uncommon for designers to be forced to abandon work because the specification of the project has gone through huge changes which have exhausted their client's original budget but left the project uncompleted. The ability for the designer to get the business to approve content at certain specified stages in the development is important as, once passed, the Agreement will usually state that no further changes may be made by the business unless these fall outside the scope of the original work. This will inevitably mean further fees.

If the business decides to make changes to its proposed virtual world during the design process or after completion of the environment, then there should be a clear process to follow in the Agreement. This issue is quite significant given the dynamic nature of computer system design. For example, it may be that the business discovers an innovative approach featured in a competitor's world or one of the open worlds. It may thus wish to make rapid changes to its own world. Any further costs associated with the changes requested by the business would be notified to the business first, under the terms of the change request procedure, although the designer may also suggest changes.

In most instances the business will simply assume that the designer has appropriate personnel with the necessary degree of skill to develop its virtual environment. However, it is a good idea to include a provision in the Agreement confirming that the designer will, at all times, have sufficient personnel to perform its contractual obligations under the Agreement. This can be a somewhat nebulous issue. There are no recognised standards in terms of skills in the field of developers. They may well utilise industry standard software or processes but in the last analysis they are usually either good or not so good. Nonetheless, it is as well to include a provision of this kind.

It is common for staff in design companies to move to other companies in the industry and often those staff are key in terms of their particular skills in certain aspects of virtual design or, indeed, the ongoing relationship between the business and the development company.

As the whole issue of virtual world participation is a new phase in Internet development, it is likely that the business' requirements of its designers will be ongoing and constantly evolving. The business might simply engage the developer to act on a retainer and introduce and implement new ideas into the virtual world as they become apparent.

A business could find itself facing a delay in construction of its world or worse, the inability of desired features to be capable of completion in the absence of appropriate personnel on the part of the developer. The Agreement should include a clause giving the business the right to terminate the Agreement if this situation occurs.

As most software development work is undertaken in stages, there are testing intervals which serve as useful opportunities to review progress and performance of the virtual world developer. The Agreement should contain provisions which allow the business to terminate the contract if, at those stages, work is not satisfactory. However, the right to terminate would only arise following an agreed notification process to enable the developer to respond to any legitimate concerns the business has over the construction process.

The duration of the Agreement must be stated. This can be for a fixed term, for example one year, and then run on a rolling basis until terminated by either party. This is more usual where the developer is to provide ongoing services to the business such as consultancy support for the virtual world, for example, recommending new features as they become apparent from general experience of virtual world use. There must also be express provisions in the Agreement dealing with the circumstances in which the Agreement can be terminated early. This usually revolves around a significant breach by one of the parties of its obligations under the Agreement.

For example, the business itself may be in breach of the Agreement if it fails to furnish, in a timely manner, all necessary written instructions, briefing materials and content, including any images, photographs, illustrations, graphics, audio clips, video clips or text. The business must usually deliver such items to the developer in an electronic file format specified and accessible by the developer. Another example might be if the business has warranted that it is the sole owner of, or is duly authorised by the owner to use, any trademark or name requested or allocated as the name of the Virtual world and further that, neither its use or registration constitutes or will constitute an infringement of any third party's Intellectual Property rights. In each of these cases a breach by the business could entitle the developer to terminate the Agreement for cause.

Conversely, if the level of service achieved by the developer falls below a minimum acceptable standard, which may be specified in the Agreement, then that could constitute a material breach by the developer, incapable of remedy, entitling the business to exercise its rights to terminate. Usually in such situations there is an agreed specified period in which the party in breach has to remedy the breach (if capable of remedy) such as within 30 days of a written notice to do so.

Another standard clause would provide the ability to terminate if the other party becomes insolvent or such a prospect is threatened.

The consequences of termination must be made clear. If the developer is in breach, the business will want to be able to recover material supplied to the developer or which is central to the successful function of the virtual world. This might include all software documentation to enable a third party developer subsequently appointed by the business to load onto another server and ensure continuity of the virtual world.

There is always a need to maintain confidentiality with regard to each party's business. During the development phase and even thereafter as long as there is commercial dialogue between the developer and the business, certain information will be revealed which is, by its nature, confidential. The business may well only be moving to a virtual world platform because it wishes to explore some highly sensitive strategies which it believes could be given better treatment in the confines of a virtual environment.

The developer would usually be under an obligation to use all reasonable endeavours to preserve the integrity of the corporate data which the business may supply as part of the build process.

One point to consider is what financial consequences may flow from a breach of the Agreement by either party. This is important because if the Agreement is terminated for cause there may be severe financial consequences for the other party. Those costs may well extend well beyond the pure costs of losing the contracted for original virtual world. For example, the business may have intended to invite participation of key suppliers or clients into its virtual world once completed. If the developer is in breach, causing the business to terminate the Agreement, then the true costs to the business may include lost business opportunities with certain clients. It is with this in mind that most agreements seek to place a cap on the total liability of a party in breach. Often this is achieved by expressly excluding liability for consequential loss as it is known, that is, losses which arise as a consequence of the breach beyond those easily envisaged. Usually, the financial liability is limited by the developer, to the total value of the fees it will have received for the project. The business may want to try and resist that limitation in negotiation. However, likewise, the business may want to limit its liability to the amounts it has already paid to the developer for the virtual world in the case where it is the party in breach. These issues are always a matter of negotiation between the parties, but it can be seen they are of vital importance.

It is inevitable, however, that disagreements can arise in any business relationship. The costs of going to court can be prohibitive and so, even where there is dispute which cannot be resolved by discussion between the business and the developer, court proceedings should be avoided where possible. One way is to enable an Alternative Dispute Resolution procedure to be included in the Agreement. This is where both parties agree to appoint a mediator in the event of dispute in an attempt to reach agreement. It is a way to seek resolution without the costs of going to court. If the mediation cannot be concluded or if one party refuses to proceed on that route then the other party can still sue in the courts for redress.

9.3 The Virtual World Hosting Agreement

The adoption by the general public of the Internet in the UK and around the world has led to the medium becoming an indispensable feature of modern life. A brief review of the Internet population in the larger EU states, for example, is telling. In the UK, Internet connections number 40.4 million, in Germany 53.2m, France 34.8m, Spain 22.8 m, Italy 33.1m, Sweden 7m, and Finland 3.3m.[1]

It is clear, that with this huge increase in Internet usage fuelled by high levels of broadband penetration, stress on the servers operated by the ISPs is acute. Now that most of the broadcast channels including ITV, BBC and Channel 4 are placing large elements of their broadcast content online, the Internet networks are being hit significantly, threatening continuity of service. This trend of offering broadcast and film content online is only going to increase as compression technologies improve. The change will also be hastened by the availability of Laptop Notebooks which can now be characterised as media centres and not merely computer devices. As the PC market undergoes churn in terms of people replacing their PCs and laptops every two to three years, the ability to watch film and television programmes on laptops with high quality screens is greater. Peer to peer Internet traffic now consumes around 70 per cent of bandwidth and promises to increase with the entertainment industry embracing peer to peer for content distribution and the increasing popularity of personal audio and video players. The growth in popularity of virtual world environments will add to the mix of Internet consumption. Many in the Internet industry predict that as online content becomes ubiquitous so it is inevitable that a two tier Internet evolves. This would mean that in order to reduce pressure on the networks, users might pay a standard rate for mainstream Internet access but a premium rate if they want to access media rich websites such as a virtual world environment.

We have considered the key features in the relationship between the operator of a virtual world and its website designer. The next essential contract is that between the virtual world operator and the ISP which hosts the online environment. We will refer to that provider in this section as the Hosting Company. Virtual world hosting services comprise the storage of the environment and its content on a service provider owned or leased server.

There is potential for platform owners such as ISPs and mobile phone companies. Over and above the revenue which can be achieved by, for example, a Hosting Company for the provision of the service, those companies also have a broader commercial objective. They need customers. The same is true of mobile phone service providers. They have the means to deliver content rich material via their networks. What they are always in need of is that content and virtual worlds offer an interesting prospect. Each require products which will drive consumers to their service. Likewise, the virtual world operator will have essential demands of the platform owner.

1 The EU Internet Statistics were updated from various sources by Nielsen/Net Ratings.

Clearly, the virtual world must be capable of being supported continually. It is likely that a range of services will be offered through it which each demand uninterrupted availability and access by inhabitants. It is, therefore, of critical importance that the virtual world operator has in place an Agreement with the provider of the hosting services which sets out clearly the service levels to be expected of that Hosting Company.

In this next section we will focus on the primary issues the virtual world operator is likely to face and review the matters to be covered in the Hosting Agreement.

Despite the importance of continuous service, the fact is that such environments rely on software and hardware systems for their presentation and, in common with any infrastructure, those systems will periodically require maintenance. The virtual world operator will, despite the need for continuity, be asked by the Hosting Company to acknowledge that from time to time its systems, servers and equipment will be inoperative or partly operational due to mechanical breakdown, maintenance, hardware or software upgrades or other causes beyond its control. In each case proper notification by the Hosting Company must be given to the virtual world operator. Occasional problems of this kind might be tolerated by that operator. However, the seamless delivery of in-world content by the operator from its environment is vital to its reputation and, therefore, repeated instances would be cause for termination of the relationship as discussed below.

The Hosting Company will almost certainly include a clause stating that it will not warrant that the hosting services are fit for the particular purposes the virtual world operator may require. Clearly, it will be obvious that the very nature of simulated environments call for the Hosting Company to be equipped to meet the content rich characteristics of the same. However, the Hosting Company will want this limitation in the Agreement because the operator may want to introduce features in-world which are not typical of such environments. Perhaps a new functionality which will impact on server capacity. Despite this concern, the above clause should be resisted by the operator if presented as part of the negotiations.

The Hosting Company will usually attempt to limit and restrict its legal and financial exposure to its client virtual world provider. Usually, it will seek to limit its total financial liability to the value of the hosting services provided in relation to the performance of its obligations under the contract. Moreover, it may exclude liability for consequential loss which the virtual world operator might suffer as a result of interruption to the hosting services. An example might be if the operator has a commercial relationship with a third party company in connection with the in-world environment. If the website is not operational due to the Hosting Company's error, the financial consequences to the operator may not simply be its own losses, but also those of the third party company who would look in the first instance to the operator for recovery of its losses. The virtual world operator must therefore look carefully at the contract to see if it contains exclusions of this kind.

The Hosting Company will want to exclude liability for the in-world content provided by the operator.

The Agreement will make clear that it does not constitute any transfer of intellectual property rights which the operator owns in the virtual content it requires to be hosted. As we have considered at Chapter 5 on IPR virtual worlds comprise a huge array of content which attracts intellectual property protection. The mere hosting of that content does not give rise to any proprietary rights on the part of the Hosting Company.

The Hosting Company might perhaps wish to use the operator's logo. The Hosting Company may want to include reference to the same in the marketing of its own services. If this is the case, then the Agreement should state it clearly.

The Hosting Company should be asked to warrant that its services will be provided by appropriately qualified and experienced personnel using all reasonable skill and care.

For its part, the virtual world operator will usually be under a contractual obligation to confirm that it will install and maintain industry standard Computer Virus protection software and will take reasonable steps to ensure that any software it uses in conjunction with the hosting services will not damage or corrupt any system of the Hosting Company.

The operator will be requested to be solely responsible for dealing with any complaints about its in-world content and that its inhabitants will not be directed to the Hosting Company in the event of any such complaints.

One very important aspect of the relationship though surprisingly sometimes overlooked, perhaps amid the enthusiasm at the start of the relationship, is how the parties can get out of the relationship. Each party's right to terminate the contract must be set out. The operator will be required to meet the hosting charges and all other obligations imposed by the contract. If it fails to do so, the Hosting Company will seek to terminate the contract. Likewise, the operator should insist on very tight service level obligations upon the Hosting Company and if these are breached by it then a right to terminate on the part of the operator should be included. Usually the failure of service level obligations is addressed by way of service level credits for failure. These may be expressed in financial terms in the form of stipulated amounts which trigger to varying degrees, based on the time during which service is interrupted. This issue will, in most cases, be negotiated according to the relative commercial standing each party possesses. At this stage in the development of virtual worlds, very few such businesses have the commercial leverage, which for example a major television broadcaster has. In other words a major television broadcaster can insist on very high levels of continuity on the part of the Hosting service.

For example, interactive programmes are very popular now. They often call for viewer participation by way of votes which are a central element of the programme format. The television company may be offering a simultaneous online broadcast or other related interactive facility via its website whilst the programme is broadcast to the television audience in the usual way. Any failure of the service could render the programme success problematic which itself may prejudice valuable programme sponsorship or advertising support. The level of continuity therefore demanded by the television company would be flawless and it will impose punitive penalties upon the Hosting Company if the service were to fail. The ability for smaller virtual world operators to leverage such penalties from a Hosting company is likely to be far less.

As is usual in any commercial agreement between businesses, if either party goes into liquidation or threatens to be wound up, such event will permit termination of the contract by the other party.

There will be an obligation on both the virtual world or social network and the Hosting Company to maintain the confidentiality of the other's business information which has been revealed during the negotiation of the relationship and during the hosting arrangement.

As with all key commercial relationships between a virtual world or social network and its strategic partners, full specialist legal advice should first be obtained. Remember, whoever the virtual world or social network deals with are themselves commercial entities and will seek to exclude or limit their own liability in the relationship as much as possible. In many cases it will be a question of bargaining power as to the extent such restrictions may govern.

CHAPTER 10 Strategic Agreements between Virtual Worlds and Aggregators of the Service

10.1 Background

Virtual world environments are still new. Whilst their conceptual basis is becoming more widely known to the general public, their more widespread adoption will require a combination of greater perceived value of the virtual experience which will come in time. It will also demand effective marketing strategies by operators of the service. In Chapter 6 we examined the methods and legal governance of online advertising and promotion. In this chapter, we will consider a different, though very important process of generating inhabitants of a virtual world. Since it is the Internet which plays host to virtual worlds, it is the Internet which is the natural medium to attract users of the service. The way this can be achieved is by the provider of the service identifying other website operators who might constitute effective aggregators of the virtual world and drive would-be inhabitants to the environment.

This strategy has appeal to the partner website operators who, may equally wish to improve the experience of their own online consumers. Companies are seeking to leverage new platforms and online audiences and are investing heavily in interactive development. The only issue at this stage of development is how long will it take for consumer habits to change.

Some televisual genres can be tailor-made to cross over to new media platforms. For example, a film download service called *FilmOn.com* offers its users more than simply the ability to select, download or stream film titles. It also provides an in-world experience to its users where they may operate, through the figure of an avatar, in various virtual world settings. These include Sunset Boulevard in Hollywood. Inhabitants can interact in the form of a social network with other users of *FilmOn.com* who share an interest in movies. Thus, the virtual world complements the company's principal activity and in turn helps drive users of the download service.

Gameshows, talent shows and reality shows are all naturally interactive and ideal for cutting down into bite-sized chunks for websites or mobile phones. Interactive television engages the viewers in a dialogue and takes them beyond the passive experience of watching television. It allows them to take part and make choices. The audience of a gameshow or a reality show expects to interact with the programme. All of these genres lend themselves to virtual world applications which cannot only replicate the interactive characteristic, but take it to new levels.

Everyone associated with new media recognises that change is inevitable but quantifying that change is difficult. This means that placing a value on virtual services is also uncertain. Content platforms such as Internet Service Providers (IPSs) or mobile phone service providers are likely to offer the virtual world provider revenue share deals where the values can be ring fenced more easily.

Undoubtedly, larger, perhaps better known, virtual world services will have more commercial power to exploit their environments with major IPSs but the real test will simply be the quality of the virtual content that determines the deals that can be secured.

At the time of writing there are significant moves by some mobile phone operators to link to social networking websites. Orange offers its pay-as-you-go subscribers free access to *Facebook* and *MySpace*. The operator is keen to build on the growth of traffic to its portal by attracting more pre paid users on the basis that it believes there is a correlation between its pay-as-you-go customers and the social network demographic. There are a range of social networking websites on Orange and it offers free access tariffs to customers so that they may use all the features associated with the social networks. It means that users can connect to the social networks online and can remain connected from their mobile phone too.

The virtual world or social network thus needs to explore new commercial opportunities.

In this chapter we will consider some strategic commercial relationships which the virtual world or social network might enter into in order to maximise revenue from its presence.

10.2 Linking and Revenue Share Agreement (The Click Through Revenue Deal)

The very nature of the Internet is such that computers across the world are linked. It is an established feature of websites to contain hyperlinks to other related websites. With the efficiency of broadband connections the visitor can seamlessly move from one website to another gathering a wealth of information. For websites offering a commercial service, there is much to be gained by the monetising of those relationships to other websites. The virtual world operator might well explore strategic relations with other online parties providing different but perhaps complementary services.

The model for this form of online revenue generation is clear. It is usually referred to as click through revenue share.

As we have noted elsewhere in this book, virtual worlds contain in-world retailers who will occupy an island presence in the environment. Those retailers may well have hyperlinks to their own e-commerce websites to facilitate the easy completion of a purchase by the inhabitant of goods or services. The revenue generated by such retailers does not form the subject of this section of our review. The retailer will already have paid the virtual world operator for its occupation in the environment and any sales thus secured via the world will reflect the effectiveness of the retailer's presence. The relationship we examine here is between the virtual world operator and other commercial entities which may not feature in the environment but which nonetheless could have a valuable role in aggregating users of the world. If those online businesses are to be recruited in furtherance of generating inhabitants of the virtual world service, they will want to be compensated for such activity. Similarly, if the virtual world operator wishes to earn monies by driving its inhabitants to websites of its partner businesses it will establish a revenue share deal in the same manner.

The virtual world operator wishing to establish formal links with another commercial entity must embody the commercial basis of that relationship in a Linking and Revenue Share Agreement. In addition, there are a number of legal considerations which should also form the content of that Agreement.

There might be any number of commercial scenarios relating to the relationship between a virtual and real world online partnership. In this section, for ease of explanation, we will take as an example such an online relationship between a virtual world website and a film company website. The example supposes the in-world feature of a new film title release in the form of virtual depiction of characters in the film production. The film company would regard such a presence as a part of its overall marketing and promotion of the new release. The virtual world might permit the inhabitant to interact with characters in the film outside the scope of the screenplay. However, the film company will in the last analysis wish to sell the film either by download to own, download to rent, or online DVD sale from its website.

We have assumed that the virtual world operator will take a commission percentage on all sales of film titles achieved by the film company via the link from the virtual world website.

Typically the virtual world operator (V) will agree to set up, with the film company (F), assistance, a connection with V's software to F's website. This link will provide a seamless connection and enable V's inhabitants to connect to perhaps the 'Order' section or shopping basket of F's website.

The Agreement will confirm that both V and F will be entitled to refer to each other as 'Alliance Partners' or a similar description to highlight their commercial connection in all their advertising and marketing material.

In our example we have envisaged that V will receive commission on sales of F's film titles however delivered, that is, by download or DVD sale. The Agreement will therefore deal with this arrangement and specify the commission rate. It will state that F will have the sole right and responsibility for processing all orders made by V's inhabitants. V will acknowledge that all contracts for the sale of the film titles to that audience are between F and the consumers and not V and the consumers.

It may well be that F is free to set the price of the games and films although possibly in such a key relationship there could be some agreement between V and F on the matter of pricing. Either way the actual pricing model needs to be set down in the Agreement.

F will be under an obligation to identify those of its online customers who are inhabitants of V and originate from its website and log them as 'V&F Customers' or an appropriate designation to reflect their nature.

There needs to be full disclosure of transactions. F will also be required to supply a monthly statement of all such transactions. The statement would need to show clearly all sales, refunds or deferred sales during that month. The statement would set out full details of the revenue achieved, the gross profit generated and of course the commission payable to V.

F would probably commit to paying V following receipt of an invoice from V which invoice might be rendered on the first day of the calendar month for the previous calendar month. There would be an express exclusion of liability for F to make a payment to V in cases where full payment has not been made by a 'V&F Customer' or where a refund has been given by F in relation to the same. The usual payment terms might apply, for example 30 days from receipt of V's invoice.

It is important to set the term of the strategic relationship from the outset. An Agreement of this kind, by its nature, would doubtless be for a limited period. The nature of virtual worlds is such that new content is of great importance. Virtual environments will become increasingly competitive and so an operator must maintain attractive contemporary features of its environment. The term of the Agreement therefore needs to be made clear. It might be for a fixed term of six months. The Agreement must be capable of being brought to an end sooner in certain specified circumstances by either party. An obvious termination trigger would be if either V or F is in material breach of an obligation under the Agreement. Or perhaps if V or F enter into liquidation or threatened liquidation or some other form of insolvency related arrangement. In such circumstances termination needs to be immediate. The Agreement would state that all commission payments due to the date of termination must be met by F.

The matter of intellectual property is very important to both the new media and mainstream media industries. With the increased convergence of the two examined elsewhere in this book, it is important to set clear the ownership rights of the various intellectual property elements which combine to perfect the relationship between V and F. This is particularly so if, as we have suggested for the purpose of review, some form of adaptation or film character or scene depiction is featured in-world.

First, the treatment of each other's existing intellectual property rights must be addressed. Both V and F will retain all right, title, and interest in their names, logos, trademarks, service marks, copyrights and proprietary technology. The Agreement will provide for the granting of a revocable, non-exclusive, wordwide licence to use, reproduce and transmit their respective names, trademarks and proprietary software on their respective websites solely for the purpose of creating the links between the websites.

The Agreement will also, on the matter of intellectual property rights, state that neither V nor F shall copy, distribute, modify, reverse engineer or create derivative works from the other's works. For example, F will not do this as regards the virtual environment software content provided by V, and V will not seek to feature extensive actual footage of F's films in the virtual environment.

Each will offer a warranty and an indemnity to the other that they have not infringed the intellectual property of any third party in the creation of their respective works. Further, that they are not in violation of any applicable law or regulation. This issue is important. The Internet's global reach can mean that it would not be lawful to make certain products available in certain countries. It might be that the content of certain works would be offensive to a particular region or jurisdiction. There could be issues of libel in both the film and virtual world depiction of that content. Other commercial considerations where an indemnity should govern include misleading advertisement laws (see Chapter 6) or unfair competition laws. Given that both parties are operating their strategic relationship using Internet technology, there would be an indemnity for computer viruses, and other destructive programs.

It is possible that as F and V seek to promote their joint arrangement they make statement about each other's product to other commercial or media organisations. The precise ambit of what they each might say in relation to the promotion of the product would be dealt with under the terms of a joint marketing agreement rather than this Linking Agreement. However, in this Agreement there would be an indemnity against all liability, losses, damage and professional fees, brought by a third party, arising out of a breach or a representation made either by F or V about either the film or the games.

V might seek to restrict its total financial exposure to F for any breach F is responsible for, to the total amount of commission paid by V to F in the calendar year of the date of the legal claim.

There would be a need to maintain confidentiality in relation to any information imparted or made available to the other as a result of the commercial relationship. This would be amplified in the Linking Agreement. Confidential Information would be defined to include all non public information concerning the business, technology and structures of the disclosing party. The receiving party would agree to keep the same in confidence and not permit any employee, agent or other person working under its direction to disclose or disseminate the information. Reasonable steps must be taken to secure confidential information by both F and V where storage is to be achieved by electronic means which will almost certainly be the case.

Neither F nor V will be able to assign (transfer) the benefit of the Linking Agreement to any third party without the prior consent of the other party.

Finally, the Agreement will be expressed to be governed by English law.

An agreement of this kind will contain many more specific commercial terms agreed as between a film company and video games company based on the actual deal struck. However, the above review sets out some principal provisions a virtual world or social network should address if considering a strategic Internet linking deal with another party.

10.3 The Virtual World Environment Licence Agreement

In this section we will consider the position in which a company wishes to operate a virtual world environment. Perhaps for internal training purposes, or to offer an interactive platform for collaborative projects with business partners. Rather than appoint a software developer to design and build the environment for ownership by the company, it instead simply takes a licence to operate a system whose infrastructure is 'off the peg'. In this model, the software developer will retain ownership of intellectual property rights in the underlying software, and licence its use to the company.

There are competing requirements for such a model from a legal perspective between the developer of the virtual world as licensor, and the company as licensee. These issues must be addressed at the outset. They are essentially commercial considerations, but as will be seen, have a strong legal dimension. All these issues, once settled, will be embodied in a legal agreement which will be The Virtual world environment Licence Agreement.

It should be stated that our review of issues to consider to a large extent relies supposes that the use of the virtual world environment by the company licensee has some material benefit to its overall operations thus giving rise to a more serious analysis of the issues. If the virtual world is simply a useful, though strategically unimportant, feature of the business then much of the discussion below will not have the same significance.

The first issue to address is that of rights clearance. The company may want to use content of its own within the virtual world. The Licensor will need to ensure that the company is not required to obtain third party rights clearance, or if it is, then they must be sought by the licensee. The Licensor should be wary of broad representations of ownership of rights in content made by the licensee. This is particularly the case for audio visual content which may contain many layers of rights. Perhaps the company wishes to use such content in its virtual world and asks the developer to adopt it in the design. The licensor will want this contractual assurance from the licensee that it has all rights in that content. Similarly, however, the company as licensee will want to be certain that the developer is not required to obtain third party clearances for its work, or if they are needed, that they are sought. This might arise in relation to software licensing because the developer may well need to incorporate third party software into its software construction of the virtual world. The licensor must ensure that what it licences is limited to that which it owns.

The company should check what is being licensed by the developer. The company should consider all rights which may exist in the content. There is potential for ownership issues in different territories. This is particularly relevant for online exploitation which may be accessible worldwide. The company should seek warranties and indemnities from the licensor regarding licensed content ownership.

It is then necessary to define the scope of the permitted acts licensed. The developer will be designing an environment for use by the company. The developer as licensor must consider a closed, limited list of permitted acts. For example, it might define permitted acts under relevant legislation. It may specify the permitted technical activity, or specify the permitted delivery and storage media. It may impose device limitations or impose timing restrictions on use of the virtual environment. Conversely, the company as licensee should consider if there is any limitation to reception by device as convergence is rendering devices as interchangeable by users. For example, will the company require virtual world access by mobile phone? The company will want to 'future proof' where possible by reference to technology whether now known or invented after the date of the Licence Agreement. If the licensor seeks to create an exclusive list of permitted media, the licensee should consider adding the words 'including but not limited to' so as to increase its options.

The developer may want to limit the term of the virtual world licence. The licensee will want a longer term. It is a question of balancing the term and royalty rate. From the licensor's perspective it may be advantageous to link royalties generated by the licensee to options to renew the term. However, the licensee should balance the risk of technology convergence or changing users' habits which may dilute the exclusivity or value of the rights negotiated with the developer.

The matter of territory must be considered. The licensor should be careful only to licence and potentially warrant or indemnify use of the virtual world in the territories in which it owns rights. This is a particular risk when online rights are granted and the parties may be considered to be aware that online use may be accessed worldwide. However, from the licensee's perspective, worldwide licences are better because they reduce enforcement difficulties which may be problematic with online territorial restrictions. If the licensor does cite the worldwide nature as the reason for the licensor resisting the grant of warranties and indemnities, this could potentially be split to give the warranties and indemnities only for the territory in which the licensor feels able to do so, but to retain the broader grant of rights.

On the matter of warranties and indemnities, clearly the developer, as licensor, will want to limit as far as possible. The licensee will conversely regard warranties and indemnities as desirable to potential third party rights infringement for online use but these may be difficult to obtain.

Assignment and sub-licensing is often an important issue for consideration by the parties. From the developer of the virtual worlds perspective, attention needs to be given to the terms on which the licensee may make the virtual world environment available to third party users. For maximum control and risk management, the licensor may set out the terms of a third party user's licence agreement in a schedule. Alternatively it may specify some of the critical terms to be included in the third party licence agreement. The company user of the virtual world, as licensee, should consider what is required on a practical level to enable third party users to use the environment as anticipated. The company should consider whether it will be able to enforce any restrictions imposed on those third parties. The licensor may instead specify what acts will be permitted by the third parties. This may be supplemented by obligations to implement steps necessary to prevent third party users from doing anything else.

Another issue to address relating to assignment arises from the developer licensor point of view from how important the identity of the company licensee is to its decision to grant the licence of the virtual world. For example, if the licensee is a company of some repute or a well known brand, then the developer may have considered that central to its decision to grant the licence. It will not, therefore, be keen to allow the licensee to then assign its ability to use the virtual world environment to another company which does not have the same attraction to the licensor. It may, therefore, include restrictive assignment provisions in the licence agreement. In any event, it will usually only allow assignment with its consent. Another mechanism which the licensor might employ is a change of control requirement. This means that the licensee must not change control in its ownership without notifying the licensor who might then object to the continuation of the licence. The licensee will want to resist such change of control provisions as they will restrict its ability to sell its own business.

Termination of the relationship must be addressed by the parties who must consider how the licence may end for both positive and negative reasons. The licensor will require an ability to terminate if the licensee breaches a major provision in the licence. The company, as licensee, may want to ensure that the ability to terminate by the licensor is not extended to circumstances where it merely suspects a risk of breach of the licence.

It is likely that the company will amass useful data during its operation of the virtual world environment. This might include in-world user behaviour patterns. Such information is very helpful to the developer as licensor and it may want to insert a provision that useful information so generated, together with adaptations of the licensed content be licensed back to it by the licensee. Conversely, the licensee may attribute value to new data or content created through its exploitation of the environment, in particular, tracking data and statistics of usage. One approach which the licensee may take to this issue is to negotiate a reduction in price for use of the environment or obtain other benefits from the licensor if such data is to be relinquished to the licensor.

On the question of data gathered from the in-world experience of the licensee company the issue of personal data arises. At Chapter 7 we examined the legal obligations in relation to personal data handling. The licensor may want access to the customer names of the licensee, whereas this is not automatically permitted under data protection laws. If access to the customer names at the end of the licensed term or even during the licensed term is important to the licensor, the licence agreement should include specific provisions compelling the licensee to include specified opt-in/opt-out questions for the users as this will give the highest chance of being able to transfer in compliance with the Data Protection Act. From the company's perspective it should be wary of a request from the licensor for customer data because, unless certain conditions are met, the licensee is not going to be able to transfer such data without taking specific measures to enable such transfer. Indeed, if the licensee does not wish to provide this data, it might cite Data protection laws as a reason for refusing the request.

CHAPTER **11**

Protecting Corporate and Individual Reputations in Virtual Worlds and Social Networks

11.1 Background

We are concerned in this book with the law which relates to a 21st century technology and expression of that technology in the form of virtual worlds. We will observe how, despite the modernity of such environments, they are subject to legal principles which, in the case of defamation, have their origin in millennia past. The earliest evidence in recorded history of any sanction for defamatory statements is in the Mosaic code. In Exodus XXII 28 it is stated 'Thou shalt not revile the gods nor curse the ruler of thy people' and in Exodus XXIII 1 'Thou shalt not raise a false report: put not thine hand with the wicked to be an unrighteous witness'.

When these entreaties were passed there was very little written matter and most of what was exchanged in communication was by word of mouth. The Internet represents the most efficient and prolific means of mass communication in the modern era and not simply of the spoken word, but of images and audiovisual content. Virtual worlds take that process still further and permit communication of all these through an apparently anonymous means. Whereas in the physical world, generally one can identify with relative ease the source of a statement, be it oral or in writing, which might be regarded as damaging to an individual or company, this is not so with the Internet.

Indeed, the power of the Internet to disseminate messages is immense and if those messages are defamatory the damage which may be done is considerable. The problem is compounded by the global nature of the medium which at once permits international distribution of the adverse statements, and the difficulties which arise from tracing and enforcing rights against the source of those statements. Moreover, we have already witnessed the destructive potential of Internet blogs which may generate negative statements about individuals and companies, often well known brand retailers. A company may find itself on the receiving end of a sustained onslaught of very public criticism voiced by unseen bloggers. Damage to reputation and business can be the result. Indeed many brands actively engage in their own blog environments with consumers in order to gather valuable data about perspectives on their own products or services, but also to head off any significant adverse comments before the same become widespread. The Internet has thus changed the dynamics of how people relate to each other and companies with their consumers.

Virtual worlds and social networks overcome the gap between people from different countries, permitting them to exchange opinions and information in environments that eliminate cultural and social restrictions.

These globalised societies are networks which resemble what we do in real life. Participants in virtual worlds use words on screens to exchange courtesies, argue, engage in discourse, and conduct business. In many ways, people create avatars that are idealised versions of themselves. However, their avatar is symbolic and relates to who they are in the real world. Making a computer into a second self, finding a soul in the machine can be a substitute for human relationships. Virtual worlds connect like-minded others worldwide. However, at the click of a mouse, a defamatory statement can be communicated to all the participants in the virtual world. In many ways creating and changing one's avatar creates a curious emotional bond between one and that avatar. It is a curious phenomenon but inhabitants of virtual worlds will testify that compliments to and failures of their avatar may each be taken personally.

Celebrity figures have found themselves embarrassed by social network websites. Hugh Grant was photographed with a number of young women. The image was posted on *Facebook* and found its way to the newspapers. The important thing to recognise is that the things one posts online are there for a very long time. They are not transient. The days of anonymity are coming to an end. The ease with which statements or images can be promoted within online networks is astonishing. The length of time those statements or images reside in virtual environments is surprising. One can see the obvious heightened risk of defamation in virtual worlds. It may be that, given the immaturity of virtual worlds at present, users will learn how better to conduct themselves. Virtual worlds and social networks will find a balance between being invasive and being helpful.

Given this merging of real life characters with virtual avatars, the potential for depiction of individuals or even corporate brands in an unfavourable light is clear.

However, like many other principles of law, libel has not caught up with the digital age. Social networking websites, by their very nature, receive thousands of postings a day. Essentially, the law expects the operator of such a website to act when faced with alleged defamatory statements published in the environment, as the publisher of a newspaper must in similar circumstances. The dynamic characteristics of social networks and virtual worlds means that the ability of the operator to remove allegedly libellous material swiftly is very limited. The problem, of course, lies in the impracticability of constant monitoring of the network content by the operator. Instead, most systems rely on reporting of offending statements made in the environment usually by the person or organisation claiming to have been defamed. If, some contend, one tries to apply what is expected if a newspaper publisher to the operator of a social network website, it is rather like trying to use a set of railway signals to control the air traffic over Heathrow Airport.

Different forms of communication thus require a different legal approach. Existing libel laws were drawn in an age when a publisher was someone who played an integral part in the creation of the content. In today's social networks, there is a division between the creator of the content and those who are merely passive hosts.

There must always be a prudent perspective when considering the terms of a statement which at first causes alarm. For one thing, whilst the dissemination of the statement may be global, there may not be a corresponding harm. A company, for example, may enjoy a reputation in the UK but not be heard of around the world and therefore find it difficult to allege damage as a consequence of an adverse statement if that statement is published via the Internet in Singapore. In addition, sometimes the source of the statement is so obviously misguided that others would not attribute much credence to their opinions. In such cases it might be better to simply ignore the statements since any damage may be limited in any event. The law also affords a number of defences to a claim for defamation and these will apply to in-world activity just as they do real world, additionally, something that is complimentary in one environment could be defamatory in another

11.2 The Defamation Act 1996

The Defamation Act 1996 was introduced to amend the law of defamation and to amend the law of limitation with respect to actions for defamation or malicious falsehood.

It is useful to review its principal provisions because they form the bedrock upon which questions of defamation in virtual world environments rest.

11.2.1 RESPONSIBILITY FOR PUBLICATION

Section 1 of the Act sets forth who is responsible for the publication of a defamatory statement. A statement means words, pictures, visual images, gestures or any other method of signifying meaning. The definition has clear application to virtual world activity. The Acts states that:

Responsibility for publication in defamation proceedings a person has a defence if he shows that:

a) he was not the author, editor or publisher of the statement complained of;
b) he took reasonable care in relation to its publication; and
c) he did not know, and had no reason to believe, that what he did caused or contributed to the publication of a defamatory statement.

For the purposes of the Act 'author' means the originator of the statement, but does not include a person who did not intend that his statement be published at all.

'Editor' means a person having editorial or equivalent responsibility for the content of the statement or the decision to publish it; and

'Publisher' means a commercial publisher, that is, a person whose business is issuing material to the public, or a section of the public, who issues material containing the statement in the course of that business.

Suppose, for the purpose of illustration, that an inhabitant of a virtual world makes what constitutes a defamatory statement about a person or company and does so through the medium of their own avatar, most likely in the form of text content uttered through the avatar. Or, perhaps that the defamatory conduct is the depiction of a person in the form of an avatar which distorts the physical characteristics of that person in a manner which is grossly unfair.

The individual or individuals who create the grotesque depiction or who make the defamatory statement will most likely be treated as authors within the meaning of the Act.

It may be seen that the operator of a virtual world, whilst not perhaps falling into the definition of author of a statement, may well be regarded as editor or publisher.

The Act then goes on to make clear that a person shall not be considered the author, editor or publisher of a statement if he is only involved:

a) in printing, producing, distributing or selling printed material containing the statement;
b) in processing, making copies of, distributing, exhibiting or selling a film or sound recording (as defined in Part I of the [1988 c. 48.] Copyright, Designs and Patents Act 1988) containing the statement;
c) in processing, making copies of, distributing or selling any electronic medium in or on which the statement is recorded, or in operating or providing any equipment, system or service by means of which the statement is retrieved, copied, distributed or made available in electronic form;
d) as the broadcaster of a live programme containing the statement in circumstances in which he has no effective control over the maker of the statement.

Once again, an examination of these provisions demonstrates that the operator of a virtual world may not be liable under the law of defamation simply by virtue of the fact they operate and make available the environment. The exceptions in (b), (c), and (d) may well provide alternative basis which the operator may rely upon to avoid such liability.

Further protection of the operator lies in section 3(e) of the Act which provides 'as the operator of or provider of access to a communications system by means of which the statement is transmitted, or made available, by a person over whom he has no effective control.'

At the time of writing there are no reported cases in English law which apply the Defamation Act 1996 to defamatory content published in virtual worlds. Thus, our review necessarily entails the application of the Acts provisions to the characteristics of a virtual environment to assess how the law may treat such environments. However, the Act does provide for a scenario where the circumstances of a defamatory statement do not easily fit into one of the above exceptions. It states that in a case not within paragraphs (a) to (e) the court may have regard to those provisions by way of analogy in deciding whether a person is to be considered the author, editor or publisher of a statement.

The Act also provides for a basis to determine whether a person took reasonable care, or had reason to believe that what he did caused or contributed to the publication of a defamatory statement. The following must be taken into account:

a) the extent of his responsibility for the content of the statement or the decision to publish it;
b) the nature or circumstances of the publication; and
c) the previous conduct or character of the author, editor or publisher.

11.2.2 OFFER TO MAKE AMENDS

There is a procedure under the Act for a person, having made a defamatory statement, to then make amends. The Act says that a person who has published a statement alleged to be defamatory of another may offer to make amends.

The offer may be in relation to the statement generally or in relation to a specific defamatory meaning which the person making the offer accepts that the statement conveys. The latter is called a qualified offer.

There are certain requirements which the offer must meet. It must be in writing. It must be expressed to be an offer to make amends under section 2 of the Defamation Act 1996, and must state whether it is a qualified offer and, if so, set out the defamatory meaning in relation to which it is made.

The question then arises, what constitutes an offer to make amends? The Act states that it must be an offer:

a) to make a suitable correction of the statement complained of and a sufficient apology to the aggrieved party;
b) to publish the correction and apology in a manner that is reasonable and practicable in the circumstances; and
c) to pay to the aggrieved party such compensation (if any), and such costs, as may be agreed or determined to be payable.

The operator of a virtual world may, therefore, have open to it this ability to make an offer of amends to a person or organisation which has been defamed by the actions of an inhabitant or inhabitants of the environment. The need to publish the correction raises an interesting issue. How might that apology be published? If, for example, a newspaper has been responsible for a defamatory statement and then makes the above offer, it may publish the apology in the pages of its publication. However, it is more difficult to see how a virtual world or social networking website can accommodate such an apology and where it might feature. It might perhaps be made in the form of an email to all subscribers to the environment. The fact remains however that one way or other the apology must be published.

It is important to note that an offer to make amends under this section may not be made by a person after serving a defence in defamation proceedings brought against him by the aggrieved party in respect of the publication in question. Thus, the offer has to made before any legal proceedings are brought, not after.

An offer to make amends may however be withdrawn before it is accepted; and a renewal of an offer which has been withdrawn shall be treated as a new offer.

11.2.3 ACCEPTING AN OFFER TO MAKE AMENDS

If an offer is made before proceedings have been issued against for example the operator of the virtual world, there is then a procedure for acceptance of that offer.

The party accepting the offer may not bring or continue defamation proceedings in respect of the publication concerned against the person making the offer, but he is entitled to enforce the offer to make amends, as follows:

1. If the parties agree on the steps to be taken in fulfilment of the offer, the aggrieved party may apply to the court for an order that the other party fulfil his offer by taking the steps agreed.
2. If the parties do not agree on the steps to be taken by way of correction, apology and publication, the virtual world operator may take such steps as it thinks appropriate,

and may in particular:

a) make the correction and apology by a statement in open court in terms approved by the court; and
b) give an undertaking to the court as to the manner of its publication.

If the parties do not agree on the amount to be paid by way of compensation, it will be determined by the court on the same principles as damages in defamation proceedings. The Act states that the court will take account of any steps taken in fulfilment of the offer and (so far as not agreed between the parties) of the suitability of the correction, the sufficiency of the apology and whether the manner of their publication was reasonable in the circumstances, and may reduce or increase the amount of compensation accordingly.

In any litigation, the question of costs is always of great importance. Legal costs are significant. Parties to disputes may incur hourly rates for firms of Solicitors of anywhere between £200–£500. Then, there are likely to be Barrister's fees on top of that, of similar fee range. If one then appreciates that those costs will likely be doubled because the party paying the costs will also have to meet the other side's legal costs if it were to lose the case at trial. The terms of any settlement offer would always be agreed but would probably require the virtual world operator to meet the costs of the defamed person or organisation. The Act states that if the parties do not agree on the amount to be paid by way of costs, it shall be determined by the court on the same principles as costs awarded in court proceedings.

The acceptance of an offer by one person to make amends does not affect any cause of action against another person in respect of the same publication. So, for example, the person or organisation which has been defamed by the actions of someone in a virtual world may accept an offer of amends from the virtual world operator, but may still pursue the action against the individual or individuals responsible for the original defamatory statement. Those individuals would need to be identifiable however but there are legal procedures to enable the identity to be disclosed for such purposes, there are constraints under the Act for such dual claim:

a) the amount of compensation paid under the offer shall be treated as paid in bona fide settlement or compromise of the claim; and
b) where another person is liable in respect of the same damage (whether jointly or otherwise), the person whose offer to make amends was accepted is not required to pay by virtue of any contribution, a greater amount than the amount of the compensation payable in pursuance of the offer.

11.2.4 FAILURE TO ACCEPT OFFER TO MAKE AMENDS

We have seen that the operator of a virtual world, for example, having recognised it is responsible for a defamatory statement, may make an offer of amends to the person or organisation so defamed. The question now arises, what happens if the aggrieved party fails to accept that offer?

The Act provides that if an offer to make amends, duly made and not withdrawn, is not accepted by the aggrieved party, the following provisions apply.

First, the fact that the offer was made is, broadly a defence to defamation proceedings in respect of the publication in question by that party against the person making the offer. There is no such defence if the person by whom the offer was made knew or had reason to believe that the statement complained of:

a) referred to the aggrieved party or was likely to be understood as referring to him; and
b) was both false and defamatory of that party, but it shall be presumed until the contrary is shown that he did not know and had no reason to believe that was the case.

If, continuing our example of a virtual world operator, that operator makes an offer, it need not rely on it by way of defence, but if it does, it may not rely on any other defence.

However, that offer may be relied on in mitigation of damages whether or not it was relied on by the virtual world operator as a defence.

11.2.5 TIME LIMITS IN WHICH LEGAL ACTION MUST BE BROUGHT

In common with all legal action, the law imposes time limits by which the case alleging defamation must be brought. The Act states that no such action shall be brought for libel or slander, or slander of title, slander of goods or other malicious falsehood, after the expiration of one year from the date on which the cause of action accrued. Thus, if an individual or organisation claims that they have been defamed by some activity emanating from a virtual world environment or social network, they must progress their legal claim speedily. This, of course, is not unreasonable. Either that party has suffered damage or they have not. The period of one year provides a sensible time frame for that party to make the decision to take action.

There is, despite this time limit, a discretionary exclusion of time limit for actions for defamation or malicious falsehood open to the court. If it appears to the court that it would be equitable to allow an action to proceed having regard to the degree to which:

a) the operation of the one year time limit prejudices the claimant or any person whom he represents; and
b) any decision of the court would prejudice the defendant or any person whom he represents;
c) the court may direct that the limit shall not apply to the action or shall not apply to any specified cause of action to which the action relates.
d) In acting under this section the court shall have regard to all the circumstances of the case and in particular to:

- the length of, and the reasons for, the delay on the part of the claimant;
- where the reason or one of the reasons for the delay was that all or any of the facts relevant to the cause of action did not become known to the claimant until after the end of the one year period, the court will consider:

i) the date on which any such facts did become known to him; and

ii) the extent to which he acted promptly and reasonably once he knew whether or not the facts in question might be capable of giving rise to an action; and
iii) the extent to which, having regard to the delay, relevant evidence is likely:

- to be unavailable; or
- to be less cogent than if the action had been brought within the period of one year.

11.2.6 THE FACILITY FOR IMMEDIATE JUDGMENT BY THE COURT

Court action in general is a significant undertaking and, despite the best efforts at progressing a case to trial quickly, the tactics which may be employed by lawyers, for example, to the defendant, can delay the action substantially. This can mean that a claimant can suffer prejudice and it is not uncommon for claimants to run out of money before their case ever reaches trial. In addition, the trial date itself is subject to court listing diaries and a trial may be at least 18 months after the legal action was launched. For the most part this is simply the operation of the system and it allows for both parties to fully ventilate their position in the period leading to trial. The court then makes its decision having considered all the evidence amassed in the period up to trial. In defamation proceedings however, the court may dispose summarily of the claimant's legal action. Summarily means that the court does not make its decision at the trial but comes to an immediate conclusion at the start of the case. The following provisions though will apply.

First, the court may dismiss the claimant's case if it appears to the court that it has no realistic prospect of success and there is no reason why it should be tried.

The court may, conversely, give judgment for the claimant and grant him summary or immediate relief if it appears to the court that there is no defence to the claim which has a realistic prospect of success, and that there is no other reason why the claim should be tried.

Unless the claimant asks for summary relief, the court shall not do this unless it is satisfied that immediate relief will adequately compensate him for the wrong he has suffered.

In considering whether a claim should be tried the court shall have regard to:

a) whether all the persons who are or might be defendants in respect of the publication complained of are before the court;
b) whether summary disposal of the claim against another defendant would be inappropriate;
c) the extent to which there is a conflict of evidence;
d) the seriousness of the alleged wrong (as regards the content of the statement and the extent of publication); and
e) whether it is justifiable in the circumstances to proceed to a full trial.

Unlike the full trial, these summary proceedings are heard and determined without a jury.

11.2.7 WHAT CONSTITUTES SUMMARY RELIEF?

The Act states that summary disposal of claim or 'summary relief' means any of the following as may be appropriate:

a) a declaration that the statement was false and defamatory of the claimant;
b) an order that the defendant publish or cause to be published a suitable correction and apology;
c) damages not exceeding £10,000 or such other amount as may be prescribed by order of the Lord Chancellor;
d) an order restraining the defendant from publishing or further publishing the matter complained of.

The Act specifies that the content of any correction and apology, and the time, manner, form and place of publication, shall be for the parties to agree. Once again, in the context of a virtual world which had featured a defamatory statement, the parties may have some difficulty in agreeing this detail. The aggrieved party may want a very prominent in-world apology, whereas the party rendering the apology may prefer a more discreet statement in the environment.

If they cannot agree on the content, the court may direct the defendant to publish or cause to be published a summary of the court's judgment agreed by the parties or settled by the court in accordance with rules of court.

If they cannot agree on the time, manner, form or place of publication, the court may direct the defendant to take such reasonable and practicable steps as the court considers appropriate.

The Act sets out the law in relation to defamation proceedings but recognises that the detailed procedure governing summary disposal of an action may be left to what are known as rules of court. These are the practical procedural steps which must be followed in the conduct of any litigation involving defamation. Provision may be made by rules of court as to the summary disposal of the claimant's claim in defamation proceedings.

Provision may be made:

a) authorising a party to apply for summary disposal at any stage of the proceedings;
b) authorising the court at any stage of the proceedings:

    i) to treat any application, pleading or other step in the proceedings as an application for summary disposal; or
    ii) to make an order for summary disposal without any such application.

c) as to the time for serving pleadings or taking any other step in the proceedings in a case where there are proceedings for summary disposal;
d) requiring the parties to identify any question of law or construction which the court is to be asked to determine in the proceedings;
e) as to the nature of any hearing on the question of summary disposal, and in particular:

i) authorising the court to order affidavits or witness statements to be prepared for use as evidence at the hearing, and
ii) requiring the leave of the court for the calling of oral evidence, or the introduction of new evidence, at the hearing.

f) authorising the court to require a defendant to elect, at or before the hearing, whether or not to make an offer to make amends.

It can be seen that the court has wide ranging power to have this issue of summary disposal addressed at all stages of the case.

11.2 8 QUALIFIED PRIVILEGE

The 1996 Act provides for certain exemptions from what might otherwise constitute publishing of defamatory material. The first of these is Qualified Privilege. There are a number of circumstances where for example, online publication perhaps via a social networking website, would fall within this exemption. The exemption has two limbs;

Part I – Statements having qualified privilege without explanation or contradiction

These include but are not limited to:

1. A fair and accurate report of proceedings in public of a legislature, for example proceedings in the House of Commons, anywhere in the world.
2. A fair and accurate report of proceedings in public before a court anywhere in the world.
3. A fair and accurate report of proceedings in public anywhere in the world of an international organisation or an international conference.
4. A fair and accurate copy of, or extract from, any register or other document required by law to be open to public inspection.

Part II – Statements privileged subject to explanation or contradiction

These include but are not limited to:

1. A fair and accurate copy of, or extract from, a notice or other matter issued for the information of the public by or on behalf of:

a) a legislature in any member State or the European Parliament;
b) the government of any member State, or any authority performing governmental functions in any member State or part of a member State, or the European Commission;
c) an international organisation or international conference.

As the heading suggests, these statements may have to be explained and are capable of being contradicted which may give rise to liability for defamation if not done so satisfactorily. In explaining these exemptions it is important to emphasise that they apply in general but are addressed here in the context of their being published via an Internet social network or possibly virtual world. One can foresee such reporting in a social network if the issue which came before a legislature was of sufficient interest to participants in social networks. For example, an issue of some public controversy might be ventilated in a social network and extracts of a Parliamentary debate featured as part of the discussion. If they do appear in such environments they still attract the qualified privilege as directed by the 1996 Act.

Other exemptions within this category include a fair and accurate report of proceedings at any public meeting or sitting in the UK of:

a) a local authority or local authority committee, a commission, tribunal, committee or person appointed for the purposes of any inquiry by any statutory provision, by Her Majesty or by a Minister of the Crown, or a person appointed by a local authority to hold a local inquiry in pursuance of any statutory provision;
b) any other tribunal, board, committee or body constituted by or under, and exercising functions under, any statutory provision.

This issue of publishing issues of public concern within Internet environments includes a fair and accurate report of proceedings at any public meeting held in a Member State of the European Union. A 'public meeting' means a meeting bona fide and lawfully held for a lawful purpose and for the furtherance or discussion of a matter of public concern, whether admission to the meeting is general or restricted. In addition, a fair and accurate report of proceedings at a general meeting of a UK public company, or a fair and accurate copy of or extract from any document circulated to shareholders of a UK public company:

a) by or with the authority of the board of directors of the company;
b) by the auditors of the company; or
c) by any shareholder of the company in pursuance of a right conferred by any statutory provision.

A fair and accurate copy of or extract from any document circulated to members of a UK public company which relates to the appointment, resignation, retirement or dismissal of directors of the company, also falls within the qualified privilege subject to explanation exemption.

Fair and accurate reports of any finding or decision of certain forms of association, formed in the UK or another European Member State, or of any committee or governing body of such an association also attract qualified privilege. Such associations include those formed for the purpose of promoting or encouraging the exercise of or interest in any art, science, religion or learning. Associations formed for the purpose of promoting or safeguarding the interests of any trade, business, industry or profession, or of the persons carrying on or engaged in any trade, business, industry or profession, and associations formed for the purpose of promoting or safeguarding the interests of a game, sport or pastime to the playing or exercise of which members of the public are invited or admitted.

One can see why the qualified privilege exemption is of direct relevance to a review of statements made within social networks because the very nature of what constitutes the privilege is likely content for such networks. In an age of Internet blogging where the affairs of large public companies are transmitted across networks and around the globe, often by pressure or special interest groups, these exemptions are very important. If for example, members of the environmental lobby promote their objectives by means of Internet social networks and use extracts from shareholders' meetings of a major public company connected with the airline industry, that lobby group could use the material in the context of their online activity. Such use would attract qualified privilege.

11.2.9 DEFENCES TO DEFAMATION

For a defendant to be liable for defamation, he must be a publisher of the defamatory statement and this covers both primary publishers who exercise direct editorial control over published statements. For example, authors, editors and publishing houses are primary publishers. Secondary publishers are those who do not take an active role but still make the defamatory comments available to third parties. Whilst ISPs are secondary publishers they are usually the first target of claimants wishing to remove a defamatory statement from the Internet.

A person has a defence to an action for defamation if he can show that he was not the author, editor or publisher (as defined in section 1(2) of the Defamation Act 1996) of the statement complained of; took reasonable care in relation to its publication, and did not know, and had no reason to believe, that what he did caused or contributed to the publication of a defamatory statement – the Internet defence.

It is clear that ISPs and other intermediaries are intended to benefit from the Internet defence, but in practice the requirements to show care and lack of knowledge represent considerable barriers to its application.

11.2.10 INJUNCTIONS TO PREVENT VIDEO BEING SHOWN ON A WEBSITE

Whenever a claimant seeks the assistance of the courts in a defamation action, usually part of the remedy sought includes an injunction against further publication of the offending material. An injunction is the form of relief granted by a court which has the effect of restraining a defendant from some activity. It may be accompanied by an award of damages but typically it is to limit the damage done to a claimant by restraining further publication of the material complained of. It is by and large a draconian step because, of necessity, it involves the prevention of specific activity and the standard the courts adopt when considering whether to grant an injunction is thus high. A recent case in the High Court suggests how difficult it is for a claimant to obtain an injunction in circumstances where the claimant alleges defamation and seeks to prevent the material which causes the complaint from being made available on a website. In *Mosley v News Group Newspapers Limited, 9 April 2008* the High Court refused to grant an injunction to prevent video footage of Max Mosley, the head of Formula 1 motor-racing, being shown on the *News of the World* website. The court held that the material was so widely accessible on other websites that granting an injunction would make very little practical difference and would be a futile gesture. However the court dismissed the newspaper's public-interest arguments under Article 10 of the European Convention on Human Rights but held that no injunction should be granted because anyone searching the Internet could find the video. The decision illustrates the difficulty of obtaining an injunction to prevent publication of material that is widely available on the Internet. However, publishers should note that the courts may look unfavourably on public-interest arguments in support of the publication of salacious photographs and video material.

11.3 Case Law Relating to Defamation and Internet Use

It is cases decided in the higher courts which serve as authority on points of law and act as precedents for subsequent disputes on similar issues. In these cases the judges usually have to interpret particular legislative provisions. Clearly, statutes cannot be framed to expressly every circumstance and therefore when new developments in technology or manner of dealing come into existence the judges have to consider how (if at all) the Act of Parliament either envisaged the development, or if it did not, how it might be safely applied to the new facts. So it is with the evolution of the commercial Internet that the courts have had to determine issues which come before them that the original legislation could not have foreseen. This is the position with regard to defamation. The Internet is a very difficult medium for the law of defamation not least because of its global nature bringing into play problems of which legal jurisdiction applies, and because of the vast content which resides online. It is this issue of abundant content which has been the focus of much legal deliberation and usually in the context of ISPs. We examine below some of the principal cases which have come before the courts to chart how the courts have approached issues of online defamation. In this way we can gain an insight into how the courts will view online social networks and virtual worlds.

GODFREY V DEMON INTERNET LTD 1999 (TIMES LAW REPORTS/1999/APRIL/(1999))

This case decided that where an ISP which had received and stored a posting on its news server and then transmitted that posting to its subscribers who wished to download it, the ISP was a publisher of the posting at common law, but not for the purposes of section 1(2), and (3) of the Defamation Act 1996.

The court had to consider the facts of the case against the Defamation Act 1996 and in particular section 1of the Act which has been described above. The High Court held that the defendants were an ISP. The court considered the process by which postings are disseminated. It said that via the Internet, a worldwide computer network, a person who subscribed to an ISP could submit an article known as a posting to the news server based at his ISP which would disseminate the posting via the Internet, and it would ultimately reach the news servers of other ISPs around the world. Internet users could access and read the posting by connecting to their local ISP's news servers and requesting it. The ISP would then transmit the posting to the user who could download it on to his computer.

The court heard evidence that a posting defamatory of the claimant, made by an unknown person which was posted on an American ISP, eventually reached and was stored by the ISP of the defendants. The claimant informed the defendants that the posting was defamatory and asked them to remove it immediately from the defendant's news server.

The court said that at common law, the defendants, whenever they transmitted and whenever there was transmitted, from the storage of their news server, a defamatory posting, actually published that posting to any subscriber to their ISP who accessed the newsgroup containing that posting and saw it. The situation was analogous to that of the bookseller who sold a book defamatory of the claimant.

The defendants' argument that they played a passive role and were merely the owners of an electronic device through which postings were transmitted, was rejected. The defendants chose to receive and store the news group containing the posting which could be accessed by subscribers, and could obliterate it, as they later did.

The court went on to say that the defendants were clearly not commercial publishers of the posting for the purposes of section 1(2) and 1(3) of the 1996 Act and were therefore able to satisfy the requirement of section 1(1)(a), the first part of the defence under section 1 of the 1996 Act set out above.

However, after the posting was published, as from the date that the defendants became aware of the defamatory content of it, they could not satisfy the additional requirements of section 1(1)(b) and (c) and could not therefore obtain the protection provided by section 1 of the 1996 Act.

The plaintiffs therefore succeeded. The decision in Godfrey makes clear that in order to rely on the Internet defence, ISPs and other intermediaries must now remove allegedly defamatory postings as soon as they are put on notice of their existence, known as the notice and take down procedure. The ISP cannot investigate the merits of the allegations. It cannot assess the availability of other libel defences before removing the allegations, unless it suspends access to the posting while it does so.

It can be seen that, in the context of a virtual world, the same considerations will come into play. If someone complains that another, acting by their avatar, has made defamatory statements which, given the statements are likely to be by email text exchange, will be libel, then the sequence of events will be as follows. The party alleging the harm will contact the operator of the virtual world. The operator will not immediately have knowledge of the statements and so will need to investigate the issue. However, to allow that investigation to take place the operator should suspend further access on the part of the alleged defamer.

However, the issue is usually not so clear cut. Whether a statement is defamatory may not be easy to determine. If the virtual world operator takes down material from its servers it is at risk of being in breach of its subscriber contract (see Chapter 3 on specimen virtual world terms). In addition, removing the allegations by take down denies individuals their right of free speech and, in a commercial context, also threatens the individual's ability to participate in the virtual environment.

TOTALISE PLC V THE MOTLEY FOOL LTD 2002 (TIMES LAW REPORTS/2002/ JANUARY/(2002))

The claimants were a company called Totalise Plc. A company called Interactive Investor Ltd was the second defendant. The first defendant did not even appear at court but the issue to be appreciated in this case really relates only to Interactive. That company operated a business which was the provision of financial information to individual investors through their website. One service they offered consisted of a series of discussion boards relating to particular companies on which users of the website posted information and opinions likely to be of interest to other investors. Before a user could make a posting on Interactive's discussion boards, the user had to register and enter into a contract containing Interactive's standard terms. On 31 January 2001 Interactive were sent a letter by solicitors acting on behalf of Totalise. That letter complained about the content of a number of postings on Interactive's website by a person using the name 'Zeddust'.

The letter alleged that the postings contained defamatory statements and were maliciously designed to call into question the competency and integrity of Totalise's management team and their solvency and generally to cause as much damage to Totalise's reputation as possible.

The letter requested confirmation that the postings would be removed, that Zeddust's posting rights be immediately withdrawn and that the identity and registration details of Zeddust be disclosed. Interactive replied stating that the postings would be removed and that Zeddust's account had been suspended but they stated that they were unable to disclose personal details about any account to a third party.

On the same day, Totalise's solicitors wrote stating that they had instructed counsel to advise on and conduct a '*Norwich Pharmacal*' application. This is a legal application compelling the defendant to disclose the identity of the Internet user.

It was contended by lawyers for Interactive that The Data Protection Act 1998 was difficult to construe and arguably prevented disclosure without a court order. While the Act might not prevent disclosure of Zeddust's name, it strongly indicated that personal data should not be disclosed without the consent of the data subject, save in exceptional circumstances. Further, Interactive was contractually obliged not to reveal the identity of its users.

The court, when considering its order as to costs, after a successful *Norwich Pharmacal* application, should consider all the circumstances. In a normal case the applicant should be ordered to pay the costs of the party making the disclosure including the costs of making the disclosure.

There might be cases where the circumstances required a different order, but they did not include cases where:

1. The party required to make the disclosure had a genuine doubt that the person seeking the disclosure was entitled to it;
2. The party was under an appropriate obligation not to reveal the information, or where the legal position was not clear, or the party had a reasonable doubt as to the obligations; or
3. The party could be subject to proceedings if disclosure was voluntary; or
4. The party would or might suffer damage by voluntarily giving the disclosure; or
5. The disclosure would or might infringe a legitimate interest of another.

The court held that where an innocent party (in this case Interactive) was involved in the act of others and thereby became under a duty to assist by disclosing full information were not the typical court proceedings, where the general rule is that the unsuccessful party pays the costs of the successful party. The court held that in general, in such applications the costs should be recovered from the wrongdoer rather than from the innocent party. The case decided that identification of website users must not be ordered if it unjustifiably invades their right to privacy.

BUNT V TILLY & OTHERS 2006 [2006] EWHC 407 (QB)

This case also concerned ISPs. The claimant alleged that statements hosted on websites, were the responsibility of a number of defendants who had authored them. However the claimant also sought remedies against their respective ISPs. The ISP Defendants which included AOL, BT and Tiscali, all applied, on grounds which overlapped to a large extent, for orders that the claims against them be struck out or dismissed on a summary basis.

The court noted that it was important that it was not pleaded that any of the three ISP Defendants had at any stage 'hosted' any website relevant to the claims. The basis upon which the Claimant sought to establish his causes of action is that the individual Defendants published the offending words 'via the services provided' by their ISPs. The claim therefore raises points of general significance as to the basis upon which a provider of such services could, if at all, be liable in respect of material which is simply communicated via the services which they provide.

Neither the pleaded case nor the evidence disclosed any role on the part of the ISP Defendants other than that of affording connection to the Internet. On this basis, it was argued by them that the necessary ingredients for publication were missing.

The court further stated that when considering the Internet, it is often necessary to resort to analogies which, in the nature of things, are unlikely to be complete because the Internet is a new phenomenon. Nevertheless, an analogy was drawn in this case with the postal service. That is to say, ISPs do not participate in the process of publication as such, but merely act as facilitators in a similar way to the postal service. They provide a means of transmitting communications without in any way participating in that process.

The court considered the decision in *Godfrey v Demon Internet Ltd* (see p. 215) upon which the Claimant relied. In that case, the Defendant ISP, had received and stored a defamatory article on its news server which had been posted by an unknown person via another ISP. Mr Godfrey informed Demon of the defamatory nature of the article and requested its removal from their news server but it remained available.

The court also considered the remarks made in the Court of Appeal in *Totalise plc v The Motley Fool* (see p. 217) 2001 and noted that the ISP in that case was not penalised in costs (having adopted the policy that it would not reveal the name and address of one of its customers without a court order) since it was an innocent party. It was recognised that the position might have been different if they were in some way implicated or involved in the wrongful act.

The court said that in determining responsibility for publication in the context of the law of defamation, it is important to focus on what the person did, or failed to do, in the chain of communication. It is clear that the state of a defendant's knowledge can be an important factor. If a person knowingly permits another to communicate information which is defamatory, when there would be an opportunity to prevent the publication, there would seem to be no reason in principle why liability should not accrue.

Of course, to be liable for a defamatory publication it is not always necessary to be aware of the defamatory content, still less of its legal significance. Editors and publishers are often fixed with responsibility, notwithstanding such lack of knowledge. On the other hand, for a person to be held responsible there must be knowing involvement in the process of publication of *the relevant words*. It is not enough that a person merely plays a passive instrumental role in the process.

The court found that in all the circumstances there was no realistic prospect of the Claimant being able to establish that any of the ISP Defendants, in any meaningful sense, knowingly participated in the relevant publication. The court also turned its attention to the Electronic Commerce (EC Directive) Regulations 2002 (see Chapter 8). The Regulations, it will be recalled, define the circumstances in which Internet intermediaries should be held accountable for material which is hosted, cached, or carried by them, but which they did not create. However, the protection which the Regulations afford is not confined to the publication of defamatory material. They embrace other illegal material, such as child pornography or the infringement of intellectual property rights.

MICHAEL LEITH-SMITH V TRACEY WILLIAMS 2006 [2006] ALL ER (D) 297 (MAR)

This case once again involved an Internet chatroom service. The claimant signed up to an Internet discussion group which allowed for his identity and other details about him to be ascertained. The defendant was also a member of the group, though operated through a pseudonym or pseudonyms. Her identity could not be ascertained through the discussion group website. Although one had to be a member of the group in order to join in the discussions, anyone could access the site via the Internet and read the material which was posted there. After some time, the defendant started referring to the claimant as, inter alia, a 'nonce', a sexual offender, a racist bigot and a Nazi. In particular, she alleged that he was a sexual deviant of the most perverted kind. Having obtained an order requiring the operator of the site to disclose the defendant's identity, the claimant issued proceedings in libel. Following the service of proceedings, the defendant continued to make similar allegations via the Internet concerning the claimant. The claimant appeared in person. The defendant did not appear and was not represented. Judgment on liability was therefore entered in default and the claimant sought both general and aggravated damages and injunctive relief.

The court ruled in the circumstances of the case, the appropriate figure for damages was £10,000. The claimant was also entitled to a prohibitory injunction preventing the defendant from re-publishing the libels or publishing similar libels.

SHEFFIELD WEDNESDAY FOOTBALL CLUB LIMITED AND OTHERS V NEIL HARGREAVES 2007 [2007] EWHC 2375 (QB)

This case provides insight into how the courts approach the matter of defamatory statements posted on Internet chatroom websites and thus helps us assess how the courts may treat virtual worlds and social networks which feature similar statements. The first claimant was a football club. The second claimant was the chairman and director of a company which owned 100 per cent of the shares in the first claimant. The defendant owned and operated a web site on which fans of the football club could post messages on matters relating to it. The website was accessible, upon registration as members, by providing an email address and password. The user names were usually pseudonyms and were used to identify individuals who posted messages. When an individual registered for the website he agreed that he would not use the bulletin board to post any material which, inter alia, was knowingly false or defamatory. Members were warned in the website terms and conditions (see Chapter 3) that the operators of the website would have the ability to remove objectionable messages and that they would make every effort to do so within a reasonable time frame if they determined that removal was necessary.

The claimants alleged that the defendant had permitted some users to pursue a sustained campaign of vilification, in the course of which users had posted false and defamatory messages on the website, and as a result the defendant had facilitated and become mixed up in the wrongdoing of those users. The claimant sought Norwich Pharmacal relief to assist it to discover the source of the leak.

The football club argued in court that all the postings were arguably defamatory, so that wrongs had been committed. They also alleged that the defendant had plainly facilitated the alleged wrongdoing by giving users the means to address other users and that there was no other way of finding out the identity of the authors.

The court had first to determine the question whether an order should be granted to enable action to be brought against the ultimate wrongdoer. It decided it could because there was no other possible means by which the claimants could have made an identification of the authors of the statements. Equally, there was no doubt that the defendant had facilitated any wrongdoing, because he had provided the means for the users to post their messages. Moreover, the defendant was likely to be able to provide the information necessary to enable any wrongdoers to be sued.

Having decided that the defendant should answer for the remarks made online the court had then to determine whether the statements were in fact defamatory. The court had to assess whether the words complained of by the football club were arguably defamatory and at the least were arguably false.

Some of the Internet postings which concerned the claimants, bordered on the trivial, and in that context, it would not have been right to have made an order for disclosure of the identities of users who had posted messages which were barely defamatory or little more than abusive or likely to have been understood as jokes. That would have been disproportionate and unjustifiably intrusive.

The postings which were more serious were those which might have reasonably been understood to have alleged greed, selfishness, untrustworthiness and dishonest behaviour on the part of the claimants. In the case of those postings, the football club's entitlement to have taken action to protect their right to reputation outweighed the right of the authors to maintain their anonymity and their right to express themselves freely.

The court took into account the restrictions on the use of defamatory language which the rules of the defendant's bulletin board imposed, restrictions which in the case of those postings had appeared to have been breached. In those circumstances, Norwich Pharmacal relief would be granted in respect of the users responsible for postings which might have reasonably been understood to have alleged greed, selfishness, untrustworthiness and dishonest behaviour.

The courts will approach the balance between freedom of expression and culpability for damaging online statements in the following manner. The identity of online posters can be revealed if their right to freedom of expression and privacy is outweighed by the reputation rights of their target.

The most recent case at the time of writing which has a bearing on the issue of defamatory postings on Internet forums is:

SMITH V ADVFN PLC 2008 (ALL ENGLAND REPORTER/2008/MARCH/SMITH V ADVFN PLC – [2008] ALL ER (D) 193 (MAR))

The facts of the case were as follows.

The claimant was the coordinator of an action group, which alleged that its members, who had been shareholders of a company listed on the Alternative Investment Market, had suffered losses due to the fraudulent direction of its directors. The defendant was a website providing financial information. It allowed registered members to post their contributions anonymously under pseudonyms known as 'avatars' (the term also used to describe the computer animated characters in a virtual world) on its bulletin board. That bulletin board was free to access, upon registration as a member, by providing a name, address, username and password. Upon registration, the IP address of users was captured by the defendant's system.

The claimant alleged that the defendant had permitted some users to post defamatory messages on the website, which focused on the concerns of the action group. As a consequence, the claimants said that the defendant had facilitated and become mixed up in the wrongdoing of those users. As is now standard, he applied for Norwich Pharmacal relief to assist him in the discovery of the sources of the messages. He sought relief in terms requiring the defendant to provide full contact details of 23 avatars, to include the registered name, address, email address and IP address of all the users concerned.

When the case came before a judge he granted the application in the terms requested by the claimant. The court order was duly complied with. However, it was common ground that the claimant became dissatisfied with the information which he recovered. Therefore, he sought to extend the Norwich Pharmacal relief, by requiring the defendant to provide the IP address, at the time each defamatory message was posted, of 64 avatars in relation to 252 different messages, or in relation to 64 avatars who had posted 100 messages and who had been the subject of the previous relief.

The court decided that the claimant's additional request for an extension of the Norwich Pharmacal relief should be allowed, despite the fact that it was of a complex and ambiguous nature. It was clear that some of the contributions on the bulletin board had arguably been defamatory of the claimant, however, there had been a doubt whether others had arguably been defamatory. The claimant had cast his net too wide in seeking an order requiring the defendant to provide the IP address, at the time each defamatory message was posted, of 64 avatars in relation to 252 different messages. In that regard the appropriate order was to require to defendant to provide the IP address of 64 avatars who had posted 100 messages and who had been the subject of the previous relief. Therefore, the Norwich Pharmacal relief would be granted.

11.4 The Liability or Otherwise of Virtual World or Social Network Operator's and Balancing the Defamation Act 1996 and the Electronic Commerce Regulations 2002

We have noted in Chapter 4 that the Electronic Commerce Regulations, in addition to setting minimum standards for commercial websites, also set out liability of ISPs in general for content which passes their networks. We have noted also how since the Regulations were introduced (as recently as 2002) technological advances have made certain Internet services now commonly used, unclear in terms of where they sit within the E-commerce Regulations. This includes the development of social networks and virtual worlds. In this chapter we have also noted how the Defamation Act 1996 operates in the context of the Internet and how the courts have approached online defamatory material. It is now useful to assess the position of liability of operators of virtual worlds and social networks by summarising for the sake of explanation many of the arguments which have been put to the courts in cases relating to ISP's in general and liability for defamation.

It is important to emphasise that the following commentary is only intended to rehearse some interesting concepts. Specific legal advice should always be taken by the operators of virtual worlds and social networks on the question of liability for alleged defamatory postings within the environment.

The proposition is sometimes advanced to the effect that there is an obligation on the operator of a virtual world or social network to 'gatekeep' its conduit. The line runs that an operator providing the Internet service to an inhabitant has an extremely good argument under both the Defamation Act 1996 and also the Electronic Commerce Directive 2002 that it is no more than a 'conduit', that it has no knowledge or control over what passes through that 'conduit', and that the entire responsibility for what does pass through that 'conduit' rests with the inhabitant who uses the service, as it is the inhabitant and not the operator who acts as a 'gatekeeper' for that 'conduit'.

The argument continues that an operator providing a social network or virtual world package to an inhabitant has no possible hope of successfully arguing that it is a mere 'conduit' and therefore immune from that law, as all content originates from within their own environment, instead of merely passing through it in 'via' fashion from one network to another.

In such circumstances not only is the operator acting as sole 'gatekeeper' between the source of the defamatory material and the Internet, they also provide a bundle of other services, each of which clearly falls foul of the other provisions of the Electronic Commerce Directive 2002 which, for example, only allows the minimum level of caching technically necessary for the underlying technology of message transmission to function.

It is important to note that the term 'gatekeeper' is one often used to describe the position of an operator but is nowhere to be found in the Electronic Commerce Regulations.

The above argument is challenged by another view which is that it flies in the face of the fundamental policy underlying the Regulations.

The Electronic Commerce Regulations do not preclude the grant of an injunction where a person or company claims they have been defamed online in a proper case. It is provided in Regulation 20(b) that nothing should affect the rights of a party to apply for relief to prevent or stop infringement of any rights.

Does this guarantee a claimant's right to apply for relief and his right to a trial? The answer is almost certainly not because injunctive relief sought by the claimant against the operator of a virtual world or social network may be wholly disproportionate to any conceivable legitimate advantage. The effect could be that an order is made by the court preventing any supply of services to a defendant against whom defamation is alleged. That would be draconian and to a large extent pointless, since the individual defendant would be able to obtain such Internet services with ease elsewhere by subscribing to another social network.

Further, even if the claim for an injunction as part of an action for defamation were formulated along conventional lines to prevent the publication of the same or similar words defamatory of the Claimant, this may be unworkable and disproportionate. The operator of the virtual world or social network may not have the ability or power to amend or modify any content. Thus, granting an injunction against a defendant might be pointless in that an operator may have no way of ensuring compliance with its terms.

Section 1 of the Defamation Act 1996 is sometimes called upon by potential Claimants and in particular its relationship with Regulation 17 of the Electronic Commerce Regulations. It is contended that there may be circumstances in which the application of the section 1 defence and of Regulation 17 would lead to inconsistent outcomes.

In addition, the relationship between Regulation 18 and the section 1 could well give rise to occasions when the operator of a social network or virtual world would be protected under Regulation 18 from liability for damages following transmission of a web page which had been temporarily stored for the purpose of more efficient access – and yet fail in respect of a section 1 defence if publication was made of the offending web page to subscribers after its existence had been brought to the operator's attention.

If we consider once more the terms of section 1 itself:

1. (1) In defamation proceedings a person has a defence if he shows that:

a) he was not the author, editor or publisher of the statement complained of;
b) he took reasonable care in relation to its publication; and
c) he did not know, and had no reason to believe, that what he did caused or contributed to the publication of a defamatory statement.

2. (2) For this purpose 'author', 'editor' and 'publisher' have the following meanings, which are further explained in subsection (3):

    a) 'author' means the originator of the statement, but does not include a person who did not intend that his statement be published at all;
    b) 'editor' means a person having editorial or equivalent responsibility for the content of the statement or the decision to publish it; and
    c) 'publisher' means a commercial publisher, that is, a person whose business is issuing material to the public, or a section of the public, who issues material containing the statement in the course of that business.

3. (3) A person shall not be considered the author, editor or publisher of a statement, if he is only involved:

a) in printing, producing, distributing or selling printed material containing the statement;
b) in processing, making copies of, distributing, exhibiting or selling a film or sound recording (as defined in Part I of the Copyright, Designs and Patents Act 1988) containing the statement;
c) in processing, making copies of, distributing or selling any electronic medium in or on which the statement is recorded, or in operating or providing any equipment, system or service by means of which the statement is retrieved, copied, distributed or made available in electronic form;
d) as the broadcaster of a live programme containing the statement in circumstances in which he has no effective control over the maker of the statement;
e) as the operator of, or provider of, access to a communications system by means of which the statement is transmitted, or made available, by a person over whom he has no effective control.

In a case not within paragraphs (a) to (e) the court may have regard to those provisions by way of analogy in deciding whether a person is to be considered the author, editor or publisher of a statement.

It is likely that the operator of a social network or virtual world may be said to have fallen foul of section 1(1)(c) above, in circumstances where the operator has been notified of an alleged defamatory statement.

However, any notification of an offending statement would need to be very clear. There have been cases where such notifications did not effectively put an ISP on notice, and its staff thus given no reason to believe that they were causing or contributing to the publication of the rogue postings. In such cases, section 1 would provide a complete defence to any claim in respect of those postings, whether for damages or an injunction. A notice to the operator of a social network or virtual world might, therefore, include full information of where on its servers the defamatory posting is located, which news group it is posted upon, or the e-mail address of the person responsible.

Moreover, if the operator of a social network or virtual world takes reasonable care having regard to its contractual terms binding those who use its services, then liability on its part may be more difficult to establish. Most social network service terms and conditions of use broadly provide that the customer must take all reasonable precautions to ensure that no one uses the service to send, knowingly receive, upload, download or use any material which is defamatory or in breach of any other right.

Section 1(5) of the Defamation Act states it is necessary, in determining whether persons took reasonable care, or had reason to believe that what they did caused or contributed to the publication of a defamatory statement, to have regard to certain specific matters. These include the extent of the person's responsibility for the content of the statement or the decision to publish it, the nature or circumstances of the publication, and the previous conduct or character of the author, editor or publisher. On the face of it these factors should all enable an ISP to rely upon the provisions of section 1.

Clearly, operators of virtual worlds and social networks host inhabitant's content on their servers and those postings are stored for a period of time, usually amounting to a few weeks, to enable other inhabitants to access them. The operator does not operate the in-world discussions, but it has the ability to remove postings from its server, although they might still be viewed via other servers. In these circumstances it is necessary to consider the terms of Regulations 19 and 22 of the Electronic Commerce Regulations.

In so far as it is relevant, the terms of regulation 19 are as follows: 'Where an information society service is provided which consists of the storage of information provided by a recipient of the service, the service provider (if he otherwise would) shall not be liable for damages or for any other pecuniary remedy or for any criminal sanction as a result of that storage where:

a) the service provider:

i) does not have actual knowledge of unlawful activity or information and, where a claim for damages is made, is not aware of facts or circumstances from which it would have been apparent to the service provider that the activity or information was unlawful; or
ii) upon obtaining such knowledge or awareness, acts expeditiously to remove or to disable access to the information; and

b) the recipient of the service was not acting under the authority or the control of the service provider.'

11.5 Drawing Together How the Courts View the Process of Caching and other Internet Techniques

As has been noted, the courts, in addition to the Defamation Act, have to consider the legislative framework which governs Internet dealings. The E-commerce Regulations are central to this review when considering the matter of bulletin board postings and web pages.

To briefly recap on the principal provisions of the E-commerce Regulations:

Regulations 17 to 19 create a defence for intermediary service providers from any liability incurred from the activities of mere conduits, caching and hosting in the circumstances set out in the regulations. Regulation 20 provides that regulations 17 to 19 do not preclude the agreement of different contractual terms or affect the rights of any party to apply to a court for relief. Regulation 22 makes provision in relation to matters which a court should have regard to when determining whether a service provider has actual knowledge for the purposes of regulations 18(b)(v) and 19(a)(i). Usually Regulation 17 will apply to Internet intermediaries who operate computer systems through which particular bulletin board postings and web pages happen to pass en route from one computer to another. This is subject to the proviso that the intermediary does not store the constituent Internet Protocol (IP) datagrams for any period longer than is reasonably necessary for the transmission. One question which arises is whether, in order to attract the protection of Regulation 17, an intermediary would need to configure its computer system to delete any copies of the relevant datagrams immediately after receiving an acknowledgment that they have been received by the intended recipient. Whether if the datagrams are stored for a longer period, the intermediary would be likely to be deemed to have 'cached' or 'hosted' them?

The purpose of Regulation 18 of the E-commerce Regulations is to protect Internet intermediaries in respect of material for which they are not the primary host but which they store temporarily on their computer systems for the purpose of enabling the efficient availability of Internet material. Many ISPs and other intermediaries regularly cache, or temporarily store, commonly accessed web pages on their computer systems, so that those pages will be more quickly accessible to their subscribers. This has been described by Internet commentators as in effect a form of halfway house between mere transmission and 'hosting'.

The process might be described as follows; the ability to view web pages quickly is an attractive attribute for users of the Internet. The huge volume of requests for web pages generated by Internet users has led to the development of technical solutions by network providers and ISPs to enable more efficient transmission of that information across the Internet.

Caching is one such solution. It is a technical process which enables ISPs, such as AOL, to speed up the delivery of web pages to Internet users by making a temporary copy of a web page that is requested by a user. When a subsequent request is made for the same page, the user can be provided with that content from the local 'cached' copy made by the ISP, rather than having to go back to the original web site which is the source of that page. This process enables the more efficient onward transmission of web pages to Internet users. However, a web cache is not a copy of the Internet – that is neither the purpose of a web cache, nor would it be commercially or technically feasible. In order for web caches not to have to expand in memory size indefinitely the actual content in a web cache is designed to be overwritten in accordance with automatic defined rules ensuring that (i) cached content is up to date and (ii) cached content which is not being searched for (or has been removed or altered) is overwritten.

An example of how caching works might be the pages of a well known Internet Social Network such as *Facebook* located at www.facebook.com. The content forming that page may be hosted by *Facebook*, that is, that content sits on computers controlled by *Facebook*. A popular site such as *Facebook* will have several hundred thousand visitors per day. When a person using an ISP such as AOL connects to the Internet via the AOL UK Propriety Service (an 'AOL User') navigates to *Facebook*, a request is sent from that user's personal computer, via AOL, to the *Facebook* computer hosting Facebook.com. The requested page is then sent back to the AOL User, via their AOL connection.

When *Facebook* computers receive high volumes of requests within short time periods, delivery of the relevant *Facebook* page may be affected and a queue may form for the relevant *Facebook* computers to become free to respond to an individual's request. The *Facebook* computers may simply become too busy. To help alleviate this problem, ISPs use a so-called 'web cache' to make the onward transmission of information of content such as *Facebook* more efficient to users of the ISP when they request such information. The ISP's web cache consists of a computer system which sits between (in this case) *Facebook's* computers, on which the *Facebook* page is stored, and the home computers of individuals wishing to view *Facebook*.

The web cache effectively watches requests for web pages made by individuals and then saves copies of the responses from *Facebook's* computers. If there is a subsequent request for the *Facebook* page from the ISP user then that request is fulfilled by delivery of the *Facebook* page from the ISP web cache, rather than via the original location on *Facebook* computers. As the request for the *Facebook* page is delivered from the ISP web cache, rather than the *Facebook* servers, it takes less time for the ISP to retrieve the images and text on the *Facebook* page and display it to the ISP user wishing to view it.

The mechanism of storage by the ISP web cache is completely automatic. Providers of web sites set automated 'rules' or conditions specifying whether a page may be cached and if it may be cached, at what time that cached material should expire; and whether the cache computers should revalidate with the original source web site as to whether a page sitting on the ISP's web cache has been updated or deleted. These rules are embedded in instructions which exist 'behind' web pages and the rules are applied by, and are readable by, web browser software in accordance with industry standards. This ensures that users of the Internet reach the most up to date versions of web pages available.

The storage of such material on the ISP's web cache is temporary because permanent storage would be inherently contradictory to the purpose and aim of the ISP web cache, which is to enable more efficient transmission of information to Internet users. It is core to the function of web caches that they do not modify the content of the information they transmit. It will subsequently be overwritten when either (a) no users of the ISP request the *Facebook* page within a specified period or (b) the source material is altered after it is stored in the cache – if *Facebook* altered the content on the *Facebook* page, or removed it entirely, then that content would be labelled for deletion as soon as another user of the ISP requested that page.

CHAPTER 12 *Disability Discrimination Considerations with Virtual Worlds and Social Networks*

12.1 The Disability Discrimination Act 1995 and Web Accessibility Best Practice

If one stops to consider for a moment it is obvious that a website will be subject to issues such as the concerns of disability. A website should be capable of being accessed by someone with, perhaps, sight impairment. That may well mean the website must be designed in a manner so as not to exclude visitors with a disability. This requirement is, in fact, a matter of law and the source of that law is the Disability Discrimination Act 1995. The date of the legislation should be noted because when it was introduced it did not contemplate the Internet and specifically websites as within its ambit. At that time whilst those in the new media sector were well aware of the Internet and its commercial potential, legislators were not.

In essence the Act makes it unlawful for a service provider to discriminate against a disabled person by refusing to provide any service which it provides to members of the public. A service provider would include a website development company and the operator of a virtual world or social network.

It is useful to examine the background to this important aspect of an online presence. In 2004 The Disability Rights Commission in the UK launched an investigation into 1,000 websites of which over 80 per cent were next to impossible for disabled people to use. They warned firms they could face legal action under the Disability Discrimination Act.

In most cases where a website is found to be in breach, usually the Disability Rights Commission would warn the website operator first rather than simply proceed to court action. Therefore, legal action would probably not be pursued as the website would be corrected following the warning.

The W3C is the Internet governing body. It is widely believed that if a case comes before the courts that the W3C accessibility guidelines will be used to assess a website's accessibility and decide the outcome of the case. The W3C offers levels of compliance. Priority 1 guidelines, which must be satisfied according to the W3C, and Priority 2, which should be satisfied and are the EU recommended level of compliance.

In 2008 a report by national computing and disability charity AbilityNet[1] claimed that social network websites are excluding disabled users. It surveyed five of the most popular networks – *Bebo, Facebook, MySpace, Yahoo!* and *YouTube* to find that many prevent disabled people from registering.

The report found the websites were shunning many disabled users as none mentions the importance of subtitles when uploading videos. In addition, none of the websites included an accessibility page providing information for disabled users.

The report found, for example, that many users could not register at the websites because interpreting the Captcha image – a random selection of distorted numbers or letters – is difficult for the visually impaired.

In 2004 the Disability Rights Commission prepared a report based on their investigation of websites. Whilst the report does not have the force of law, it is a useful guide to the kind of problems faced by disabled or impaired people in accessing websites. At the time of writing there are no reported legal cases on breach of accessibility of a website let alone a virtual world or social network website. However, the principles referred to in this chapter will certainly govern such websites.

The impairment groups represented in the user testing for the report were:

- Blind people who use screen readers with synthetic speech or Braille output.
- Partially sighted people who may use screen magnification.
- People who are profoundly deaf and hard of hearing.
- People with specific learning difficulties such as dyslexia.
- Physically impaired people whose use of the web may be affected by their lack of control of arms and hands, by tremor and by lack of dexterity in hands and fingers.

The report makes a number of recommendations to improve the position and these include the following:

- Websites commissioners should formulate written policies for meeting the needs of disabled people. This might include ensuring that disabled people with a range of sensory, cognitive and mobility impairments are involved from early on in the process of website design and development.
- Those who provide and oversee education and training of web developers, including those who sell web-authoring tools, should promote an understanding that good practice entails attending and responding to the needs of disabled people. This might include ensuring that modules form an integral part of any continuing professional development or product support.
- Web designers themselves should accept that good practice entails attending and responding to the needs of disabled people. This would involve taking steps to familiarise themselves with how disabled people use the web and with their needs in web accessibility.
- The Government should raise awareness. For example, by a publicity campaign aimed at web designers and commissioners.
- Website designers involving disabled people in the design and testing of websites at an early stage.

1 Source: AbilityNet, January 2008.

- Web designers should not rely exclusively on automated accessibility training.
- Developers of automated accessibility checking tools should enhance their functionality to make them more useful to website commissioners and website developers.
- The designers and providers of assistive technology should enable and encourage users to keep their products up to date.

It is helpful to consider the key problems experienced by impairment groups according to the Disability Rights Commission report findings. Such a review should assist the operator of a virtual world or social network in properly developing its website to ensure the website meets Disability Guidelines. The report however did not concentrate on such online environments but rather websites across a range of activities. We will apply the findings to how a virtual world is designed.

12.1.1 BLIND USERS

- There must not be problems of incompatibility between screen reading software and web pages. For example the assistive technology not detecting some links or it proving impossible to highlight text when using text to speech software.
- There must not be incorrect or non-existent labelling of links, form elements and frames, nor cluttered and complex page structures.
- ALT tags on images should be clear and there must not be confusing and disorienting navigation mechanisms within the virtual world.

12.1.2 PARTIALLY SIGHTED USERS

- There should not be inappropriate use of colours and poor contrast between content and background.
- There should not be any incompatibility between accessibility software, for example magnification of web pages.
- The layout of each webpage must not be unclear and confusing.
- The graphics and text featured in the virtual world must not be too small. The environment must not contain confusing and disorienting navigation mechanisms.

12.1.3 PHYSICALLY IMPAIRED USERS

Similar issues of design apply to this category of users. Thus, there must not be confusing and disorienting navigation mechanisms, unclear and confusing layout of webpages, in-world graphics and text sizes must not be too small.

Once again, the virtual world must not feature inappropriate use of colours and poor contrast between content and background.

12.1.4 HEARING IMPAIRED USERS

- Unclear and confusing layout of pages.
- Confusing and disorienting navigation mechanisms.
- Lack of alternative media for audio-based information and complex terms/language.

- Inappropriate use of colours and poor contract between content and background.
- Graphics and text too small.

12.1.5 DYSLEXIC USERS

- Unclear and confusing layout of pages.
- Confusing and disorienting navigation mechanisms.
- Inappropriate use of colours and poor contrast between content and background.
- Graphics and text too small.
- Complicated language and terminology.

There are many other pointers for the virtual world or social network to adopt best practice in its website.

These include:

- Provide a text equivalent for every non-text element.
- Ensure foreground and background colour combinations provide sufficient contrast when viewed by someone having colour deficits or when viewed on a black and white screen.
- Until user agents allow users to freeze moving content, avoid movement in pages.
- Divide large blocks of information into more manageable groups where natural and appropriate.
- Clearly identify the target of each link.
- Use the clearest and simplest language appropriate for a website's content.

CHAPTER 13 Employment Law Issues and Employees' Participation in Virtual Worlds

The issue of employees using the Internet has received some extensive focus in the media in recent times. That attention tends to be centred on the wasting of company time and the impact on productivity. Whilst these are certainly real concerns, there are other potential problems when employees participate in Internet forums whilst at work and these issues are writ large in the context of virtual worlds. In this chapter we will examine some very practical matters which should govern a company's approach to its personnel entering into the virtual environment.

It is estimated that currently 12 per cent of Internet minutes are spent on the social network website *MySpace*. Clearly, some of this time must be being occupied whilst people are at their workplace. However, fears of lost productivity are already being dismissed with the recognition that, in fact, social networks could benefit business. Employers might look at how they can connect into this world rather than try to dictate how their employees connect. On one level, employees can become a source of networking for business opportunities. There are a number of social networks which, for example, comprise mainly professional and business people. The links which can be made within these environments can generate business activity which otherwise would not have presented itself. Business networking is a long established model for growth so why not use the ultimate means of networking to further that goal?

We refer here to the situation whereby the company either operates its own virtual world environment or in which its employees are free to participate for business orientated reasons, or where its employees simply access other virtual worlds whilst at work.

Employers, of course, have business interests to protect. There is the essential need to safeguard its client or customer base, maintain confidentiality of its business affairs and processes and generally to uphold its good reputation.

The particular problem which virtual worlds present is the fact that they necessarily involve communication from one person, in this case the employee, with many others. In addition, typically, that in-world dialogue will be by email text communication and such message exchanges can be forensically retrieved from the data records as a matter of evidence.

The greatest risk, therefore, to a company is one of liability rather than lost productivity. These risks have become clear since the advent of email in the office environment. People still send messages by email to one another which they would never dream of sending in the form of a letter. They regard email as much more informal and benign and its immediacy makes it an easy channel for ill-considered comments which, on any mature reflection, or, had the technology not existed, could not be sent in haste. There have been cases which have involved employees sending inappropriate material by email both to each other and to external recipients.

The legal liability can take many forms. One issue is derogatory statements made about fellow employees which might lead to claims for harassment or racial or sexual discrimination. Similarly, comments made about competitor companies can be hugely damaging and might give rise to claims for corporate defamation or malicious falsehood.

These risks are raised also by the very nature of email text. The matter of interpretation is important. When a comment is made face-to-face it can be obviously intended in jest which is apparent from the facial expression of the person making the statement or their physical demeanor. In addition, they may be well known to other employees and thus statements they make in conversation can be placed in the context of understood characteristics of the person which everyone knows to be inoffensive at heart. However, when committed to the written word, the same message can take on a very different construction. Thus, the problems of legal liability arise not merely in cases of deliberate harm, but also in cases of inadvertent harm.

There is a form of action available to an employee who claims that their working lives are being made intolerable by the activity of others in the company which is called constructive dismissal. This arises where the employee resigns as a result of the alleged abuse and then claims that the employer is responsible for the resignation by allowing the continuance of the intolerable behaviour of the fellow employees. In other words, but for the harassment they would not have given up their job and the loss which arises as a consequence may form the claim against the employer business.

Other risks flowing from harassment can include the health of the employee deteriorating, resulting in long periods of absence from work due to illness and then to a claim for damage to health. Such claims may attach against the employer even if the employer has no knowledge of the matter as the employer may be vicariously liable for the actions of their employees where the action complained of is in the course of employment.

It is for these reasons that companies now adopt Internet and email use policies within the organisation to which employees are required to adhere.

A typical provision in such a policy would be not to bring the company into disrepute. It is likely that most companies will regard such action as gross misconduct because the employee ought to have a loyalty to the employer company.

The same concerns will inevitably impact on virtual environments. Clearly, an in-world company will want to ensure that employees who participate in virtual worlds do not use the forum for invective against their employer.

Caution should be noted, however, as to the extent a company can control such action. A recent case involving an employee's use of an Internet weblog to make comments about his employer offers some guidance on the degree to which companies can reasonably control Internet – as thus virtual world exchanges. In 2005, a Waterstones' employee, was dismissed for gross misconduct by Waterstones, who alleged he had brought the company into disrepute by referring to them occasionally as 'Bastardstones'. The employee appealed and was offered reinstatement which he actually declined. The employee's view was that the employer had been unduly heavy handed and that his comments should have been taken in the context of the overall tone of his weblog rather than as a definitive criticism of his employer.

In another case in 2006, Dixon Wilson dismissed an employee in France. The employee kept a weblog, La Petite Anglaise, which mainly discussed her life as an expatriate in France and, on occasion, she referred to the environment at her workplace and the attitude of her bosses. She referred to the senior partner as being old school and recounted how he calls secretaries 'typists'. However, the firm itself was not named. It was only when the employee posted photographs of herself online that the employer believed that their firm could be identified. The firm dismissed the employee under a French law for 'loss of confidence' and 'dismissal with real and serious cause' alleging that her entries brought the firm into disrepute. The employee appealed against her dismissal and the French tribunal found in her favour and awarded her £30,000.

Despite this being a French case, there would probably be a similar outcome in the UK. This means that UK employers need to act with care if they believe that the in-world activities of employees are a problem. The employer needs to act reasonably and be aware that terminating a contract of employment where an employee posts what the employer deems to be inappropriate content could lead to a claim for wrongful dismissal. The best advice is, therefore, for a company which operates in a virtual world to adopt clear guidelines to overcome ambiguities in this area as far as possible.

Whilst the issue of in-world comments by an employee which have the potential to harm the reputation of the employer is not always clear, there is another issue where the law provides the employer more certainty.

The position regarding confidential information is clearer. Most employers will have provisions in their employment contracts relating to confidentiality as well as having a policy in relation to confidential information.

At first view this is an obvious matter for concern but in practical terms the legal position can still present difficulties. An employee may reveal company secrets in-world such as information about the business and, given that at law, disclosure generally destroys the nature of confidential information, employers may in addition, wish to reinforce any policy with a reminder as well as training of staff in measures to protect confidential information.

In 2008 an excellent report was published which examined the impact Internet social networks are having on employee capacity. In this section we will briefly examine some of the findings of that report entitled the *Demos Report: Network Citizens – Power and Responsibility at Work*[1] as they assist in placing virtual world and social network issues in further context.

Networks are not a new social phenomenon. People have sought such relationships for centuries and certainly the attraction to business of networks to generate commercial activity and leads is beyond question. However, it is the advent of the Internet and, more recently, Internet social networks which have made Networks significantly more powerful.

The effect of this is manifold but certainly it is leading to a loosening of organisational structures. There is a shift to a people-centred service economy. Individuals have far

1 Demos Report – *Network Citizens – Power and Responsibility at Work*. Peter Bradwell and Richard Reeves. First published in 2008.

more capacity to take control of their own networks in a social context but also within their employment arrangements. For employers there are challenges. Should they ban *Facebook*? Or open their own *Facebook* group? Start their own *Twitter* feed?

Social networks have become impossible for organisations to ignore. Different organisations, big, small, at the leading edge of network innovation or responding to external changes, are making sense of social networks in different ways. The report finds that organisations are paying serious attention to the collaborative ethic that networks demand.

Businesses should recognise that 'social' networking is not so very different from 'professional' networking. Therefore, attempts to control employees' use of social networking software in the office may end up damaging the organisation in the long run by depleting its network capital. Of course, bans on *Facebook* or *YouTube* are in any case almost impossible to enforce. Companies might just as well try to put a time limit on the numbers of minutes allowed each day for gossiping. A network permissive culture requires a degree of trust on the part of managers and responsibility on the part of employees; but to the extent that networks add internal economic value, the report found that this is usually a risk worth taking. Second, a greater value ought to be placed on developing networks with people outside the company. Too often, it is only senior staff who are encouraged to build relationships with people outside the organisation. However, the power of horizontal networks across organisational boundaries is clear, and growing. In particular, companies should consider how to keep former employees in the network. Ex-employees often retain strong network links to their former colleagues. These links can act to bring in information and experience from outside. Companies that pay attention to alumni management are likely to keep some of the value of internally created networks even when some of the network members move on. Nurturing and hosting networks can bring benefits in terms of productivity, innovation and workplace democracy.

Bibliography

The Internet and Intellectual Property
Jonathan Cornthwaite
2nd Edition, Monitor Press 2000, ISBN 1 871241 87 1

Music the Business – The Essential Guide To The Law And The Deals
Ann Harrison
2nd Edition, Virgin Books 2003, ISBN 1 85227 013 6

The Law of Internet and Mobile Communications –The EU and US Contrasted
Andrew Sparrow
TFM Publishing Ltd, 2004, ISBN 1 903378 18 4

The E Commerce Handbook
Andrew Sparrow
Fitzwarren Handbooks, 2001, ISBN 0-9524812 9 4

Music Distribution and the Internet – A Legal Guide for the Music Business
Andrew Sparrow
Gower Publishing, 2006 ISBN 10 0 566 08709 X

Copyright Law Update, The College of Law Programme 1323
Contributors; Michael Hicks, Peter Groves, Michael Shepherd and Clive Thorne

E-Contracts
Rex Nwakodo and Susan Singleton
Tottel Publishing Ltd, 2005, ISBN 1 84592 980 2

The Laws of the Internet (2nd Edition)
Clive Gringras
Butterworths, 2002, ISBN 0 406 908 087

Distance Selling Changes, Kolvin Stowe, *E Commerce Law and Policy* August 2005, Volume 07 Issue 08.

Department For Culture, Media and Sport Consultation on the proposal by the European Commission for the revision of the Television Without Frontiers Directive. December 2006.

Entertainment Law: A Guide to Contracts in the Film Industry
Anthony Mosawi
Published by Butterworths, 1997, ISBN 0 406 406 00253 3

Demos Report – Network Citizens – Power and responsibility at Work
Peter Bradwell and Richard Reeves
First published in 2008
© Demos. Some rights reserved
Magdalen House, 136 Tooley Street,
London, SE1 2TU, UK
ISBN 978-1-906693-04-6
Copy edited by Susannah Wight, London

Index

Enterprise 2.0:
How Social Software Will Change the Future of Work
Niall Cook
Hardback: 978-0-566-08800-1

Integrated Intellectual Asset Management:
A Guide to Exploiting and Protecting your Organization's Intellectual Assets
Steve Manton
Hardback: 978-0-566-08721-9

Law for Project Managers
David Wright
Hardback: 978-0-566-08601-4

Music Distribution and the Internet:
A Legal Guide for the Music Business
Andrew Sparrow
Hardback: 978-0-566-08709-7

Film and Television Distribution and the Internet:
A Legal Guide for the Media Industry
Andrew Sparrow
Hardback: 978-0-566-08736-3
E-book: 978-0-7546-8190-8

Visit **www.gowerpublishing.com** and

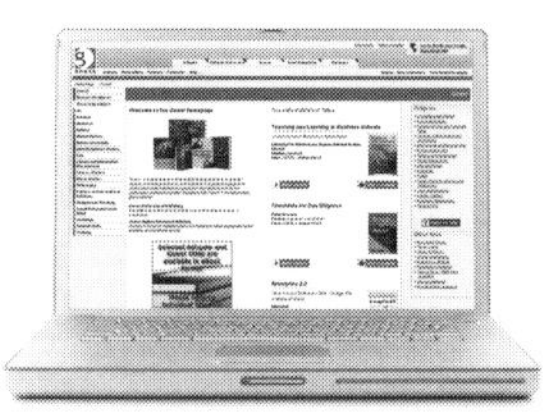

- search the entire catalogue of Gower books in print
- order titles online at 10% discount
- take advantage of special offers
- sign up for our monthly e-mail update service
- download free sample chapters from all recent titles
- download or order our catalogue